taste of home CHURCH SUPPER desserts

taste of home
BOOKS

REIMAN MEDIA GROUP, LLC. • GREENDALE, WISCONSIN

taste of home

Reader's Digest

A TASTE OF HOME/READER'S DIGEST BOOK

visit us at tasteofhome.com

For more Reader's Digest products and information,
visit rd.com (in the United States)
or see rd.ca (in Canada).

Editor in Chief: **Catherine Cassidy**
Vice President, Executive Editor/Books:
Heidi Reuter Lloyd
Creative Director: **Howard Greenberg**
North American Chief Marketing Officer: **Lisa Karpinski**
Food Director: **Diane Werner RD**
Senior Editor/Books: **Mark Hagen**
Editor: **Janet Briggs**
Art Director: **Edwin Robles, Jr.**
Content Production Supervisor: **Julie Wagner**
Design Layout Artist: **Catherine Fletcher**
Proofreaders: **Linne Bruskewitz, Amy Glander**
Recipe Asset System Manager: **Coleen Martin**
Premedia Supervisor: **Scott Berger**
Recipe Testing & Editing:
Taste of Home Test Kitchen
Food Photography: **Taste of Home Photo Studio**
Administrative Assistant: **Barb Czysz**

The Reader's Digest Association, Inc.
President and Chief Executive Officer:
Mary G. Berner
President, North American Affinities:
Suzanne M. Grimes
President/Publisher Trade Publishing:
Harold Clarke
Associate Publisher:
Rosanne McManus
Vice President, Sales and Marketing:
Stacey Ashton

Cover Photography
Photographer: **Lori Foy**
Food Stylist: **Kaitlyn Besasie**
Set Stylist: **Doene Jahnke, Jennifer Bradley Vent**

Additional Photography
Photographer: **Mark Derse**

Special thanks to
St. Charles Borromeo Parish,
Milwaukee, Wisconsin
For other Taste of Home books and products,

International Standard Book Number (10): 0-89821-893-4
International Standard Book Number (13): 978-0-89821-893-0
Library of Congress Control Number: 2010932789

Pictured on front cover: Chocolate Strawberry Torte, p, 97.
Pictured on top of the front cover from left to right: Chocolate Jubilees, p.13;
Peanut Butter Cupcakes, p.136; Raspberry Dreams, p. 36;
and Fresh Raspberry Pie, p. 202.

Pictured on back cover (clockwise from top left): Oatmeal Kiss Cookies, p. 40;
Pink Velvet Cupcakes, p. 148; and Cappuccino Torte, p. 127.

Printed in China
1 3 5 7 9 10 8 6 4 2

table of contents

Share a Heavenly Treat at Your Next Church Supper

At the end of a church supper, potluck or block party, the dessert table is a beehive of activity with both kids and adults hovering over the variety of home-baked delights. If you want to make sure your sweets are the first to disappear, then serve any of the 386 crowd-pleasing goodies in **Taste of Home Church Supper Desserts.**

This collection is your ticket to wowing your church group, neighbors, friends and family with a fabulous dessert...every time!

Turn here for a wealth of recipes sure to inspire you to bake up a spectacular contribution for a potluck, bake sale or church dinner. To start, there is a variety of cookies with flavors such as chocolate, oatmeal, spice and peanut butter. If you are tight on time, try one of the slice-and-bake cookies. Since the dough needs to be refrigerated, you can simply mix it one night and bake it the next!

The recipes in "Bars and Brownies" are an easy way to make at least two dozen treats, and you can use the baking pan to carry them to the function.

The cakes featured here are sure to satisfy any partygoer. There are luscious layer cakes, popular sheet cakes and simple Bundt cakes. You'll also find heavenly angel food, light chiffon and rich butter cakes. And for cupcake lovers, an entire chapter is devoted to those fun-loving delights.

Count on cheesecakes to receive a warm welcome at any event. Included are cute individual servings, such as Apricot Cheesecake Tarts and Jam-Topped Mini Cheesecakes to decadent sensations, such as Peaches and Cream Torte and scrumptious Caramel Apple Cheesecake.

Fruit, cream, nut and custard pies…there's a type to tickle every sweet tooth. You'll find classics like Pumpkin and Coconut Meringue and to tasty fruit pies, such as Apple Blackberry Pie and Crumb-Topped Cherry Pie.

We all scream for ice cream and other frosty delights, and "Frozen Treats" has a delicious assortment. These desserts are great for family, potlucks or events you're hosting in your own home.

"More Desserts" has a smorgasbord of items from gelatin-based desserts and fluffs to pastries and trifles. Any one of these sweet sensations makes a perfect ending to a gathering.

You'll see heads turn and receive recipe requests when you dish up an irresistible creation from Taste of Home Church Supper Desserts.

cookies

Tiny Tim Sandwich Cookies • Cherry Kisses • Salted Peanut Cookies • Yummy Cracker Snacks • Chocolate Jubilees • Triple Chocolate Browni Cookies • Oatmeal Sandwich Cookie • Coconut Clouds • Chocolate-Min

Sandwich Cookies • Cinnamon Almond Strips • Nutty Butter Munchies • Finnish Butter Cookies • Dipped Gingersnap • Buttery Walnut Cutouts • Holida Spritz • Apricot Filled Triangles • Cherr Bonbon Cookies • Two-Tone Christma Cookies • Maple Pecan Cookies Mocha Logs • Hazelnut Shortbrea

tiny tim sandwich cookies

I have many special Christmas memories of my mother and I in the kitchen preparing these cute bite-sized cookies for family and friends. Vary the food coloring for events throughout the year.

Eudora Delezenne • Port Huron, Michigan

1 cup sugar, divided

2 to 3 drops red food coloring

2 to 3 drops green food coloring

1/2 cup butter, softened

1/2 cup shortening

1/4 cup confectioners' sugar

1 teaspoon almond extract

2-1/3 cups all-purpose flour

FROSTING:

2 cups confectioners' sugar

3 tablespoons butter, softened

4-1/2 teaspoons heavy whipping cream

3/4 teaspoon almond extract

Red and green food coloring, optional

» In a small bowl, combine 1/2 cup sugar and red food coloring; set aside. In another small bowl, combine remaining sugar with green food coloring; set aside.

» In a large bowl, cream the butter, shortening and confectioners' sugar until light and fluffy. Beat in extract. Gradually add flour and mix well. Shape into 1/2-in. balls.

» Place 1 in. apart on ungreased baking sheets. Coat bottom of two glasses with cooking spray, then dip one in red sugar and the other in green sugar. Flatten cookies alternately with prepared glasses, redipping in sugar as needed.

» Bake at 375° for 8-10 minutes or until edges are lightly browned. Remove to wire racks to cool completely.

» For frosting, in a small bowl, combine the confectioners' sugar, butter, cream and extract. If desired, tint half of the frosting red and the other half green. Frost the bottoms of half of the cookies; top with remaining cookies.

Yield: 5 dozen.

salted peanut cookies

1-1/2 cups shortening

1 cup sugar

1 cup packed brown sugar

3 eggs

1 teaspoon vanilla extract

3-3/4 cups all-purpose flour

2 teaspoons baking soda

1 teaspoon salt

1-1/2 cups semisweet chocolate chips

1-1/2 cups salted peanuts

» In a large bowl, cream shortening and sugars until light fluffy. Add eggs, one at a time, beating well after each addition. Beat in vanilla. Combine the flour, baking soda and salt; gradually add to creamed mixture and mix well. Stir in chocolate chips and peanuts.

» Drop by tablespoonfuls 2 in. apart onto greased baking sheets. Bake at 350° for 10-12 minutes or until lightly browned. Remove to wire racks.

Yield: 10 dozen.

Instead of walnuts or pecans, this chocolate chip cookie recipe calls for salted peanuts. Whenever I bake these, friends and family are eager to sample them.

Charleen Block • Hutchinson, Minnesota

Cookies that melt in your mouth and are practically fat-free...is it any wonder these crispy meringue morsels disappear as fast as I can whip them up? People love them.

Jo Ann Blomquest • Freeport, Illinois

cherry kisses

4 egg whites

1-1/4 cups sugar

1/3 cup chopped walnuts

1/3 cup chopped pitted dates

1/3 cup chopped candied cherries

» Place egg whites in a large bowl; let stand at room temperature for 30 minutes. Beat on medium speed until soft peaks form. Gradually beat in sugar, 1 tablespoon at a time, on high until stiff glossy peaks form and the sugar is dissolved. Fold in the walnuts, dates and cherries.

» Drop by teaspoonfuls 2 in. apart onto lightly greased baking sheets. Bake at 300° for 20-30 minutes or until firm to the touch. Cool for 1 minute before removing to a wire rack. Store in an airtight container.

Yield: 6 dozen.

yummy cracker snacks

These treats are a hit with my group, and it seems no matter how many I make, they always disappear too quickly.

D. Weaver • Ephrata, Pennsylvania

96 butter-flavored crackers

1 cup creamy peanut butter

1 cup marshmallow creme

2 pounds milk chocolate candy coating, melted

Holiday sprinkles, optional

» Spread half of the crackers with peanut butter. Spread remaining crackers with marshmallow creme; place creme side down over peanut butter crackers, forming a sandwich.

» Dip sandwiches in melted candy coating, allowing excess to drip off. Place on waxed paper-lined pans; refrigerate for 15 minutes or until set. If desired, drizzle with additional candy coating and decorate with sprinkles. Store the cookies in an airtight container.

Yield: 4 dozen.

triple-chocolate brownie cookies

My gang of chocolate lovers gets triply excited when these cookies come out of the oven. They have the texture and taste of a scrumptious fudge brownie and are topped off with tempting chocolate drizzle.

Linda Robinson • New Braunfels, Texas

4 ounces unsweetened chocolate, chopped

3/4 cup butter, cubed

4 eggs

2 cups sugar

1-1/2 cups all-purpose flour

1/2 cup baking cocoa

2 teaspoons baking powder

1/2 teaspoon salt

2 cups (12 ounces) semisweet chocolate chips, divided

2 teaspoons shortening

» In a microwave melt chocolate and butter; stir until smooth. Cool slightly. In a large bowl, beat eggs and sugar. Stir in chocolate mixture. Combine the flour, cocoa, baking powder and salt; gradually add to chocolate mixture and mix well. Stir in 1-1/2 cups chocolate chips. Cover and refrigerate for 2 hours or until easy to handle.

» Drop by tablespoonfuls 2 in. apart onto greased baking sheets. Bake at 350° for 7-9 minutes or until edges are set and tops are slightly cracked. Cool for 2 minutes before removing from pans to wire racks to cool completely.

» In a microwave, melt remaining chips and shortening; stir until smooth. Drizzle over cookies. Let stand for 30 minutes or until chocolate is set. Store in an airtight container.

Yield: 6 dozen.

mixing it up

Drop cookie dough is usually so thick that it can be dropped from a spoon and requires no shaping. If while you're mixing the dough the mixer begins to strain, use a wooden spoon to stir in the last of the flour or all of the nuts, chips and dried fruit. Drop cookies are also great for little bakers because no cutting is involved. They can even help you mix up the dough!

butter pecan roll-ups

This is my variation of traditional lace cookies. Enjoy them alone or alongside scoops of ice cream. The recipe makes a lot, so the roll-ups are just perfect for potlucks, cookie exchanges, charity bake sales or any bring-a-dish get-together where a dessert is needed. Best of all, you can prepare a big batch long ahead of time and store them in the freezer. What could be easier?

Stella Wartmann • Port Charlotte, Florida

6 tablespoons butter, softened

1/2 cup sugar

1/2 cup packed brown sugar

1 egg

1/2 teaspoon vanilla extract

6 tablespoons all-purpose flour

1/8 teaspoon salt

1 cup ground pecans

» In a small bowl, cream butter and sugars until light and fluffy. Beat in egg and vanilla. Combine flour and salt; gradually add to creamed mixture and mix well. Stir in pecans.

» Drop by teaspoonfuls, six at a time, onto a well-greased baking sheet. Bake at 400° for 4-5 minutes or until edges begin to brown. Cool for 1 minute.

» Loosen each cookie and curl around a wooden spoon handle. Cool on a wire rack. Repeat with remaining dough.

Yield: about 6 dozen.

toffee almond sandies

I knew after sampling some of these sandies that I just had to add the cookie recipe to my bulging files!

Vicki Crowley • Monticello, Iowa

1 cup butter, softened

1 cup canola oil

1 cup sugar

1 cup confectioners' sugar

2 eggs

1 teaspoon almond extract

4-1/2 cups all-purpose flour

1 teaspoon baking soda

1 teaspoon cream of tartar

1 teaspoon salt

2 cups sliced almonds

1 package (8 ounces) toffee bits

» In a large bowl, cream the butter, oil and sugars until light and fluffy. Add eggs, one at a time, beating well after each addition. Beat in extract. Combine the flour, baking soda, cream of tartar and salt; gradually add to the creamed mixture and mix well. Stir in almonds and toffee bits.

» Drop by teaspoonfuls 2 in. apart onto ungreased baking sheets. Bake at 350° for 10-12 minutes or until golden brown. Remove to wire racks to cool.

Yield: 9 dozen.

glazed pfeffernuesse

Our version of the classic German cookie is nice to have on hand for the holiday season. They stay fresh—and become more intense in flavor—when stored in an airtight container for a few weeks.

Taste of Home Test Kitchen

1-1/4 cups butter, softened

1-1/4 cups packed brown sugar

3/4 cup molasses

1/2 cup water

1 teaspoon anise extract

6 cups cake flour

1/2 teaspoon baking soda

1/2 teaspoon salt

1-1/2 teaspoons ground cinnamon

1/2 teaspoon ground allspice

1/2 teaspoon ground cloves

1/4 teaspoon ground nutmeg

1/4 teaspoon ground mace

1/8 teaspoon ground cardamom

1/8 teaspoon pepper

2 cups finely chopped nuts

GLAZE:

1 cup confectioners' sugar

3 tablespoons 2% milk

1/4 teaspoon vanilla extract

Additional confectioners' sugar

» In a large bowl, cream butter and brown sugar until light and fluffy. Beat in the molasses, water and extract. Combine the flour, baking soda, salt and spices; gradually add to creamed mixture and mix well. Stir in nuts. Cover and refrigerate for 1 hour.

» Roll dough into 1-in. balls. Place 2 in. apart on greased baking sheets. Bake at 375° for 10-12 minutes or until golden brown.

» Meanwhile, in a shallow bowl, combine the confectioners' sugar, milk and vanilla. Place additional confectioners' sugar in another shallow bowl. Remove cookies to wire racks; cool 5 minutes. Dip tops of warm cookies in glaze, allow excess to drip off; dip in confectioners' sugar. Cool completely on wire racks. Store in an airtight container.

Yield: about 10 dozen.

EDITOR'S NOTE: This recipe does not use eggs.

chocolate jubilees

Rich and fudgy, these cookies appear in many of the care packages I send. I combined several recipes and added maraschino cherries to come up with this winning recipe.

LaVera Fenton • Colorado Springs, Colorado

1 cup butter, softened

1 cup shortening

2 cups packed brown sugar

1 cup sugar

4 eggs

2 to 3 teaspoons almond extract

4 cups all-purpose flour

1 cup quick-cooking oats

1 cup baking cocoa

2 teaspoons baking soda

2 teaspoons salt

3 cups (18 ounces) semisweet chocolate chips

1 jar (16 ounces) maraschino cherries, drained and chopped

1 cup sliced almonds, optional

» In a large bowl, cream butter, shortening and sugars until light and fluffy. Add eggs, one at a time, beating well after each addition. Beat in extract. Combine the flour, oats, cocoa, baking soda and salt; gradually add to the creamed mixture and mix well. Transfer to a larger bowl if necessary. Stir in chocolate chips, cherries and almonds if desired.

» Roll into 1-1/2-in. balls. Place 3 in. apart on ungreased baking sheets. Bake at 375° for 12-14 minutes or until the edges are firm. Remove to wire racks to cool.

Yield: about 5-1/2 dozen.

oatmeal sandwich cookies

These fun treats put a sweet fluffy filling between two chewy oatmeal cookies. They are perfect for snacking and to carry in lunch boxes. Best of all, they sell instantly at bake sales.

Jan Woodall • Indianapolis, Indiana

1-1/2 cups shortening

2-2/3 cups packed brown sugar

4 eggs

2 teaspoons vanilla extract

2-1/4 cups all-purpose flour

2 teaspoons ground cinnamon

1-1/2 teaspoons baking soda

1 teaspoon salt

1/2 teaspoon ground nutmeg

4 cups old-fashioned oats

FILLING:

3/4 cup shortening

3 cups confectioners' sugar

1 jar (7 ounces) marshmallow creme

1 to 3 tablespoons milk

» In a large bowl, cream shortening and brown sugar. Add eggs, one at a time, beating well after each. Beat in vanilla. Combine flour, cinnamon, baking soda, salt and nutmeg; add to creamed mixture. Stir in oats.

» Drop by rounded teaspoonfuls 2 in. apart onto lightly greased baking sheets. Bake at 350° for 10-12 minutes or until golden brown. Remove to wire racks to cool.

» For filling, in a small bowl, cream the shortening, sugar and marshmallow creme. Add enough milk to achieve a spreading consistency. Spread filling on the bottom of half of the cookies; top with remaining cookies.

Yield: about 4-1/2 dozen.

apricot-filled triangles

It's a good thing this recipe makes a big batch because no one can stop eating just one! These crisp, buttery cookies truly do melt in your mouth. If you like, make the apricot filling and the cookie dough a day ahead and refrigerate it overnight. The next day, all you'll need to do is roll out the dough, bake and then enjoy these delectable triangles.

Mildred Lorence • Carlisle, Pennsylvania

1 pound dried apricots (2-1/2 cups)

1-1/2 cups water

1/2 cup sugar

DOUGH:

2/3 cup shortening

3 tablespoons 2% milk

1-1/3 cups sugar

2 eggs

1 teaspoon lemon extract

4 cups cake flour

2 teaspoons baking powder

1 teaspoon salt

» In a small saucepan, cook apricots and water over low heat for 45 minutes or until the water is absorbed and apricots are soft. Cool slightly.

» Transfer apricots to a blender. Cover and process until smooth. Add sugar; cover and process until blended. Set aside.

» In a large saucepan over low heat, melt shortening and milk. Remove from the heat; stir in sugar. Add eggs, one at a time, whisking well after each addition. Stir in extract.

» Combine the flour, baking powder and salt; gradually add to the saucepan and mix well. Cover and refrigerate for 4 hours or until easy to handle.

» On a lightly floured surface, roll out to 1/8-in. thickness. Cut with a floured 3-in. round cookie cutter.

» Place 1 teaspoon apricot filling in the center of each. Bring three edges together over filling, overlapping slightly (a small portion of filling will show in the center); pinch edges gently. Place 1 in. apart on ungreased baking sheets.

» Bake at 400° for 8-10 minutes or until golden brown. Remove to wire racks to cool.

Yield: 6 dozen.

chocolate-mint sandwich cookies

If you ask me, refreshing mint filling sandwiched between two chocolate cookies makes for some tasty nibbling.

Monica Kneuer • Peconic, New York

3/4 cup butter, softened

1 cup sugar

1 egg

1/2 teaspoon vanilla extract

2 cups all-purpose flour

3/4 cup baking cocoa

1 teaspoon baking powder

1/2 teaspoon baking soda

1/2 teaspoon salt

1/4 cup 2% milk

FILLING:

3 tablespoons butter, softened

1-1/2 cups confectioners' sugar

1 tablespoon 2% milk

1/4 teaspoon peppermint extract

2 to 3 drops green food coloring, optional

» In a large bowl, cream butter and sugar until light and fluffy. Beat in egg and vanilla. Combine the flour, cocoa, baking powder, baking soda and salt; gradually add to creamed mixture alternately with milk, beating well after each addition.

» Shape into two 10-1/2-in. rolls; wrap each in plastic wrap. Refrigerate overnight.

» Unwrap dough and cut into 1/8-in. slices. Place 2 in. apart on lightly greased baking sheets. Bake at 325° for 9-11 minutes or until edges are set. Remove to wire racks to cool.

» Combine filling ingredients; beat until smooth. Add food coloring if desired. Spread on the bottom of half of the cookies; top with remaining cookies.

Yield: 5 dozen.

1 teaspoon coconut extract

1 teaspoon vanilla extract

2 cups flaked coconut, toasted

» In a large bowl, cream the butter, shortening and sugars until light and fluffy. Beat in eggs and extracts. Stir in sour cream. Combine the flour, salt and baking soda; gradually add to creamed mixture and mix well. Fold in coconut.

» Drop by tablespoonfuls 2 in. apart onto lightly greased baking sheets. Bake at 375° for 8-10 minutes or until set. Remove to wire racks to cool.

» In a small heavy saucepan, cook butter over medium heat for 5-7 minutes or until golden brown. Pour into a small bowl; beat in the confectioners' sugar, milk and extracts. Frost cookies; dip in coconut. Let stand until completely dry. Store in an airtight container.

Yield: about 5-1/2 dozen.

coconut clouds

Coconut lovers will have an extra reason to celebrate when they taste these cake-like drop cookies. The generous frosting and coconut topping make them a welcomed addition to any dessert buffet.

Donna Scofield • Yakima, Washington

1/4 cup butter, softened

1/4 cup shortening

1 cup sugar

1/2 cup packed brown sugar

2 eggs

1 teaspoon coconut extract

1 teaspoon vanilla extract

1 cup (8 ounces) sour cream

2-3/4 cups all-purpose flour

1 teaspoon salt

1/2 teaspoon baking soda

1 cup flaked coconut, toasted

FROSTING:

1/3 cup butter, cubed

3 cups confectioners' sugar

3 tablespoons evaporated milk

cinnamon almond strips

These rich, buttery cookies are proof that sometimes the most simple ingredients can result in the most delicious treat.

Fred Grover • Lake Havasu City, Arizona

1-1/2 cups butter, softened

1 cup sugar

3 eggs, separated

3 cups all-purpose flour

TOPPING:
1-1/2 cups sugar

1 cup finely chopped almonds

1-1/2 teaspoons ground cinnamon

» In a large bowl, cream butter and sugar until light and fluffy. Beat in egg yolks. Gradually add flour and mix well.

» Using a cookie press fitted with a bar disk, press dough 1 in. apart into long strips onto ungreased baking sheets. In a small bowl, beat the egg whites until stiff peaks form; brush over the dough.

» Combine topping ingredients; sprinkle over strips. Cut each strip into 2-in. pieces (there is no need to separate the pieces).

» Bake at 350° for 8-10 minutes or until edges are firm (do not brown). Cut into pieces again if necessary. Remove to wire racks to cool.

Yield: about 10 dozen.

candied fruit cookies

These no-fuss drop cookies are both nutty and fruity, so they are always a hit wherever I take them.

Florence Monson • Denver, Colorado

1/2 cup butter, softened

3/4 cup sugar

1 egg

1-1/4 cups all-purpose flour

1/2 teaspoon baking soda

1/2 teaspoon salt

1/2 teaspoon ground cinnamon

2-1/2 cups pitted dates, chopped

1/2 cup each chopped candied cherries and pineapple

3/4 cup coarsely chopped Brazil nuts, toasted

3/4 cup chopped almonds, toasted

» In a large bowl, cream butter and sugar until light and fluffy. Beat in egg. Combine the flour, baking soda, salt and cinnamon; gradually add to the creamed mixture and mix well. Fold in fruits and nuts.

» Drop by teaspoonfuls 2 in. apart onto greased baking sheets. Bake at 375° for 8-10 minutes or until lightly browned. Remove to wire racks.

Yield: 7 dozen.

delicate mint thins

When I was newly married, I needed something fancy to impress my relatives at a family reunion, and came up with these crisp cookies. I received many compliments on their subtle flavor.

Kristine McDaniel • Kettering, Ohio

1/2 cup butter, softened

1/2 cup sugar

1 egg yolk

1/2 teaspoon vanilla extract

1-1/2 cups all-purpose flour

1-1/2 teaspoons baking powder

1/8 teaspoon salt

3 tablespoons 2% milk

1 cup fresh mint, finely chopped

1-2/3 cups semisweet chocolate chips

1 tablespoon shortening

» In a large bowl, cream butter and sugar until light and fluffy. Beat in egg yolk and vanilla. Combine the flour, baking powder and salt; add to creamed mixture alternately with milk, mixing well after each addition. Stir in mint. Shape into two 8-in. rolls; wrap each in plastic wrap. Chill for 2 hours or until firm.

» Unwrap and cut into 1/4-in. slices. Place 1 in. apart on greased baking sheets. Bake at 350° for 8-12 minutes or until edges are golden. Remove to wire racks to cool.

» In a microwave, melt chocolate chips and shortening; stir until smooth. Dip each cookie halfway; allow excess to drip off. Place on waxed paper; let stand until set.

Yield: about 4-1/2 dozen.

finnish butter cookies

The delicate texture and wonderful flavor of these crispy Finnish cookies make them a great little treat for afternoon gatherings.

Audrey Thibodeau • Gilbert, Arizona

3/4 cup butter, softened

1/4 cup sugar

1 teaspoon almond extract

2 cups all-purpose flour

1 egg white

2 tablespoons sugar

1/3 cup finely chopped almonds

» In a small bowl, cream butter and sugar until light and fluffy. Beat in extract. Gradually add 1-1/4 cups flour. Knead in remaining flour. Cover and chill for at least 2 hours.

» On a lightly floured surface, roll out dough to 1/4 in. thickness. Cut with a 1-1/2- to 2-in. cookie cutter; place on ungreased baking sheets. Beat egg white until foamy; brush over cutouts. Sprinkle with sugar and almonds.

» Bake at 350° for 7-8 minutes or until edges begin to brown. Cool on wire racks.

Yield: 4 dozen.

surprise crinkles

I created this cookie by trial and error using many different kinds of candy. Milky Ways were the secret surprise my gang liked best.

Lola Fensky • Moundridge, Kansas

1 cup shortening

1/2 cup butter, softened

2 cups packed brown sugar

1 cup sugar

3 eggs

1-1/2 teaspoons vanilla extract

4-1/4 cups all-purpose flour

1-1/2 teaspoons baking soda

1/4 teaspoon ground cinnamon

1/8 teaspoon salt

2 packages (13.3 ounces each) fun-size Milky Way candy bar

» In a large bowl, cream the shortening, butter and sugars until light and fluffy. Add eggs, one at a time, beating well after each addition. Beat in vanilla. Combine the flour, baking soda, cinnamon and salt; gradually add to the creamed mixture and mix well.

» Roll into 1-1/2-in. balls. Cut each candy bar into fourths; push one portion into the center of each ball, completely covering candy with dough. Place 2 in. apart on ungreased baking sheets.

» Bake at 350° for 12-14 minutes or until golden brown and surface cracks. Remove to wire racks to cool.

Yield: 9 dozen.

buttery walnut cutouts

Chopped walnuts add flavor and crunch to these rich vanilla slice-and-bake cookies. Plus, the nuts give them a pretty golden color.

Grace Simons • Orange City, Florida

1 cup butter, softened

3/4 cup sugar

1 egg

1 teaspoon vanilla extract

2-1/2 cups all-purpose flour

2 teaspoons baking powder

1/2 teaspoon salt

1 cup finely chopped walnuts

» In a large bowl, cream butter and sugar until light and fluffy. Beat in egg and vanilla. Combine the flour, baking powder and salt; gradually add to creamed mixture and mix well. Stir in walnuts. Cover and refrigerate the dough for 1 hour or until easy to handle.

» On a floured surface, roll out to 1/8-in. thickness. Cut with floured 2-in. cookie cutters. Place 1 in. apart on ungreased baking sheets. Bake at 375° for 6-8 minutes or until edges are golden brown. Remove to wire racks to cool.

Yield: 4 dozen.

holiday spritz

I tried substituting rum extract for vanilla in a classic spritz recipe, and the end result was a cookie that tasted a lot like eggnog.

Lisa Varner • Charleston, South Carolina

1 cup butter, softened

1 cup confectioners' sugar

1 egg

1-1/2 teaspoons rum extract

2-1/2 cups all-purpose flour

1/4 teaspoon salt

Colored sugar

» In a large bowl, cream butter and confectioners' sugar until light and fluffy. Beat in egg and extract. Combine flour and salt; gradually add to creamed mixture and mix well.

» Using a cookie press fitted with the disk of your choice, press cookies 1 in. apart onto ungreased baking sheets. Sprinkle with colored sugar.

» Bake at 375° for 6-9 minutes or until lightly browned. Cool for 2 minutes before removing from pans to wire racks.

Yield: 7 dozen.

> For filling, in a large bowl, beat peanut butter, confectioners' sugar, vanilla and enough milk to achieve spreading consistency. Spread on half of the cookies and top each with another cookie.

Yield: 44 sandwich cookies.

peanut butter sandwich cookies

I'm a busy mother of two. I work in our school office and help my husband on our hog and cattle farm. When I find time to bake a treat, I like it to be a special one like this. The creamy filling gives traditional peanut butter cookies a new twist.

Debbie Kokes • Tabor, South Dakota

1 cup butter-flavored shortening

1 cup creamy peanut butter

1 cup sugar

1 cup packed brown sugar

3 eggs

1 teaspoon vanilla extract

3 cups all-purpose flour

2 teaspoons baking soda

1/4 teaspoon salt

FILLING:

1/2 cup creamy peanut butter

3 cups confectioners' sugar

1 teaspoon vanilla extract

5 to 6 tablespoons milk

> In a large bowl, cream the shortening, peanut butter and sugars until light and fluffy. Add eggs, one at a time, beating well after each addition after each addition. Add vanilla. Combine the flour, baking soda and salt; add to creamed mixture and mix well.

> Shape into 1-in. balls and place 2 in. apart on ungreased baking sheets. Flatten to 3/8-in. thickness with fork. Bake at 375° for 7-8 minutes or until golden. Remove to wire racks to cool.

dipped macaroons

I always get praise from my entire family—from my kids to great-grandkids—on these elegant cookies. Dipping macaroons in chocolate makes them uncommonly good!

Lillian McDivitt • Rochester Hills, Michigan

2-2/3 cups flaked coconut

2/3 cup sugar

6 tablespoons all-purpose flour

1/4 teaspoon salt

4 egg whites

1/2 to 1 teaspoon almond extract

2 cups milk chocolate chips

1 tablespoon shortening

> In a large bowl, combine the coconut, sugar, flour and salt. Stir in egg whites and almond extract; mix well. Drop by rounded teaspoonfuls onto greased baking sheets. Bake at 325° for 15-20 minutes or until golden brown. Cool for 2 minutes before removing to wire racks.

> In a microwave, melt chips and shortening; stir until smooth. Dip half of each cookie in mixture; allow excess to drip off. Place on waxed paper; let stand until set.

Yield: about 3 dozen.

placing dough on baking sheets

Unless the recipe states otherwise, place cookie dough 2 to 3 inches apart on a cool baking sheet. This allow the hot oven air to circulate around each cookie for more even baking.

» In a large bowl, cream shortening and sugars until light and fluffy. Add eggs, one at a time, beating well after each addition. Beat in molasses. Combine the flour, baking soda, ginger, cinnamon and salt; add to the creamed mixture alternately with water, beating well after each addition. Cover and refrigerate for 3 hours or until easy to handle.

» On a lightly floured surface, roll out to 1/4-in. thickness. Cut with 2-1/2-in. cookie cutters dipped in flour. Place 1 in. apart on greased baking sheets.

» Bake at 350° for 8-10 minutes or until edges are firm. Remove to wire racks to cool. Frost or dust with confectioners' sugar if desired.

Yield: about 6-1/2 dozen.

almond-edged butter cookies

I know you will love these delicate goodies—everyone does! The crunchy, buttery flavor melts in your mouth.

Diane Nelson • Apple Valley, California

1 cup butter, softened

1-1/3 cups plus 6 tablespoons sugar, divided

2 eggs, separated

1/4 cup half-and-half cream

1 teaspoon vanilla extract

3 cups all-purpose flour

2 teaspoons baking powder

1/2 teaspoon salt

1 cup sliced almonds, toasted and chopped

» In a large bowl, cream butter and 1-1/3 cups sugar until light and fluffy. Beat in the egg yolks, cream and vanilla. Combine the flour, baking powder and salt; gradually add to creamed mixture and mix well.

» Shape into four 1-1/2-in. rolls; wrap each in plastic wrap. Refrigerate for 1 hour or until firm.

» In a shallow bowl, combine almonds and remaining sugar. In a small bowl, lightly beat egg whites. Unwrap dough; brush with egg whites. Roll in almond mixture, pressing firmly into dough. Cut into 1/4-in. slices.

» Place 2 in. apart on lightly greased baking sheets. Bake at 400° for 7-8 minutes or until edges are lightly browned. Remove to wire racks. Store in an airtight container.

Yield: about 7-1/2 dozen.

soft molasses cutout cookies

I received this recipe years ago, when my husband and I managed a retirement home. We put out homemade cookies for morning and afternoon coffee, and these were the first ones to disappear.

Vivian Person • Balaton, Minnesota

1 cup shortening

1/2 cup sugar

1/2 cup packed brown sugar

2 eggs

1 cup dark molasses

5-1/2 cups all-purpose flour

3 teaspoons baking soda

1 teaspoon ground ginger

1 teaspoon ground cinnamon

3/4 teaspoon salt

1/2 cup water

Frosting or confectioners' sugar, optional

mocha logs

My mom made these cookies for the holidays when I was a child, and now they are one of my favorite recipes to make. I often pass them out to friends.

Gayle Tarkowski • Traverse City, Michigan

1 cup butter, softened

2 tablespoons instant coffee granules

3/4 cup sugar

1 egg

1 teaspoon vanilla extract

2-1/4 cups all-purpose flour

1/2 teaspoon salt

1/4 teaspoon baking powder

1 cup (6 ounces) semisweet chocolate chips

1-1/2 teaspoons shortening

1 cup chopped walnuts

» In a small bowl, beat butter and coffee granules for 1 minute. Add sugar; beat until light and fluffy. Beat in egg and vanilla. Combine the flour, salt and baking powder; gradually add to creamed mixture and mix well.

» Roll dough into 1/2-in.-thick logs; cut into 2-in. pieces. Place on ungreased baking sheets. Or use a cookie press fitted with a star-shaped disk to press dough into 2-in. logs 1 in. apart on baking sheets.

» Bake at 375° for 8-12 minutes or until lightly browned. Cool for 2 minutes before removing to wire racks to cool completely.

» In a microwave, melt chocolate chips and shortening; stir until smooth. Dip ends of cookies in chocolate; allow excess to drip off. Sprinkle with walnuts. Place on waxed paper; let stand until set. Store in an airtight container.

Yield: 12-1/2 dozen.

mint sandwich cookies

Chocolate-covered mint candies are the filling in these doctored-up sugar cookies. You can use colored sugar to suit any season.

Taste of Home Test Kitchen

1 tube (18 ounces) refrigerated sugar cookie dough, softened

1/4 cup all-purpose flour

1/8 teaspoon peppermint extract

Coarse sugar

40 chocolate-covered thin mints

» In a large bowl, beat the cookie dough, flour and extract until blended. Roll into 1/2-in. balls.

» Place 2 in. apart on greased baking sheets. Coat the bottom of a glass with cooking spray, then dip in coarse sugar. Flatten balls with prepared glass to 1/4-in. thickness, dipping in additional sugar as needed.

» Bake at 350° for 7-9 minutes or until set. Carefully remove one cookie from baking sheet. Immediately turn cookie over and place a mint on the bottom of the cookie; top with another cookie, pressing lightly. Repeat with remaining cookies and mints. Cool on wire racks.

Yield: 40 cookies.

cinnamon oatmeal cookies

A hint of cinnamon makes these chewy oatmeal treats stand out from all others. The recipe makes a big batch, so it's perfect when you need a snack for a crowd.

Terri Crum • Fort Scott, Kansas

2-1/2 cups shortening

5 cups sugar

4 eggs

1/3 cup molasses

1 tablespoon vanilla extract

4-3/4 cups quick-cooking oats

4-1/3 cups all-purpose flour

4 teaspoons baking powder

4 teaspoons ground cinnamon

1 teaspoon baking soda

1 teaspoon salt

» In a large bowl, cream shortening and sugar until light and fluffy. Add eggs, one at a time, beating well after each addition. Beat in molasses and vanilla. Combine the remaining ingredients; gradually add to creamed mixture and mix well.

» Drop by tablespoonfuls 2 in. apart onto greased baking sheets. Bake at 350° for 10-12 minutes or until edges are firm. Remove to wire racks to cool.

Yield: about 13 dozen.

cherry bonbon cookies

These goodies have always been part of my Christmas cookie baking. The tender bites with the surprise cherry in the center are sure to be a hit in your home, too.

Lori Daniels • Beverly, West Virginia

36 maraschino cherries

1 cup butter, softened

1-1/2 cups confectioners' sugar

1 tablespoon whole milk

3 teaspoons vanilla extract

2-3/4 cups all-purpose flour

1/4 teaspoon salt

CHRISTMAS GLAZE:

1-1/4 cups confectioners' sugar

1 to 2 tablespoons water

Red and green liquid food coloring

Colored sprinkles

CHOCOLATE GLAZE:

1 cup confectioners' sugar

1 to 2 tablespoons water

1 ounce unsweetened chocolate, melted

1 teaspoon vanilla extract

1/2 cup chopped pecans or walnuts

» Pat cherries dry with paper towels; set aside. In a large bowl, cream butter and confectioners' sugar until light and fluffy. Beat in milk and vanilla. Combine flour and salt; gradually add to creamed mixture.

» Shape a tablespoonful of dough around each cherry, forming a ball. Place 2 in. apart on ungreased baking sheets. Bake at 350° for 14-16 minutes or until bottoms are browned. Remove to wire racks to cool.

» For Christmas glaze, in a small bowl, combine confectioners' sugar and enough water to achieve a dipping consistency. Transfer half of the glaze to another bowl; tint one bowl green and the other red. Dip the tops of nine cookies in green glaze and nine cookies in red glaze, then decorate with sprinkles. Let stand until set.

» For chocolate glaze, in a small bowl, combine confectioners' sugar and enough water to achieve dipping consistency. Stir in chocolate and vanilla. Dip the tops of remaining cookies in glaze, then sprinkle with nuts. Let stand until set.

Yield: 3 dozen.

jelly-topped sugar cookies

On busy days, I appreciate this fast-to-fix drop sugar cookie. Top each gem with your favorite flavor of jam or jelly.

June Quinn • Kalamazoo, Michigan

3/4 cup sugar

3/4 cup canola oil

2 eggs

2 teaspoons vanilla extract

1 teaspoon lemon extract

1 teaspoon grated lemon peel

2 cups all-purpose flour

2 teaspoons baking powder

1/2 teaspoon salt

1/2 cup jam or jelly

» In a large bowl, beat sugar and oil until blended. Beat in eggs, extracts and lemon peel. Combine the flour, baking powder, and salt; gradually add to sugar mixture and mix well.

» Drop by rounded tablespoonfuls 2 in. apart onto ungreased baking sheets. Coat bottom of a glass with cooking spray, then dip in sugar. Flatten cookies with prepared glass, redipping in sugar as needed.

» Place 1/4 teaspoon jelly in the center of each cookie. Bake at 400° for 8-10 minutes or until set. Remove the cookies to wire racks to cool.

Yield: about 3-1/2 dozen.

triple-chocolate peppermint treats

These minty chocolate cookies are a reminder of Christmas. They make a lot and are good for classroom parties, bake sales or for sharing. They're quick and easy for the whole family to make together.

Teresa Ralston • New Albany, Ohio

1 cup butter, softened

1 cup packed brown sugar

1/2 cup sugar

2 eggs

2 teaspoons vanilla extract

2-1/2 cups all-purpose flour

3/4 cup baking cocoa

1 teaspoon salt

1 teaspoon baking soda

1 cup (6 ounces) semisweet chocolate chips

1/2 cup 60% cacao bittersweet chocolate baking chips

WHITE CHOCOLATE FROSTING:
1/2 cup white baking chips

4 ounces cream cheese, softened

3 cups confectioners' sugar

1/3 to 1/2 cup crushed peppermint candies

» In a large bowl, cream butter and sugars until light and fluffy. Beat in eggs and vanilla. Combine the flour, cocoa, salt and baking soda; gradually add to creamed mixture and mix well. Stir in the chocolate chips.

» Drop by rounded teaspoonfuls 2 in. apart onto ungreased baking sheets. Bake at 375° for 8-10 minutes or until set. Cool for 2 minutes before removing to wire racks to cool completely.

» In a microwave, melt the baking chips; stir until smooth. Cool. Meanwhile, in a small bowl, beat cream cheese and confectioners' sugar until smooth. Beat in melted chips. Frost cookies; sprinkle with peppermint candies.

Yield: about 6-1/2 dozen.

double-drizzle pecan cookies

The caramel and chocolate drizzles on these chewy treats make them doubly delectable and oh-so pretty on a serving tray.

Paula Marchesi • Lenhartsville, Pennsylvania

1/2 cup butter, softened

1-1/2 cups packed brown sugar

1 egg

1 teaspoon vanilla extract

1-1/2 cups all-purpose flour

1-1/2 teaspoons baking powder

1/4 teaspoon salt

1-1/4 cups chopped pecans, toasted

CARAMEL DRIZZLE:
1/2 cup packed brown sugar

1/4 cup heavy whipping cream

1/2 cup confectioners' sugar

CHOCOLATE DRIZZLE:
1 ounce semisweet chocolate

1 tablespoon butter

» In a large bowl, cream butter and brown sugar until light and fluffy. Beat in egg and vanilla. Combine the flour, baking powder and salt; gradually add to creamed mixture and mix well.

» Shape dough into 1-in. balls; roll in pecans. Place 2 in. apart on ungreased baking sheets; flatten slightly. Bake at 350° for 8-10 minutes or until lightly browned. Cool for 2 minutes before removing to wire racks to cool completely.

» In a small saucepan, bring the brown sugar and cream to a boil. Remove from the heat; whisk in confectioners' sugar. Immediately drizzle over cookies.

» In a microwave, melt chocolate and butter; stir until smooth. Drizzle over cookies. Let stand until set. Store in an airtight container.

Yield: about 3-1/2 dozen.

dipped gingersnaps

I get a great deal of satisfaction making and giving time-tested treats like these soft, chewy cookies. Dipping them in white chocolate makes great gingersnaps even more special.

Laura Kimball • West Jordan, Utah

2 cups sugar

1-1/2 cups canola oil

2 eggs

1/2 cup molasses

4 cups all-purpose flour

4 teaspoons baking soda

3 teaspoons ground ginger

2 teaspoons ground cinnamon

1 teaspoon salt

Additional sugar

2 packages (10 to 12 ounces each) white baking chips

1/4 cup shortening

» In a large bowl, combine sugar and oil. Beat in eggs. Stir in molasses. Combine the flour, baking soda, ginger, cinnamon and salt; gradually add to creamed mixture and mix well.

» Shape into 3/4-in. balls and roll in sugar. Place 2 in. apart on ungreased baking sheets. Bake at 350° for 10-12 minutes or until cookie springs back when touched lightly. Remove to wire racks to cool.

» In a small saucepan, melt chips with shortening over low heat, stirring until smooth. Dip the cookies halfway into the melted chips; shake off excess. Place on waxed paper-lined baking sheets until set.

Yield: about 14-1/2 dozen.

caramel tassies

Buttery cookie cups with a smooth caramel filling make a nice addition to a dessert tray. These are one of my family's favorites.

Jane Bricker • Scottdale, Pennsylvania

1 cup butter, softened

2 packages (3 ounces each) cream cheese, softened

2 cups all-purpose flour

FILLING:

1 package (14 ounces) caramels

1/4 cup plus 3 tablespoons evaporated milk

FROSTING:

2 tablespoons shortening

2 tablespoons butter, softened

1 cup confectioners' sugar

1 tablespoon evaporated milk

» In a large bowl, cream butter and cream cheese until light and fluffy. Gradually add flour and mix well. Cover and refrigerate for 1 hour or until easy to handle.

» Roll dough into 1-in. balls; press onto the bottom and up the sides of ungreased miniature muffin cups. Prick bottoms with a fork. Bake at 375° for 15-17 minutes or until golden brown. Cool for 5 minutes before removing from pans to wire racks.

» In a large heavy saucepan over low heat, melt caramels with milk. Remove from the heat; cool slightly. Transfer to a heavy-duty resealable plastic bag; cut a small hole in a corner of the bag. Pipe filling into pastry cups. Cool to room temperature.

» For frosting, in a small bowl, beat shortening and butter until smooth. Gradually beat in confectioners' sugar and milk until fluffy. Pipe onto filling. Store in the refrigerator.

Yield: 4 dozen.

» Divide dough into thirds; flatten each portion into a circle. Wrap each in plastic wrap; chill for 1 hour or until easy to handle.

» On a lightly floured surface, roll out one portion of dough to 1/8-in. thickness. Cut with a floured 1-1/2-in. cookie cutter; place 1/2 in. apart on ungreased baking sheets. Repeat with remaining dough; chill and reroll scraps.

» Bake at 375° for 6-8 minutes or until edges begin to brown. Remove to wire racks to cool.

» For filling, place 3/4 cup semisweet chocolate chips and milk chocolate chips in a small bowl. In a small saucepan, bring cream just to a boil. Pour over chocolate; whisk until smooth. Refrigerate for 1-1/2 hours or until filling reaches spreading consistency, stirring occasionally.

» Spread filling over the bottom of half of the cookies; top with remaining cookies. In a microwave, melt remaining semisweet chips; stir until smooth. Drizzle over cookies. Let stand until set. Store in an airtight container in the refrigerator.

Yield: 3 dozen.

hazelnut-espresso sandwich cookies

The inspiration for this cute cookie came from my sister's description of a hazelnut cookie she tried in Italy. She declared my version to be a wonderful approximation. I create an assembly line with my family to quickly fill the cooled cookies.

Cindy Beberman • Orland Park, Illinois

1 cup butter, softened

1-1/4 cups sugar

1 egg

1 egg yolk

4 teaspoons instant espresso granules

2 teaspoons vanilla extract

2-1/2 cups all-purpose flour

1/2 teaspoon salt

1/2 teaspoon baking powder

1 cup finely ground hazelnuts

FILLING:

1-3/4 cups semisweet chocolate chips, divided

1-1/4 cups milk chocolate chips

1 cup heavy whipping cream

» In a large bowl, cream butter and sugar until light and fluffy. Beat in the egg, yolk, espresso granules and vanilla. Combine the flour, salt and baking powder; gradually add to creamed mixture and mix well. Stir in hazelnuts.

amish raisin cookies

I found this recipe for a chewy raisin cookie in one of the many Amish cookbooks I own. I haven't seen it duplicated anywhere else.

Marcia Wagner • Berrien Springs, Michigan

1 cup raisins

1 cup water

3/4 cup butter, softened

2 cups packed brown sugar

1 egg

1 teaspoon vanilla extract

3 cups all-purpose flour

1 teaspoon baking powder

1 teaspoon baking soda

1/8 teaspoon salt

» In a small saucepan, combine raisins and water. Bring to a boil; cook until liquid is reduced to 1/2 cup. Set aside to cool.

» In a large bowl, cream butter and brown sugar until light and fluffy. Beat in egg and vanilla. Combine the flour, baking powder, baking soda and salt; gradually add to creamed mixture and mix well. Stir in raisins with liquid.

» Drop by tablespoonfuls 2 in. apart onto ungreased baking sheets. Bake at 375° for 10-12 minutes or until the surface cracks. Remove to wire racks to cool.

Yield: 6 dozen.

double chocolate sprinkle cookies

Chock-full of chocolate chips and sprinkles, these chewy treats never last long no matter where I take them. They're simply outstanding.

Barb Meinholz • South Milwaukee, Wisconsin

2 cups butter, softened

2 cups sugar

2 cups packed brown sugar

4 eggs

2 teaspoons vanilla extract

5 cups old-fashioned oats

4 cups all-purpose flour

2 teaspoons baking soda

2 teaspoons baking powder

1 teaspoon salt

4 cups (24 ounces) semisweet chocolate chips

3 cups chopped walnuts

2 cups chocolate sprinkles

» In a large bowl, cream the butter and sugars until light and fluffy. Add eggs, one at a time, beating well after each addition. Beat in vanilla.

» Place the oats in a blender; cover and process until finely ground. Combine the oats, flour, baking soda, baking powder and salt; gradually add to creamed mixture and mix well. Stir in the chocolate chips, walnuts and sprinkles.

» Roll into 1-1/2-in. balls. Place 2 in. apart on ungreased baking sheets. Flatten with a glass. Bake at 350° for 12-14 minutes or until golden brown. Remove to wire racks to cool.

Yield: about 9 dozen.

fruit-filled spritz cookies

From the first time I baked these cookies, they've been a divine success. Old-fashioned and attractive, they're just perfect.

Ingeborg Keith • Newark, Delaware

1-1/2 cups chopped dates

1 cup water

1/2 cup sugar

2 teaspoons orange juice

2 teaspoons grated orange peel

1 cup maraschino cherries, chopped

1/2 cup flaked coconut

1/2 cup ground nuts

DOUGH:
1 cup butter, softened

1 cup sugar

1/2 cup packed brown sugar

3 eggs

1/2 teaspoon almond extract

1/2 teaspoon vanilla extract

4 cups all-purpose flour

1/2 teaspoon baking soda

1/2 teaspoon salt

Confectioners' sugar

» In a small saucepan, combine the first five ingredients; bring to a boil, stirring constantly. Reduce heat; cook and stir for 8 minutes or until thickened. Cool completely. Stir in the cherries, coconut and nuts; set aside.

» In a large bowl, cream butter and sugars until light and fluffy. Beat in eggs and extracts. Combine the flour, baking soda and salt; gradually add to creamed mixture and mix well.

» Using a cookie press fitted with a bar disk, press a 12-in.-long strip of dough onto an ungreased baking sheet. Spread fruit filling over dough. Press another strip over filling. Cut into 1-in. pieces (there is no need to separate the pieces). Repeat with remaining dough and filling.

» Bake at 375° for 12-15 minutes or until edges are golden. Recut into pieces if necessary. Remove to wire racks to cool. Dust with confectioners' sugar.

Yield: about 7-1/2 dozen.

buttermilk spice crisps

These cookies were a Christmas tradition for one of the families in my childhood church. I looked forward to caroling at their house because we were rewarded with one of these tasty morsels!

Marla Mason • Cedar Rapids, Iowa

1 cup butter, softened

2 cups sugar

1 egg

1/3 cup buttermilk

4-2/3 cups all-purpose flour

2 teaspoons baking soda

2 teaspoons ground cinnamon

1 teaspoon each ground allspice, ground cloves and ground nutmeg

» In a large bowl, cream butter and sugar until light and fluffy. Beat in egg and buttermilk. Combine the flour, baking soda, cinnamon, allspice, cloves and nutmeg; gradually add to the creamed mixture and mix well. Shape into two 9-in. rolls; wrap each in plastic wrap. Refrigerate for 4 hours or until firm.

» Unwrap and cut into 1/4-in. slices. Place 2 in. apart on ungreased baking sheets. Bake at 350° for 10-12 minutes or until golden brown. Remove to wire racks to cool.

Yield: 6 dozen.

> In a large bowl, cream the shortening, butter and brown sugar until light and fluffy. Add eggs, one at a time, beating well after each addition. Beat in vanilla and maple flavoring. Combine flour and baking soda; gradually add to the creamed mixture and mix well. Stir in white chips and pecans.

> Drop by tablespoonfuls 2 in. apart onto ungreased baking sheets. Bake at 350° for 9-11 minutes or until golden brown. Cool for 2 minutes before removing to wire racks.

> In a large bowl, cream the butter, confectioners' sugar, maple flavoring and enough milk to achieve spreading consistency. Frost each cookie with 1 teaspoon frosting; top with a pecan half.

Yield: 7 dozen.

crackle cookies

This recipe falls in the oldie but goodie category. My family loves them! Kids can help by rolling the balls in confectioners' sugar and placing them on the baking sheets.

Ruth Cain • Hartselle, Alabama

1 cup sugar

1/4 cup canola oil

2 eggs

2 ounces unsweetened chocolate, melted and cooled

1 teaspoon vanilla extract

1 cup all-purpose flour

1 teaspoon baking powder

1/4 teaspoon salt

Confectioners' sugar

> In a large bowl, beat sugar and oil until blended. Beat in eggs, chocolate and vanilla. Combine the flour, baking powder and salt; gradually add to sugar mixture and mix well. Cover and refrigerate dough for at least 2 hours.

> With sugared hands, shape dough into 1-in. balls. Roll in confectioners' sugar. Place 2 in. apart on greased baking sheets. Bake at 350° for 10-12 minutes or until set. Remove to wire racks to cool.

Yield: about 3 dozen.

maple pecan cookies

When I bake cookies for the annual youth ski trip, I try at least one new recipe. When I received recipe requests for these frosted goodies, I knew I had a keeper.

Nancy Johnson • Laverne, Oklahoma

1 cup shortening

1/2 cup butter, softened

2 cups packed brown sugar

2 eggs

1 teaspoon vanilla extract

1 teaspoon maple flavoring

3 cups all-purpose flour

2 teaspoons baking soda

1 package (10 to 12 ounces) white baking chips

1/2 cup chopped pecans

FROSTING:

1/4 cup butter, softened

4 cups confectioners' sugar

1 teaspoon maple flavoring

3 to 5 tablespoons 2% milk

1-1/2 cups pecan halves

chunky drop cookies

I like to prep these sweet, salty gems ahead of time. The night before, I measure out the pretzels, peanuts, raisins and chocolate. The next day, they come together in a snap.

Kelly Ward-Hartman • Cape Coral, Florida

1 cup butter, softened

1 cup packed brown sugar

1/2 cup sugar

2 eggs

3 teaspoons vanilla extract

2-1/2 cups all-purpose flour

3/4 teaspoon baking powder

2 cups halved pretzel sticks

1 cup coarsely chopped dry roasted peanuts

1 cup semisweet chocolate chunks

1 cup raisins

» In a large bowl, cream butter and sugars until light and fluffy. Add eggs, one at a time, beating well after each addition. Beat in vanilla. Combine the flour and baking powder; gradually add to creamed mixture and mix well. Stir in the pretzels, peanuts, chocolate chunks and raisins.

» Drop by heaping tablespoonfuls 2 in. apart onto ungreased baking sheets. Bake at 350° for 10-14 minutes or until edges are golden brown. Cool for 2 minutes before removing to wire racks.

Yield: about 6-1/2 dozen.

chocolate-peanut butter cookies

Kids will love making these easy cookies with mom, dad or the grandparents. These dense, rich cookies make an absolutely perfect snack with a cup of coffee.

Elaine Stephens • Carmel, Indiana

2 cans (16 ounces each) chocolate fudge frosting, divided

1 egg

1 cup chunky peanut butter

1-1/2 cups all-purpose flour

Granulated sugar

» Set aside one can plus 1/3 cup frosting. In a large bowl, combine the egg, peanut butter and remaining frosting. Stir in flour just until moistened.

» Drop by rounded tablespoonfuls 2 in. apart on baking sheets coated with cooking spray. Flatten cookies with a fork dipped in sugar.

» Bake at 375° for 8-11 minutes or until set. Remove to wire racks. Cool completely; spread with reserved frosting.

Yield: 3-1/2 dozen.

cran-orange icebox cookies

My family looks forward to sampling these gorgeous treats during the holidays. The cran-orange flavor makes them special.

Nancy Rollag • Kewaskum, Wisconsin

1 cup butter, softened

1 cup sugar

1 egg

2 tablespoons 2% milk

1 teaspoon vanilla extract

3 cups all-purpose flour

1-1/2 teaspoons baking powder

2 teaspoons grated orange peel

2/3 cup chopped dried cranberries

1/4 cup chopped pecans

8 to 10 drops red food coloring, optional

» In a large bowl, cream butter and sugar until light and fluffy. Beat in the egg, milk and vanilla. Combine flour and baking powder; gradually add to creamed mixture and mix well.

» Transfer 1 cup of dough to a small bowl; stir in orange peel and set aside. Add the cranberries, pecans and food coloring if desired to remaining dough; divide in half.

» Line an 8-in. x 4-in. loaf pan with waxed paper. Press one portion of cranberry dough evenly into pan; top with orange dough, then remaining cranberry dough. Cover and refrigerate for 2 hours or until firm.

» Remove dough from pan; cut in half lengthwise. Cut each portion into 1/4-in. slices. Place 1 in. apart on lightly greased baking sheets.

» Bake at 375° for 8-10 minutes or until edges begin to brown. Remove to wire racks. Store in an airtight container.

Yield: 4 dozen.

cindy's chocolate chip cookies

Chocolate chip cookies are a mainstay in our cookie jar. They are most people's all-time favorites, which makes them perfect for gifts, bake sales or simply everyday snacking.

Cindy Utter • Jacksonville, Illinois

1 cup butter, softened

1 cup shortening

2 cups packed light brown sugar

1 cup sugar

4 eggs

2 teaspoons vanilla extract

4-1/2 cups all-purpose flour

2 teaspoons baking soda

2 teaspoons salt

2 cups (12 ounces) semisweet chocolate chips

1 cup chopped pecans

» In a large bowl, cream the butter, shortening and sugars until light and fluffy. Beat in eggs and vanilla. Combine the flour, baking soda and salt; add to creamed mixture and mix well. Stir in chocolate chips and nuts (dough will be sticky). Cover and chill dough for 1 hour.

» Drop by tablespoonfuls 2 in. apart onto greased baking sheets. Bake at 350° for 10-12 minutes or until lightly browned. Remove to wire racks to cool.

Yield: about 11 dozen.

two-tone christmas cookies

I dreamed up this recipe using two of my favorite flavors—pistachio and raspberry. These pink and green cookies are tasty and eye-catching, too. They're perfect for formal or informal gatherings, and everybody likes them.

Marie Capobianco • Portsmouth, Rhode Island

1 cup butter, softened

1-1/2 cups sugar

2 egg yolks

2 teaspoons vanilla extract

1 teaspoon almond extract

3-1/2 cups all-purpose flour

1 teaspoon baking powder

1 teaspoon salt

1/2 teaspoon baking soda

9 drops green food coloring

1 tablespoon 2% milk

1/3 cup finely chopped pistachios

9 drops red food coloring

3 tablespoons seedless raspberry preserves

2 cups (12 ounces) semisweet chocolate chips, melted

Additional chopped pistachios, optional

» In a large bowl, cream butter and sugar until light and fluffy. Beat in egg yolks and extracts. Combine the flour, baking powder, salt and baking soda; gradually add to creamed mixture and mix well. Divide dough in half. Stir green food coloring, milk and nuts into one portion; mix well. Add red food coloring and jam to the other half.

» Between two pieces of waxed paper, shape each portion into an 8-in. x 6-in. rectangle. Cut in half lengthwise. Place one green rectangle on a piece of plastic wrap. Top with one pink

rectangle; press together lightly. Repeat, forming a second stack. Wrap each in plastic wrap and refrigerate overnight.

» Remove one stack from the refrigerator at a time. Unwrap dough; cut in half lengthwise. Return one portion to the refrigerator. Cut remaining portion into 1/8-in. slices. Place 1 in. apart on ungreased baking sheets. Bake at 375° for 7-9 minutes or until set. Remove to wire racks to cool. Repeat with the remaining dough.

» Drizzle cooled cookies with melted chocolate. Sprinkle with additional pistachios if desired.

Yield: 6-1/2 dozen.

» Place 1 in. apart on ungreased baking sheets. Bake at 350° for 9-11 minutes or until set. Cool for 1 minute before removing to wire racks to cool completely.

» Sprinkle cookies with confectioners' sugar. In a microwave, melt chocolate chips and shortening; stir until smooth. Drizzle over cookies; let stand until set. Store in an airtight container.

Yield: 10-1/2 dozen.

brown sugar cutouts

I bake so many cookies for the holidays that I have one recipe box just for cookies alone! But of all of them, these simple cutouts are among my husband's favorites.

Norma Mueller • Wauwatosa, Wisconsin

1 cup butter, softened

2 cups packed brown sugar

3 eggs

2 teaspoons grated lemon peel

3 cups all-purpose flour

1 teaspoon baking soda

1 teaspoon ground ginger

FROSTING:

1-1/2 cups confectioners' sugar

1/2 teaspoon vanilla extract

2 to 3 tablespoons half-and-half cream

Green food coloring, optional

» In a large bowl, cream butter and brown sugar until light and fluffy. Beat in eggs and lemon peel. Combine the flour, baking soda and ginger; gradually add to creamed mixture and mix well. Cover and refrigerate for 2 hours or until easy to handle.

» On a floured surface, roll out dough to 1/8-in. thickness. Cut with lightly floured 2-in. cookie cutters. Place 2 in. apart on ungreased baking sheets. Bake at 350° for 8-10 minutes or until golden brown. Remove to wire racks to cool.

» For frosting, in a small bowl, combine the confectioners' sugar, vanilla and enough cream to achieve spreading consistency. Add food coloring if desired to some or all of the frosting. Decorate cookies.

Yield: about 6 dozen.

chocolate walnut crescents

I use a round cookie cutter to form the crescent shapes for these nutty delights. They're pretty sprinkled with sugar and drizzled with chocolate.

TerryAnn Moore • Vineland, New Jersey

1 cup butter, softened

1/2 cup sugar

1 teaspoon vanilla extract

2 cups all-purpose flour

2 cups ground walnuts

3 tablespoons baking cocoa

2 to 3 tablespoons confectioners' sugar

1 package (12 ounces) semisweet chocolate chips

2 teaspoons shortening

» In a large bowl, cream butter and sugar until light and fluffy. Beat in vanilla. Combine the flour, walnuts and cocoa; gradually add to creamed mixture and mix well. Cover and refrigerate for 1 hour or until easy to handle.

» On a lightly floured surface, roll out dough to 1/4-in. thickness. Using a floured, plain or finely scalloped 2-in. round cookie cutter, cut a semicircle off one corner of the dough, forming the inside of a crescent shape. Reposition cutter 1-1/4 in. from inside of crescent; cut cookie, forming a crescent 1-1/4 in. wide at its widest point. Repeat. Refrigerate and reroll the scraps if desired.

lemon oatmeal cookies

My grandmother always made these cookies for us at Christmas, and now I have inherited that task. With rich cream cheese in the dough and the sugary almond topping, one batch of these fabulous snacks doesn't last long at my house.

Michelle Naber • Tonawanda, New York

1 cup butter-flavored shortening

1 package (3 ounces) cream cheese, softened

1-1/4 cups sugar

1 egg yolk

2 teaspoons grated lemon peel

1 teaspoon lemon extract

1-1/3 cups all-purpose flour

1-1/3 cups quick-cooking oats

1/2 teaspoon salt

TOPPING:

1 egg

1 egg white

Sugar

1/2 cup sliced almonds

» In a large bowl, cream the shortening, cream cheese and sugar until light and fluffy. Beat in the egg yolk, lemon peel and extract. Combine the flour, oats and salt; gradually add to creamed mixture and mix well.

» Drop by heaping teaspoonfuls 2 in. apart onto greased baking sheets. Beat egg and egg white; brush over dough. Sprinkle with sugar; top with almonds.

» Bake at 350° for 10-12 minutes or until edges are lightly browned. Remove to wire racks.

Yield: 4-1/2 dozen.

malted milk cookies

My daughter substituted crushed malted milk balls in our favorite chocolate chip cookie recipe to create these crisp treats. They're so yummy fresh from the oven.

Audrey Metzger • Larchwood, Iowa

1 cup butter, softened

3/4 cup packed brown sugar

1/3 cup sugar

1 egg

2 teaspoons vanilla extract

2-1/4 cups all-purpose flour

2 tablespoons instant chocolate drink mix

1 teaspoon baking soda

1/2 teaspoon salt

2 cups malted milk balls, crushed

» In a large bowl, cream the butter and sugars until light and fluffy. Beat in egg and vanilla. Combine the flour, drink mix, baking soda and salt; gradually add to creamed mixture and mix well. Stir in malted milk balls.

» Shape into 1-1/2-in. balls. Place 2 in. apart on greased baking sheets. Bake at 375° for 10-12 minutes or until set. Cool for 1 minute before removing from pans to wire racks to cool completely.

Yield: about 3 dozen.

raspberry dreams

I made variations to my friend's recipe to come up with these wonderful sandwich cookies.

Lori Brown • Sioux Falls, South Dakota

2 cups butter, softened

1 cup sugar

4 egg yolks

2 teaspoons vanilla extract

1 drop lemon juice

5-1/3 cups all-purpose flour

1/4 teaspoon salt

FILLING:
1 jar (12 ounces) raspberry preserves

ICING:
1 cup confectioners' sugar

1 drop lemon juice

1 drop red food coloring, optional

1 to 2 tablespoons 2% milk

» In a large bowl, cream butter and sugar until light and fluffy. Add egg yolks, one at a time, beating well after each addition. Beat in vanilla and lemon juice. Combine flour and salt; gradually add to the creamed mixture and mix well. Refrigerate for 1 hour or until easy to handle.

» Divide dough into three portions. On a lightly floured surface, roll out each portion to 1/4-in. thickness. Cut with a 2-in. round cookie cutter. Place 1 in. apart on ungreased baking sheets.

» Bake at 350° for 8-10 minutes or until edges are very lightly browned. Remove to wire racks to cool.

» Spread the bottom half of the cookies with raspberry preserves; top with remaining cookies.

» For icing, combine the confectioners' sugar, lemon juice, food coloring if desired and enough milk to achieve a drizzling consistency. Drizzle over cookies.

Yield: about 4-1/2 dozen.

brownie biscotti

Daintily drizzled with white chocolate, this eye-catching biscotti is loaded with chocolate chips and crunchy almonds.

Amber Sumner • Congress, Arizona

1/2 cup butter, melted

3 eggs

2 teaspoons vanilla extract

2-1/2 cups all-purpose flour

1-1/3 cups sugar

3/4 cup baking cocoa

2 teaspoons baking powder

1/2 teaspoon baking soda

1 cup unblanched almonds, toasted and coarsely chopped

1/2 cup miniature semisweet chocolate chips

DRIZZLE:

1/2 cup white baking chips

1-1/2 teaspoons shortening

» In a large bowl, combine the butter, eggs and vanilla until well blended. Combine the flour, sugar, cocoa, baking powder and baking soda; gradually add to butter mixture just until combined (dough will be crumbly).

» Turn dough onto a lightly floured surface; knead in almonds and chocolate chips. Divide dough in half. On an ungreased baking sheet, shape each portion into a 12-in. x 3-in. log, leaving 3 in. between the logs.

» Bake at 325° for 30-35 minutes or until set and tops are cracked. Cool for 15 minutes. Carefully transfer to a cutting board; cut diagonally with a serrated knife into 1/2-in. slices.

» Place cut side down on ungreased baking sheets. Bake for 20-25 minutes or until firm and dry. Remove to wire racks to cool.

» For drizzle, in a microwave, melt white chips and shortening at 70% power for 1 minute; stir. Microwave at additional 10 to 20-second intervals, stirring until smooth. Drizzle over biscotti.

Yield: 3 dozen.

cinnamon stars

These cookies will fill your home with an irresistible aroma as they bake. My grandmother made them every Christmas when I was a child. I have fond memories of helping her in the kitchen.

Jean Jones • Peachtree City, Georgia

1 cup butter, softened

2 cups sugar

2 eggs

2-3/4 cups all-purpose flour

1/3 cup ground cinnamon

» In a large bowl, cream butter and sugar until light and fluffy. Add eggs, one at a time, beating well after each addition. Combine flour and cinnamon; gradually add to creamed mixture and mix well. Cover and refrigerate for 1 hour or until easy to handle.

» On a lightly floured surface, roll out to 1/4-in. thickness. Cut with a 2-1/2-in. star-shaped cookie cutter dipped in flour. Place 1 in. apart on ungreased baking sheets.

» Bake at 350° for 15-18 minutes or until edges are firm and bottom of cookies are lightly browned. Remove to wire racks to cool.

Yield: 5 dozen.

pistachio cranberry cookies

I came up with this recipe one year when looking for a cookie that had a little red and green in it. The combination of cranberries and pistachios is simply heavenly.

Arlene Kroll • Vero Beach, Florida

1/2 cup butter, softened

1/2 cup canola oil

1/2 cup sugar

1/2 cup packed brown sugar

1 egg

1 teaspoon vanilla extract

1-3/4 cups all-purpose flour

1/2 teaspoon baking powder

1/2 teaspoon baking soda

1/2 teaspoon salt

1 cup crisp rice cereal

1/2 cup old-fashioned oats

1/2 cup dried cranberries

1/2 cup chopped pistachios

» In a large bowl, cream butter, oil and sugars until light and fluffy. Beat in egg and vanilla. Combine the flour, baking powder, baking soda and salt; gradually add to creamed mixture and mix well. Stir in the cereal, oats, cranberries and pistachios.

» Drop by tablespoonfuls 2 in. apart onto ungreased baking sheets. Bake at 350° for 10-12 minutes or until lightly browned. Remove to wire racks to cool.

Yield: 5 dozen.

super chunky cookies

Chocolate lovers will go crazy over these cookies—they have four kinds of chocolate! When friends ask me to make "those" cookies, I know they mean this recipe. One of these will keep you going until mealtime.

Rebecca Jendry • Spring Branch, Texas

1/2 cup butter-flavored shortening

1/2 cup butter, softened

1 cup packed brown sugar

3/4 cup sugar

2 eggs

2 teaspoons vanilla extract

2-1/2 cups all-purpose flour

1 teaspoon baking soda

1/8 teaspoon salt

1 cup miniature semisweet chocolate chips

1 cup milk chocolate chips

1 cup white baking chips

4 ounces bittersweet chocolate, coarsely chopped

3/4 cup English toffee bits or almond brickle chips

1/2 cup chopped pecans

» In a large bowl, cream the shortening, butter and sugars until light and fluffy. Add eggs, one at a time, beating well after each addition. Beat in vanilla. Combine the flour, baking soda and salt; gradually add to the creamed mixture and mix well. Stir in the remaining ingredients.

» Drop batter by tablespoonfuls 3 in. apart onto ungreased baking sheets. Bake at 350° for 10-12 minutes or until lightly browned. Cool for 2-3 minutes before removing to wire racks to cool completely.

Yield: 6-1/2 dozen.

nutty butter munchies

I have a sweet tooth and I find these crisp nut-filled cookies are a great way to satisfy it.

Zenola Frazier • Tallulah, Louisiana

1 cup butter, softened

1/2 cup chunky peanut butter

1 cup sugar

1 cup packed brown sugar

3 eggs

1 teaspoon vanilla extract

1/2 teaspoon almond extract

3 cups all-purpose flour

1/2 teaspoon baking soda

1/2 teaspoon salt

1-1/2 cups chopped pecans

1/2 cup salted peanuts

» In a large bowl, cream the butter, peanut butter and sugars until light and fluffy. Add eggs, one at a time, beating well after each addition. Beat in extracts. Combine the flour, baking soda and salt; gradually add to the creamed mixture and mix well. Stir in nuts.

» Drop by tablespoonfuls 2 in. apart onto greased baking sheets. Flatten with a glass dipped in sugar. Bake at 350° for 10-12 minutes or until the edges are lightly browned. Remove to wire racks to cool.

Yield: 8-1/2 dozen.

chocolate-dipped orange cookies

These tender cookies are pretty to look at—and the delicious flavor combination of cream cheese, orange, chocolate and almonds makes them irresistible.

Linda Call • Falun, Kansas

1 cup butter, softened

1 package (8 ounces) cream cheese, softened

1 cup sugar

1/2 teaspoon vanilla extract

2 tablespoons grated orange peel

2-1/2 cups all-purpose flour

1/2 teaspoon salt

1 cup finely chopped blanched almonds

GLAZE:
5 ounces semisweet chocolate, chopped

3 tablespoons butter

1/4 cup finely chopped blanched almonds

» In a large bowl, cream the butter, cream cheese and sugar until light and fluffy. Beat in vanilla and orange peel. Combine the flour and salt; gradually add to creamed mixture and mix well. Stir in almonds.

» Roll into 1-in. balls. Place 2 in. apart on ungreased baking sheets. Flatten with a glass dipped in sugar. Bake at 325° for 20-25 minutes or until firm. Remove to wire racks to cool.

» For glaze, in a microwave, melt chocolate and butter; stir until smooth. Dip each cookie halfway into chocolate; allow excess to drip off. Immediately sprinkle with almonds. Place on waxed paper until set.

Yield: 6 dozen.

raspberry nut pinwheels

A number of years ago, I won first prize in a recipe contest with these delectable swirls. The taste of raspberries and walnuts really comes through in each bite, and they're so much fun to make!

Pat Habiger • Spearville, Kansas

1/2 cup butter, softened

1 cup sugar

1 egg

1 teaspoon vanilla extract

2 cups all-purpose flour

1 teaspoon baking powder

1/4 cup seedless raspberry jam

3/4 cup finely chopped walnuts

» In a large bowl, cream butter and sugar until light and fluffy. Beat in egg and vanilla. Combine flour and baking powder; gradually add to creamed mixture and mix well.

» Roll out dough between waxed paper into a 12-in. square. Remove top piece of waxed paper. Spread dough with jam and sprinkle with nuts. Roll up tightly jelly-roll style; wrap in plastic wrap. Refrigerate for 2 hours or until firm.

» Unwrap dough and cut into 1/4-in. slices. Place 2 in. apart on ungreased baking sheets. Bake at 375° for 9-12 minutes or until edges are lightly browned. Remove to wire racks to cool.

Yield: about 3-1/2 dozen.

oatmeal kiss cookies

This oatmeal cookie is a nice change from the usual peanut butter kiss cookie. Children enjoy unwrapping the chocolate kisses.

Anna Mary Knier • Mount Joy, Pennsylvania

1/2 cup butter, softened

1/2 cup shortening

1 cup sugar

1 cup packed brown sugar

2 eggs

2 cups all-purpose flour

1 teaspoon baking soda

1 teaspoon salt

2-1/4 cups quick-cooking oats

1 cup chopped nuts

72 milk chocolate kisses

» In a large bowl, cream the butter, shortening and sugars until light and fluffy. Add eggs, one at a time, beating well after each addition. Combine the flour, baking soda and salt; gradually add to creamed mixture and mix well. Stir in oats and nuts. Roll into 1-in. balls. Place 2 in. apart on ungreased baking sheets.

» Bake at 375° for 10-12 minutes or until lightly browned. Immediately press a chocolate kiss in the center of each cookie. Remove to wire racks.

Yield: 6 dozen.

hidden mint morsels

Is it a cookie or a candy? No matter which answer folks choose, they find these minty morsels yummy. The recipe makes so much that you can whip up dozens of gifts at once.

Adina Skilbred • Prairie du Sac, Wisconsin

1/3 cup shortening

1/3 cup butter, softened

3/4 cup sugar

1 egg

1 tablespoon 2% milk

1 teaspoon vanilla extract

1-3/4 cups all-purpose flour

1/3 cup baking cocoa

1-1/2 teaspoons baking powder

1/4 teaspoon salt

1/8 teaspoon ground cinnamon

PEPPERMINT LAYER:

4 cups confectioners' sugar

6 tablespoons light corn syrup

6 tablespoons butter, melted

2 to 3 teaspoons peppermint extract

CHOCOLATE COATING:

2 packages (11-1/2 ounces each) milk chocolate chips

1/4 cup shortening

» In a large bowl, cream the shortening, butter and sugar until light and fluffy. Beat in the egg, milk and vanilla. Combine the flour, cocoa, baking powder, salt and cinnamon; gradually add to creamed mixture. Cover and chill for 8 hours or overnight.

» On a lightly floured surface, roll dough to 1/8-in. thickness. Cut with a lightly floured 1/2-in. round cookie cutter; place on ungreased baking sheets.

» Bake at 375° for 6-8 minutes or until set. Cool for 2 minutes before removing to wire racks to cool completely.

» In a large bowl, combine all the peppermint layer ingredients. Knead for 1 minute or until smooth. Shape into 120 balls, 1/2 in. each. Place a ball on each cookie and flatten to cover cookie. Place on waxed paper-lined baking sheets; refrigerate for 30 minutes.

» In a microwave, melt chips and shortening; stir until smooth. Spread about 1 teaspoonful over each cookie. Chill until firm.

Yield: about 10 dozen.

lemon angel wings

The light, lemony flavor of these treats is wonderful. With their unique shape, they look impressive.

Charolette Westfall • Houston, Texas

1-1/2 cups all-purpose flour

1 cup cold butter, cubed

1/2 cup sour cream

1 teaspoon grated lemon peel

10 tablespoons sugar, divided

» Place flour in a large bowl; cut in butter until crumbly. Stir in sour cream and lemon peel until well blended. Place on a piece of waxed paper; shape into a 4-1/2-in. square. Wrap in plastic wrap and refrigerate for at least 2 hours.

» Cut dough into four 2-1/4-in. squares. Place one square on a piece of waxed paper sprinkled with 2 tablespoons sugar. Cover with another piece of waxed paper. Keep remaining squares refrigerated. Roll out dough into a 12-in. x 5-in. rectangle, turning often to coat both sides with sugar.

» Lightly mark center of 12-in. side. Starting with a short side, roll up jelly-roll style to the center mark, peeling paper away while rolling. Repeat rolling from other short side, so the two rolls meet in the center and resemble a scroll.

» Wrap in plastic wrap and refrigerate. Repeat with remaining squares, using 2 tablespoons sugar for each. Chill for 1 hour.

» Unwrap dough and cut into 1/2-in. slices; dip each side in remaining sugar. Place 2 in. apart on foil-lined baking sheets. Bake at 375° for 14 minutes or until golden brown. Turn cookies over; bake 5 minutes longer. Remove to wire racks to cool.

Yield: 3 dozen.

hazelnut shortbread

Traditional shortbread only contains flour, sugar and butter, resulting in a rich, crumbly cookie. This cookie gets added flavor from chopped hazelnuts, some maple syrup and a touch of chocolate.

Karen Morrell • Canby, Oregon

1 cup butter, softened

1/2 cup sugar

2 tablespoons maple syrup or honey

2 teaspoons vanilla extract

2 cups all-purpose flour

1-1/4 cups finely chopped hazelnuts

1/2 cup each white, red, green, yellow and dark chocolate
    candy coating disks

» In a large bowl, cream butter and sugar until light and fluffy. Add syrup and vanilla. Beat in flour just until combined; fold in nuts. Shape into two 1-1/2-in. rolls; wrap tightly in waxed paper. Chill for 2 hours or until firm.

» Cut into 1/4-in. slices and place 2 in. apart on ungreased baking sheets. Bake at 325° for 14-16 minutes or until edges begin to brown. Remove to wire racks to cool.

» In separate microwave-safe bowls, melt candy coating disks; stir until smooth. Drizzle over cookies. Let stand until set.

Yield: 6 dozen.

pecan crescent cookies

Rich, delicate and absolutely irresistible, these old-fashioned nut cookies were one of Mom's specialties.

Grace Yaskovic • Lake Hiawatha, New Jersey

1 cup butter, softened

1/2 cup sugar

1 teaspoon vanilla extract

2 cups all-purpose flour

1 cup finely chopped pecans

Confectioners' sugar

» In a large bowl, cream butter, sugar and vanilla until light and fluffy. Gradually add flour. Stir in pecans.

» Shape rounded teaspoonfuls of dough into 2-1/2-in. logs and shape into crescents. Place 1 in. apart on ungreased baking sheets.

» Bake at 325° for 20-22 minutes or until set and bottoms are lightly browned. Let stand for 2-3 minutes before removing to wire racks to cool. Dust with confectioners' sugar before serving.

Yield: 6 dozen.

slice 'n' bake fruitcake cookies

1 cup butter, softened

1 cup confectioners' sugar

1/2 cup sugar

1 egg

2 teaspoons vanilla extract

2-1/4 cups all-purpose flour

1/2 teaspoon baking soda

1/2 cup raisins

1/2 cup each red and green candied cherries, chopped

» In a large bowl, cream butter and sugars until light and fluffy. Beat in egg and vanilla. Combine the flour and baking soda; gradually add to creamed mixture and mix well. Fold in raisins and cherries. Shape dough into two 2-in.-thick logs; wrap each in plastic wrap. Refrigerate for 2 hours or until firm.

» Cut logs into 1/4-in. slices. Place 2 in. apart on ungreased baking sheets. Bake at 350° for 12-15 minutes or until lightly browned. Remove to wire racks to cool.

Yield: 5 dozen.

A cross between classic fruitcake and buttery cookies, these treats are perfect for Christmas. Each one is bursting with raisins and candied cherries.

Marlene Robinson • Sexsmith, Alberta

spiced christmas cookies

This wonderful cookie recipe has been passed down through six generations and was brought to America from Germany in 1846. It's a tradition in our house and one we're proud to share.

Tanya Juhasz • Newberry, Florida

2 cups molasses

1 cup butter, melted

1 cup (8 ounces) sour cream

1 tablespoon lemon juice

8 cups all-purpose flour

1 cup packed brown sugar

3 teaspoons each ground cinnamon, nutmeg and cloves

2-1/4 teaspoons baking soda

1 teaspoon grated lemon peel

3/4 teaspoon salt

3 cups chopped walnuts

1-2/3 cups raisins

1/4 cup chopped candied lemon peel

1/4 cup chopped candied orange peel

FROSTING:
4-1/2 cups confectioners' sugar

1 cup heavy whipping cream

2 tablespoons lemon juice

GARNISH:
4 cups red and/or green candied cherries, cut as desired

» In a very large bowl, beat the molasses, butter, sour cream and lemon juice until well blended. Combine the flour, brown sugar, spices, baking soda, lemon peel and salt; gradually add to butter mixture and mix well. Stir in the walnuts, raisins and candied peels. Cover and refrigerate for 30 minutes or until easy to handle.

» Divide dough into four portions. On a lightly floured surface, roll out each portion to 1/4-in. thickness. Cut with a floured 2-1/4-in. round cookie cutter. Place 1 in. apart on ungreased baking sheets. Bake at 350° for 10-12 minutes or until bottoms are lightly browned. Remove to wire racks to cool.

» Combine frosting ingredients until smooth. Frost cookies; decorate with cherries. Store in an airtight container.

Yield: 7-1/2 dozen.

ranger cookies

These golden brown cookies are crispy on the outside and cake-like on the inside. Their tasty blend of oats, rice cereal, coconut and brown sugar have made them a favorite with our family. You won't be able to eat just one.

Mary Lou Boyce • Wilmington, Delaware

1 cup shortening

1 cup sugar

1 cup packed brown sugar

2 eggs

1 teaspoon vanilla extract

2 cups all-purpose flour

1 teaspoon baking soda

1/2 teaspoon baking powder

1/2 teaspoon salt

2 cups quick-cooking oats

2 cups crisp rice cereal

1 cup flaked coconut

» In a large bowl, cream shortening and sugars until light and fluffy. Beat in eggs and vanilla. Combine the flour, baking soda, baking powder and salt; gradually add to creamed mixture and mix well. Stir in the oats, cereal and coconut.

» Drop by rounded tablespoonfuls 2 in. apart onto ungreased baking sheets. Bake at 350° for 7-9 minutes or until golden brown. Remove to wire racks.

Yield: 7-1/2 dozen.

> » Transfer to a cutting board; cut with a serrated knife into scant 3/4-in. slices. Place cut side down on ungreased baking sheets. Bake for 5 minutes. Turn and bake 5-7 minutes longer or until firm and golden brown. Remove to wire racks to cool. Store in an airtight container.

Yield: 3 dozen.

torcetti

Our Sicilian grandmother often had my sister and I roll out the dough for these tasty "Torcetti." Their melt-in-your-mouth goodness is not too sweet but oh-so delicious.

Joy Quici • Upland, California

5 cups all-purpose flour

1 cup cold butter, cubed

1 cup shortening

1 package (1/4 ounce) active dry yeast

1/2 cup warm milk (110° to 115°)

2 eggs

1 tablespoon sugar

1-1/2 teaspoons vanilla extract

2 cups confectioners' sugar

Additional confectioners' sugar

> » Place flour in a large bowl; cut in butter and shortening until mixture resembles coarse crumbs. Set aside. In a large bowl, dissolve yeast in warm milk. Add the eggs, sugar, vanilla and 2 cups of the crumb mixture; beat until well blended. Gradually beat in remaining crumb mixture.

> » Turn onto a floured surface; knead for 3-4 minutes. Place in a greased bowl, turning once to grease top. Cover and let rise in a warm place until doubled, about 1 hour.

> » Punch dough down; divide into six portions. Shape each portion into twelve 6-in. ropes, about 1/4-in. thick; roll in confectioners' sugar. Shape each rope into a loop. Holding both ends of loop, twist together three times.

> » Place 2 in. apart on greased baking sheets. Bake at 375° for 12-14 minutes or until golden brown. Roll warm cookies in additional confectioners' sugar. Cool on wire racks.

Yield: 6 dozen.

lemon anise biscotti

With the growing popularity of gourmet coffees, cappuccino and espresso, I'm finding lots of people enjoy these classic dipping cookies.

Carrie Sherrill • Forestville, Wisconsin

2 eggs

1 cup sugar

1/4 cup canola oil

1/2 teaspoon lemon extract

1/4 teaspoon vanilla extract

2 cups all-purpose flour

1 teaspoon baking powder

1/2 teaspoon salt

4 teaspoons grated lemon peel

2 teaspoons aniseed, crushed

> » In a small bowl, beat eggs and sugar for 2 minutes or until thickened. Add oil and extracts; mix well. Combine the flour, baking powder and salt; beat into egg mixture. Stir in lemon peel and aniseed.

> » Divide dough in half. On a lightly floured surface, shape each portion into a 12-in. x 2-in. rectangle. Transfer to a baking sheet lined with parchment paper. Flatten to 1/2-in. thickness.

> » Bake at 350° for 30-35 minutes or until golden and tops begin to crack. Carefully remove to wire racks; cool for 5 minutes.

white chocolate raspberry thumbprints

When I pass around the cookie tray, all eyes land on these fancy thumbprints. The white chocolate filling and dab of jewel-toned jam will satisfy the most discriminating sweet tooth.

Agnes Ward • Stratford, Ontario

3/4 cup butter, softened

1/2 cup packed brown sugar

2 eggs, separated

1-1/4 cups all-purpose flour

1/4 cup baking cocoa

1-1/4 cups finely chopped pecans or walnuts

FILLING:
4 ounces white baking chocolate, coarsely chopped

2 tablespoons butter

1/4 cup seedless raspberry jam

» In a large bowl, cream butter and brown sugar until light and fluffy. Beat in egg yolks. Combine flour and cocoa; gradually add to creamed mixture and mix well. Cover and refrigerate for 1-2 hours or until easy to handle.

» In a shallow bowl, whisk egg whites until foamy. Place nuts in another shallow bowl. Shape dough into 1-in. balls. Dip in egg whites, then roll in nuts.

» Using a wooden spoon handle, make an indentation in center of each cookie. Place 1 in. apart on greased baking sheets. Bake at 350° for 8-10 minutes. Remove to wire racks to cool.

» In a microwave, melt white chocolate and butter; stir until smooth. Spoon about 1/2 teaspoon into each cookie. Top each with about 1/4 teaspoon jam. Store in an airtight container.

Yield: about 3 dozen.

sour cream sugar cookies

I make these cookies every Valentine's Day The heart-shaped treats stay soft for at least a week, and they look so pretty frosted bright pink, then piped with lacy frosting.

Carolyn Walton • Smoot, Wyoming

1 cup shortening

1 cup sugar

1 egg

1 cup (8 ounces) sour cream

1-1/2 teaspoons vanilla extract

4 cups all-purpose flour

1-1/2 teaspoons baking soda

1/4 teaspoon salt

FROSTING:
1 cup butter, softened

9 cups confectioners' sugar

3 teaspoons vanilla extract

2/3 to 3/4 cup 2% milk

Paste food coloring

» In a large bowl, cream shortening and sugar until light and fluffy. Beat in the egg, sour cream and vanilla. Combine the flour, baking soda and salt; gradually add to creamed mixture and mix well. Cover and chill for 1 hour or until easy to handle.

» On a lightly floured surface, roll dough to 1/4-in. thickness. Cut with a floured 3-in. heart-shaped cookie cutter.

» Place 1 in. apart on baking sheets lightly coated with cooking spray. Bake at 350° for 8-10 minutes or until set. Cool for 1 minute before removing to wire racks to cool completely.

» For frosting, in a large bowl, cream butter until light and fluffy. Beat in confectioners' sugar and vanilla. Add enough milk to achieve desired consistency. Tint with food coloring. Decorate cookies as desired.

Yield: about 4-1/2 dozen.

mocha chunk cookies

I'm always on the lookout for new dishes and desserts to try. I clipped this delicious recipe years ago and have been making it ever since.

Herbert Greene • Sonoma, California

1/4 cup instant coffee granules

2 tablespoons boiling water

1/2 cup butter, softened

3/4 cup sugar

1/2 cup packed brown sugar

1 egg

1 teaspoon vanilla extract

1-1/2 cups all-purpose flour

1/4 teaspoon baking soda

Dash salt

1 package (12 ounces) semisweet chocolate chunks

1-1/2 cups chopped walnuts, optional

» In a small bowl, combine coffee and water; set aside. In a large bowl, cream butter and sugars until light and fluffy. Beat in the egg and vanilla.

» Combine the flour, baking soda and salt; add to creamed mixture alternately with reserved coffee mixture, beating well after each addition. Stir in chocolate chunks and nuts if desired. Cover and refrigerate for 30 minutes.

» Shape tablespoonfuls of dough into balls. Place 2 in. apart on greased baking sheets. Bake at 350° for 10-12 minutes or until golden brown. Remove to wire racks to cool.

Yield: 3 dozen.

» Place solid and cutout cookies 1 in. apart on greased baking sheets. Bake at 375° for 7-9 minutes or until edges are lightly browned. Remove to wire racks.

» In a small bowl, combine the confectioners' sugar, water and vanilla; brush over warm cookies with cutout centers. Immediately sprinkle with colored sugar if desired. Spread 1/2 teaspoon of jam over the bottom of each solid cookie; place cookies with cutout centers over jam.

Yield: about 3-1/2 dozen.

chocolate-dipped peanut logs

A cookie exchange introduced me to these fancy peanut butter treats. They're eye-catching for bake sales.

Patricia Grall • Hortonville, Wisconsin

1 cup creamy peanut butter

1/2 cup butter, softened

1/2 cup shortening

1 cup sugar

1 cup packed brown sugar

2 eggs

2-1/2 cups all-purpose flour

1-1/2 teaspoons baking soda

1 teaspoon baking powder

1/4 teaspoon salt

8 ounces dark chocolate candy coating, coarsely chopped

2/3 cup ground salted peanuts

» In a large bowl, cream the peanut butter, butter, shortening and sugars until light and fluffy. Add eggs, one at a time, beating well after each addition. Combine the dry ingredients; gradually add to the creamed mixture and mix well.

» Shape into 2-in. logs. Place 2 in. apart on ungreased baking sheets. Bake at 350° for 8-10 minutes or until lightly browned. Remove to wire racks to cool.

» In a microwave, melt candy coating; stir until smooth. Dip one end of each cookie into coating; allow excess to drip of. Dip into peanuts. Place on waxed paper to set.

Yield: about 8-1/2 dozen.

EDITOR'S NOTE: Reduced-fat or generic brands of peanut butter are not recommended for this recipe.

sweetheart coconut cookies

Ruby red jam and colored sugar add a festive look to these crisp sandwich cookies that are perfect for Valentine's Day.

Jo Ellen Helmlinger • Columbus, Ohio

1 cup flaked coconut

1 cup sugar

3/4 cup cold butter, cubed

2-1/4 cups all-purpose flour

2 eggs, lightly beaten

1/2 teaspoon vanilla extract

GLAZE:

3/4 cup confectioners' sugar

1 tablespoon water

1/2 teaspoon vanilla extract

Red colored sugar, optional

1/2 cup seedless raspberry jam

» Place coconut and sugar in a food processor; cover and process until coconut is coarsely chopped. In a large bowl, cut butter into flour until crumbly. Stir in coconut mixture. Stir in eggs and vanilla.

» On a lightly floured surface, roll out dough to 1/8-in. thickness. Cut with a 2-1/2-in. heart-shaped cookie cutter dipped in flour. Using a 1-in. heart-shaped cookie cutter, cut out the center of half of the cookies. Reroll small cutouts if desired.

orange-pecan icebox cookies

These slice-and-bake cookies have a pleasant orange flavor but are not overly sweet. They are chock-full of pecans for a nice crunch.

Novella Cook • Hinton, West Virginia

1/2 cup butter, softened

1/2 cup shortening

1/2 cup sugar

1/2 cup packed brown sugar

1 egg

2 tablespoons orange juice

1 tablespoon grated orange peel

1/2 teaspoon lemon extract

1/2 teaspoon vanilla extract

2-3/4 cups all-purpose flour

1/2 teaspoon salt

1/2 teaspoon baking soda

1/4 teaspoon baking powder

1 cup finely chopped pecans

» In a large bowl, cream the butter, shortening and sugars until light and fluffy. Beat in the egg, orange juice, orange peel and extracts. Combine the flour, salt, baking soda and baking powder; gradually add to the creamed mixture and mix well. Stir in pecans. Shape dough into four 5-in. rolls; wrap each in plastic wrap. Refrigerate for 3-4 hours or until firm.

» Unwrap and cut into 1/4-in. slices. Place 2 in. apart on greased baking sheets. Bake at 350° for 9-10 minutes or until edges begin to brown. Remove to wire racks to cool.

Yield: about 6 dozen.

lara's tender gingersnaps

Soft gingersnaps embody the tastes and smells of the Christmas season, but are perfect for any fall potluck. I enjoy the flavors of cloves, cinnamon and ginger blended into one delicious snack.

Lara Pennell • Mauldin, South Carolina

1 cup packed brown sugar

3/4 cup butter, melted

1 egg

1/4 cup molasses

2-1/4 cups all-purpose flour

1-1/2 teaspoons ground ginger

1 teaspoon baking soda

1 teaspoon ground cinnamon

1/2 teaspoon ground cloves

1/4 cup sugar

» In a large bowl, beat brown sugar and butter until blended. Beat in egg, then molasses. Combine the flour, ginger, baking soda, cinnamon and cloves; gradually add to brown sugar mixture and mix well (dough will be stiff). Cover and refrigerate for at least 2 hours.

» Shape dough into 1 in. balls. Roll in sugar. Place 2 in. apart on baking sheets coated with cooking spray. Bake at 350° for 9-11 minutes or until set. Cool for 1 minute before removing from pans to wire racks.

Yield: 3 dozen.

bars & brownies

peanut butter brownie bars

This simple treat will appeal to adults and children alike. Creamy peanut butter, crunchy nuts and crisp cereal make the bars fun to bite into. The recipe makes a lot so these are great for parties.

Radelle Knappenberger • Oviedo, Florida

1 package fudge brownie mix
  (13-inch x 9-inch pan size)

12 peanut butter cups, chopped

1/2 cup salted peanuts, chopped

2 cups (12 ounces) semisweet chocolate chips

1-1/4 cups creamy peanut butter

1 tablespoon butter

1/8 teaspoon salt

1-1/2 cups crisp rice cereal

1 teaspoon vanilla extract

» Prepare brownie batter according to package directions. Spread into a greased 13-in. x 9-in. baking pan. Bake at 350° for 20-25 minutes or until a toothpick inserted near the center comes out with moist crumbs.

» Sprinkle with peanut butter cups and peanuts. Bake 4-6 minutes longer or until chocolate is melted. Cool on a wire rack.

» Meanwhile, in a large saucepan, combine the chocolate chips, peanut butter, butter and salt. Cook and stir until chips are melted and mixture is smooth. Remove from the heat; stir in cereal and vanilla. Carefully spread over brownies. Cover and refrigerate for at least 2 hours before cutting.

Yield: 3 dozen.

creamy cashew brownies

My sister-in-law dubbed me the "dessert queen" because of treats like this that I take to our family get-togethers. The brownies have a fudge-like texture and a rich cream cheese topping. Cashews and a hot fudge swirl make them special.

Karen Wagner • Danville, Illinois

1 package fudge brownie mix (13-inch x 9-inch pan size)

1/3 cup water

1/4 cup canola oil

1 egg

1 cup (6 ounces) semisweet chocolate chips

2 packages (8 ounces each) cream cheese, softened

1-1/2 cups confectioners' sugar

1 teaspoon vanilla extract

1 cup salted cashews, coarsely chopped

1/2 cup hot fudge ice cream topping, warmed

» In a large bowl, combine the brownie mix, water, oil and egg. Stir in the chips. Spread into a greased 13-in. x 9-in. baking pan.

» Bake at 350° for 25-27 minutes or until a toothpick inserted near the center comes out clean (do not overbake). Cool on a wire rack.

» For topping, in a bowl, beat cream cheese, confectioners' sugar and vanilla until smooth. Spread over brownies. Sprinkle with cashews; drizzle with hot fudge topping. Refrigerate before cutting into bars. Store in the refrigerator.

Yield: 2 dozen.

My young sons are crazy about these simple, fast-fixing cookie bars. And as an on-the-go mom, easy preparation makes this one scrumptious dessert I can rely on—even at the last minute. You might want to vary the jam or jelly to suit your own family's tastes.

Carolyn Mulloy • Davison, Michigan

peanut butter 'n' jelly bars

1 tube (16-1/2 ounces) refrigerated peanut butter cookie dough

1/2 cup peanut butter chips

1 can (16 ounces) buttercream frosting

1/4 cup creamy peanut butter

1/4 cup seedless raspberry jam or grape jelly

» Let dough stand at room temperature for 5-10 minutes to soften. Press into an ungreased 13-in. x 9-in. baking dish; sprinkle with peanut butter chips.

» Bake at 375° for 15-18 minutes or until lightly browned and edges are firm to the touch. Cool on a wire rack.

» In a small bowl, beat frosting and peanut butter until smooth. Spread over bars. Drop jam by teaspoonfuls over frosting; cut through frosting with a knife to swirl the jam.

Yield: 2 dozen.

brownie mallow bars

These yummy sweets are appreciated wherever I take them. A brownie mix streamlines assembly of the chewy bars, which are topped with mini marshmallows and a decadent layer of chocolate, peanut butter and crisp cereal.

Stacy Butler • Lees Summit, Missouri

1 package fudge brownie mix (13-inch x 9-inch pan size)

1 package (10-1/2 ounces) miniature marshmallows

2 cups (12 ounces) semisweet chocolate chips

1 cup peanut butter

1 tablespoon butter

1-1/2 cups crisp rice cereal

» Prepare the brownie batter according to package directions for fudge-like brownies. Pour the batter into greased 13-in. x 9-in. baking pan.

» Bake at 350° for 28-30 minutes. Top with marshmallows; bake 3 minutes longer (marshmallows will not be completely melted). Cool on a wire rack.

» In a microwave-safe bowl, melt the chocolate chips, peanut butter and butter; stir until smooth. Stir in the cereal and spread over brownies. Refrigerate for 1-2 hours or until firm before cutting.

Yield: 2-1/2 dozen.

blueberry bars

Our three sons like these bars so much that after they were married, each of my daughters-in-law asked for the directions.

Sue Neilson • Lansdale, Pennsylvania

1 cup butter, softened

1-3/4 cups sugar

4 eggs

1 teaspoon vanilla extract

3 cups all-purpose flour

1-1/2 teaspoons baking powder

1/2 teaspoon salt

1 can (21 ounces) blueberry pie filling

1/8 teaspoon ground nutmeg

GLAZE:
1-1/4 cups confectioners' sugar

2 tablespoons lemon juice

1 tablespoon butter, melted

» In a large bowl, cream butter and sugar until light and fluffy. Add eggs, one at a time, beating well after each addition. Beat in vanilla. Combine the flour, baking powder and salt; add to creamed mixture just until combined.

» Spread half of the batter into a greased 15-in. x 10-in. x 1-in. baking pan. Spread with pie filling; sprinkle with nutmeg. Drop remaining batter by teaspoonfuls over the top.

» Bake at 350° for 40-45 minutes or until golden brown. In a small bowl, combine the glaze ingredients until smooth. Drizzle over warm bars. Cool completely on a wire rack.

Yield: 4 dozen.

cream cheese brownies

Brownies are a common dessert in our household—they're just about the only form of chocolate my husband will eat! I love this rendition that makes a big batch and has a rich cream-cheese layer in the center.

Barbara Nitcznski • Denver, Colorado

4 ounces unsweetened chocolate, chopped

1/2 cup butter, cubed

4 eggs

2 cups sugar

2 teaspoons vanilla extract

1-1/2 cups all-purpose flour

1 cup chopped nuts, optional

FILLING:
2 packages (8 ounces each) cream cheese, softened

1/2 cup sugar

1 egg

2 teaspoons vanilla extract

» In a microwave, melt chocolate and butter; stir until smooth. Cool slightly. In a large bowl, beat eggs and sugar. Stir in vanilla and chocolate mixture. Gradually add flour to chocolate mixture (batter will be thick). Stir in nuts if desired.

» Spread half of the batter evenly into a greased 13-in. x 9-in. baking pan; set aside.

» In a small bowl, beat the filling ingredients until blended. Gently spread over batter. Spoon remaining batter over filling; spread to cover.

» Bake at 350° for 45-50 minutes or until filling is set. Cool on a wire rack for 1 hour.

» Refrigerate the brownies for at least 2 hours. Cut into bars. Refrigerate leftovers.

Yield: 4 dozen.

storing bars & brownies

Cover a pan of uncut bars and brownies with foil, or place the pan in a large resealable bag. (If made with perishable ingredients, like cream cheese, store the bars, covered, in the refrigerator.) Once they are cut, store in an airtight container.

apricot date squares

Memories of my mom's fruity date bars inspired me to devise this wonderful treat. I've had great results replacing the apricot jam with orange marmalade.

Shannon Koene • Blacksburg, Virginia

1 cup water

1 cup sugar

1 cup chopped dates

1/2 cup 100% apricot spreadable fruit or jam

1-3/4 cups old-fashioned oats

1-1/2 cups all-purpose flour

1 cup flaked coconut

1 cup packed brown sugar

1 teaspoon ground cinnamon

1/4 teaspoon salt

3/4 cup cold butter, cubed

» In a small saucepan, combine the water, sugar and dates. Bring to a boil. Reduce the heat; simmer, uncovered, for 30-35 minutes or until mixture is reduced to 1-1/3 cups and is slightly thickened, stirring occasionally.

» Remove from the heat. Stir in spreadable fruit until blended; set aside. In a food processor, combine the oats, flour, coconut, brown sugar, cinnamon and salt. Add butter; cover and process until mixture resembles coarse crumbs.

» Press 3 cups crumb mixture into a 13-in. x 9-in. baking dish coated with cooking spray. Spread date mixture to within 1/2 in. of edges. Sprinkle with remaining crumb mixture; press down gently.

» Bake at 350° for 20-25 minutes or until edges are lightly browned. Cool on a wire rack. Cut into squares.

Yield: 3 dozen.

» Pour into a greased 15-in. x 10-in. x 1-in. baking pan. Bake at 350° for 18-22 minutes or until a toothpick inserted near the center comes out clean. Cool on a wire rack.

» For frosting, in a large bowl, beat cream cheese and butter until light and fluffy. Beat in vanilla. Gradually add confectioners' sugar until smooth. Spread over bars. Store in the refrigerator.

Yield: 3 dozen.

honey-oat granola bars

I found these bars in a monthly newsletter I subscribe to. We eat a few of them each day. It's a basic recipe to which you can add any of your favorite flavors—coconut, chocolate or different flavored chips, nuts or dried fruits.

Jean Boyce • New Ulm, Minnesota

4 cups quick-cooking oats

1 cup packed brown sugar

1 cup chopped salted peanuts

1 cup (6 ounces) semisweet chocolate chips

1/2 cup sunflower kernels

3/4 cup butter, melted

2/3 cup honey

1 teaspoon vanilla extract

» In a bowl, combine oats, brown sugar, peanuts, chocolate chips and sunflower kernels. Stir in butter, honey and vanilla until combined (mixture will be crumbly). Press into a greased parchment paper-lined 15-in. x 10-in. x 1-in. baking pan.

» Bake at 350° for 15-20 minutes or until browned and bubbly. Cool for 15 minutes on a wire rack; cut into squares. Cool completely before removing from pan.

Yield: 3 dozen.

banana nut bars

My sister gave me this recipe, which is always in demand with family and friends. It's amazing how fast these tempting bars vanish when I serve them!

Susan Huckaby • Smiths, Alabama

1 cup butter, cubed

1/2 cup water

1-1/2 cups sugar

1/2 cup packed brown sugar

1 cup mashed ripe bananas (about 2 medium)

1/2 cup buttermilk

2 eggs

1 teaspoon vanilla extract

2 cups all-purpose flour

1 teaspoon baking soda

1/2 cup chopped pecans or walnuts

FROSTING:
1 package (8 ounces) cream cheese, softened

1/2 cup butter, softened

1 teaspoon vanilla extract

3-1/2 cups confectioners' sugar

» In a small saucepan, bring butter and water to a boil. Remove from the heat; set aside. In a large bowl, beat the sugars, bananas, buttermilk, eggs and vanilla until blended. Combine flour and baking soda; gradually add to sugar mixture. Beat in butter mixture until blended. Stir in nuts.

triple-layer mocha bars

These blue-ribbon bars win kudos from everyone who tries them. Coconut and walnuts add fun flair, and the homemade mocha frosting just can't be beat.

Marjorie Van Riper • Ralston, Nebraska

1-3/4 cups all-purpose flour

2/3 cup packed brown sugar

3/4 cup cold butter, cubed

FILLING:

3 eggs

1/2 cup sugar

2 teaspoons vanilla extract

3/4 cup chocolate malted milk powder

1/4 cup all-purpose flour

1 teaspoon baking soda

1/4 teaspoon salt

1 cup flaked coconut

1/2 cup chopped walnuts

FROSTING:

1-1/2 cups confectioners' sugar

3 tablespoons chocolate malted milk powder

2 tablespoons brewed coffee

2 tablespoons butter, melted

1 teaspoon vanilla extract

» In a large bowl, combine the flour and brown sugar; cut in butter until crumbly. Press into a greased 13-in. x 9-in. baking pan. Bake at 350° for 8-10 minutes or until golden brown.

» In another large bowl, beat eggs until foamy. Add the sugar and vanilla; mix well. Combine the malted milk powder, flour, baking soda and salt; add to egg mixture. Fold in the coconut and walnuts.

» Spread over prepared crust. Bake for 25-30 minutes or until a toothpick inserted near the center comes out clean. Cool on a wire rack.

» In a small bowl, combine the frosting ingredients. Spread over cooled bars. Store in the refrigerator.

Yield: about 3 dozen.

peanut mallow bars

Big and little kids alike look forward to eating these snacks that have all the taste of Payday candy bars. Not only do they beat the clock when time is tight, but they make great contributions to bake sales.

Janice Huelsmann • Trenton, Illinois

1 package (18-1/4 ounces) yellow cake mix

2 tablespoons water

1/3 cup butter, softened

1 egg

4 cups miniature marshmallows

PEANUT TOPPING:

1 package (10 ounces) peanut butter chips

2/3 cup light corn syrup

1/4 cup butter, cubed

2 cups crisp rice cereal

2 cups salted peanuts

2 teaspoons vanilla extract

» In a large bowl, beat the cake mix, water, butter and egg until blended (batter will be thick). Spread into a greased 13-in. x 9-in. baking pan.

» Bake at 350° for 22-25 minutes or until a toothpick inserted near the center comes out clean. Sprinkle with marshmallows. Bake 2 minutes longer or until marshmallows are melted. Place on a wire rack.

» In a large saucepan, combine the peanut butter chips, corn syrup and butter; cook and stir over medium-low heat until smooth. Remove from the heat; stir in the cereal, peanuts and vanilla. Spread over marshmallows. Cool completely.

Yield: 2-1/2 dozen.

caramel brownies

My family can't possibly eat all of the sweets I whip up, so my coworkers are quite happy to sample them...particularly these rich brownies that are full of caramel, chocolate chips and walnuts.

Clara Bakke • Coon Rapids, Minnesota

2 cups sugar

3/4 cup baking cocoa

1 cup canola oil

4 eggs

1/4 cup 2% milk

1-1/2 cups all-purpose flour

1 teaspoon salt

1 teaspoon baking powder

1 cup (6 ounces) semisweet chocolate chips

1 cup chopped walnuts, divided

1 package (14 ounces) caramels

1 can (14 ounces) sweetened condensed milk

» In a large bowl, beat the sugar, cocoa, oil, eggs and milk. Combine the flour, salt and baking powder; gradually add to egg mixture until well blended. Fold in chocolate chips and 1/2 cup walnuts.

» Spoon two-thirds of the batter into a greased 13-in. x 9-in. baking pan. Bake at 350° for 12 minutes.

» Meanwhile, in a large saucepan, heat the caramels and condensed milk over low heat until caramels are melted. Pour over baked brownie layer. Sprinkle with remaining walnuts.

» Drop remaining batter by teaspoonfuls over caramel layer; carefully swirl brownie batter with a knife.

» Bake 35-40 minutes longer or until a toothpick inserted near the center comes out with moist crumbs (do not overbake). Cool on a wire rack.

Yield: 2 dozen.

chocolate pecan bars

These chewy, chocolaty bars are great for any special occasion...and always a big hit with everyone. They're easy to prepare and make a big batch. We find them simply irresistible!

Carole Fraser • North York, Ontario

2/3 cup butter, softened

1/3 cup sugar

2 cups all-purpose flour

FILLING:
6 ounces semisweet chocolate, chopped

1-1/4 cups light corn syrup

1-1/4 cups sugar

4 eggs, lightly beaten

1-1/4 teaspoons vanilla extract

2-1/4 cups chopped pecans

GLAZE:
4 ounces semisweet chocolate, chopped

1-1/4 teaspoons shortening

» In a small bowl, cream butter and sugar until light and fluffy. Beat in flour. Press into a greased 15-in. x 10-in. x 1-in. baking pan. Bake at 350° for 12-15 minutes or until golden brown.

» Meanwhile, in a large saucepan, melt chocolate with corn syrup over low heat; stir until smooth. Remove from the heat. Stir in the sugar, eggs and vanilla. Add pecans.

» Spread evenly over hot crust. Bake for 25-30 minutes or until firm around the edges. Cool on a wire rack.

» In a microwave, melt the chocolate and shortening; stir until smooth. Drizzle over bars.

Yield: 4 dozen.

Looking for an easy way to transform plain old refrigerated cookie dough into something special enough for guests? Try this treat! I dress up the bars with chocolate chips, coconut and nuts.

Shirley Dehler • Columbus, Wisconsin

fancy sugar cookie bars

1 tube (16-1/2 ounces) refrigerated sugar cookie dough

1 cup semisweet chocolate chips

1/2 cup flaked coconut

1/4 cup chopped pecans

» Let dough stand at room temperature for 5-10 minutes to soften. Press into an ungreased 13-in. x 9-in. baking pan. Bake at 350° for 10-12 minutes or until golden brown.

» Sprinkle with the chocolate chips, coconut and pecans. Bake 10-12 minutes longer or until golden brown. Cool in pan on a wire rack.

Yield: 2 dozen.

ginger cranberry bars

These beautiful bars were among the winners of a cranberry festival bake-off. They're tangy, chunky and unique.

Lynn Newman • Gainesville, Florida

1 cup butter, softened

1/2 cup sugar

2 teaspoons almond extract, divided

2 cups all-purpose flour

2 cans (16 ounces each) whole-berry cranberry sauce

2 tablespoons chopped crystallized ginger

3 egg whites

1/2 cup confectioners' sugar

1/2 cup sliced almonds

» In a large bowl, cream butter and sugar until light and fluffy. Stir in 1-1/2 teaspoons almond extract. Beat in flour until crumbly.

» Press into a greased 13-in. x 9-in. baking dish. Bake at 350° for 25-28 minutes or until golden brown.

» Meanwhile, in a small saucepan, heat cranberry sauce and ginger. In a small bowl, beat egg whites on medium speed until soft peaks form. Gradually beat in confectioners' sugar, 1 tablespoon at a time, and remaining extract on high until stiff glossy peaks form. Spread cranberry mixture over crust. Spread meringue over cranberry layer; sprinkle with almonds.

» Increase heat to 400°. Bake for 14-15 minutes or until lightly browned. Cool completely before cutting. Refrigerate the leftovers.

Yield: 2 dozen.

pecan pie bars

I love to cook large quantities and do most of the cooking for our church functions. People seem to enjoy this scrumptious treat even more than pecan pie.

Clara Honeyager • North Prairie, Wisconsin

6 cups all-purpose flour

1-1/2 cups sugar

1 teaspoon salt

2 cups cold butter, cubed

FILLING:

8 eggs

3 cups sugar

3 cups corn syrup

1/2 cup butter, melted

3 teaspoons vanilla extract

5 cups chopped pecans

» In a large bowl, combine the flour, sugar and salt. Cut in butter until crumbly. Press onto the bottom and up the sides of two greased 15-in. x 10-in. x 1-in. baking pans. Bake at 350° for 18-22 minutes or until crust edges are beginning to brown and bottom is set.

» For filling, combine the eggs, sugar, corn syrup, butter and vanilla in a large bowl. Stir in pecans. Pour over crust.

» Bake 25-30 minutes longer or until edges are firm and center is almost set. Cool on wire racks. Cut into bars. Refrigerate until serving.

Yield: 6-8 dozen.

raspberry nut bars

If you need a special dessert for a potluck, try this one. These bars are not overly sweet and have a wonderful crunch from the pecans.

Beth Ask • Ulster, Pennsylvania

3/4 cup butter, softened

1/3 cup packed brown sugar

1/4 cup sugar

1 egg

1 teaspoon vanilla extract

2 cups all-purpose flour

1 teaspoon baking powder

1/4 teaspoon baking soda

1/4 teaspoon salt

3/4 cup chopped pecans, divided

2/3 cup raspberry jam

2 tablespoons lemon juice

GLAZE:
1/2 cup confectioners' sugar

2 teaspoons 2% milk

» In a large bowl, cream the butter and sugars until light and fluffy. Beat in the egg and vanilla. Combine the flour, baking powder, baking soda and salt; add to the creamed mixture. Stir in 1/2 cup pecans.

» Spread half of the dough into a greased 13-in. x 9-in. baking pan. Combine jam and lemon juice until blended; spread over dough. Dollop remaining dough over top. Sprinkle with remaining pecans.

» Bake at 325° for 30-35 minutes or until lightly browned. Cool. Combine glaze ingredients; drizzle over bars.

Yield: 3 dozen.

spreading jam

If jam is too stiff to easily spread over cookie dough, you may tear the bottom of the bar. To make it spread easier, warm slightly in a microwave. It will only take a few seconds to warm…you don't want the jam to be runny.

double chocolate orange brownies

I have to give my husband credit for this idea—since we love chocolate and orange together, he suggested I create a brownie featuring both. Now they're not only his first-pick for a snack, but also my whole gang's…I'm always asked to bake them for family gatherings.

Elinor Townsend • North Grafton, Massachusetts

3/4 cup butter, cubed

4 ounces unsweetened chocolate, chopped

3 eggs

2 cups sugar

1 teaspoon orange extract

1 cup all-purpose flour

1 cup (6 ounces) semisweet chocolate chips

Confectioners' sugar

» In a microwave, melt butter and chocolate; stir until smooth. Cool slightly. In a large bowl, beat eggs and sugar. Stir in chocolate mixture. Beat in extract. Gradually add flour to chocolate mixture.

» Pour into a greased 13-in. x 9-in. baking dish. Sprinkle with chips. Bake at 350° for 30-35 minutes or until a toothpick inserted near the center comes out clean (do not overbake).

» Cool completely on a wire rack. Cut into squares. Just before serving, sprinkle with confectioners' sugar.

Yield: 2 dozen.

diamond almond bars

Making these chewy almond bars has been a tradition in our family for generations. They're especially popular at holidays. But be sure to freeze several dozen to enjoy later.

Liz Green • Tamworth, Ontario

1 cup butter, softened

1 cup plus 1 tablespoon sugar, divided

1 egg, separated

1 teaspoon almond extract

2 cups all-purpose flour

1/2 cup blanched sliced almonds

1/4 teaspoon ground cinnamon

» In a large bowl, cream butter and 1 cup sugar until light and fluffy. Add egg yolk; beat well. Stir in extract. Add flour, beating until combined.

» Press into a greased 15-in. x 10-in. x 1-in. baking pan. Beat egg white until foamy; brush over dough. Top with almonds. Combine cinnamon and remaining sugar; sprinkle over top.

» Bake at 350° for 25-30 minutes or until lightly browned (do not overbake). Cool on a wire rack for 10 minutes. Cut into diamond-shaped bars. Cool completely.

Yield: 5 dozen.

caramel cereal treats

I've received a lot of praise for these snacks. Even my husband's friends at work request the sweet, crispy treats.

Laurie Lingenfelter • Nevada, Iowa

8 cups Sugar Smacks cereal

1-3/4 cups dry roasted peanuts

1 package (14 ounces) caramels

1/2 cup sweetened condensed milk

1 tablespoon butter

1/2 cup milk chocolate chips

» In a large bowl, combine cereal and peanuts; set aside. In a large microwave-safe bowl, combine the caramels, milk and butter. Microwave, uncovered, on high for 1-2 minutes or until caramels are melted, stirring every 30 seconds.

» Pour over cereal mixture; stir to coat. With greased hands, pat mixture into a greased 15-in. x 10-in. x 1-in. pan.

» In a microwave, melt the chips; stir until smooth. Cool slightly. Drizzle the chocolate over caramels. Let stand until set. Cut into bars.

Yield: 3-1/2 dozen.

EDITOR'S NOTE: This recipe was tested in a 1,100-watt microwave.

grandma's chocolate chip bars

My grandmother made this delicious dessert with a unique meringue topping for every special occasion. She's now gone, but her wonderful recipe lives on.

Sandy Hartig • New Berlin, Wisconsin

1 cup shortening

1/2 cup sugar

1/2 cup packed brown sugar

3 egg yolks

1 tablespoon water

1 teaspoon vanilla extract

2 cups all-purpose flour

1 teaspoon baking powder

1/2 teaspoon salt

1/4 teaspoon baking soda

1 cup semisweet chocolate chips

TOPPING:
3 egg whites

1 teaspoon vanilla extract

1/8 teaspoon salt

1 cup packed brown sugar

1/4 cup chopped walnuts

» In a large bowl, cream shortening and sugars until light and fluffy. Beat in the egg yolks, water and vanilla. Combine the flour, baking powder, salt and baking soda; gradually add to creamed mixture and mix well. Stir in chocolate chips.

» Spread into a greased 13-in. x 9-in. baking pan. Bake at 350° for 15 minutes or until top is dry.

» Meanwhile, in a large bowl, beat egg whites, vanilla and salt on medium speed until soft peaks form. Gradually beat in brown sugar, 1 tablespoon at a time on high until stiff peaks form.

» Spread over warm crust to within 1 in. of edges. Sprinkle with walnuts. Bake for 25 minutes or until a toothpick inserted near center comes out clean. Cool on a wire rack. Cut into bars.

Yield: 2 dozen.

raspberry coconut bars

I've been whipping up these delectable bars for years, and now my daughter enjoys helping me. I bake them every Christmas and have received many compliments. The chocolate drizzle makes such a pretty lacy effect.

Barb Bovberg • Fort Collins, Colorado

1-2/3 cups graham cracker crumbs

1/2 cup butter, melted

2-2/3 cups flaked coconut

1 can (14 ounces) sweetened condensed milk

1 cup seedless raspberry preserves

1/3 cup chopped walnuts, toasted

1/2 cup semisweet chocolate chips

1/4 cup white baking chips

» In a small bowl, combine cracker crumbs and butter. Press into a 13-in. x 9-in. baking dish coated with cooking spray. Sprinkle with coconut; drizzle with milk.

» Bake at 350° for 20-25 minutes or until lightly browned. Cool completely on a wire rack.

» Spread preserves over the crust. Sprinkle with walnuts. In a microwave, melt chocolate chips; stir until smooth. Drizzle over walnuts. Repeat with white chips. Cut into bars. Refrigerate for 30 minutes or until chocolate is set.

Yield: 3 dozen.

apricot bars

I created this recipe last winter and have had so many favorable comments from those who have sampled it. Great apricot flavor and a sprinkling of coconut make these bars so special!

Barbara Rohlf • Spirit Lake, Iowa

1 package (16 ounces) pound cake mix

4 eggs

1/2 cup butter, melted

2 teaspoons vanilla extract, divided

1 cup chopped dried apricots

1 package (8 ounces) cream cheese, softened

2 cups confectioners' sugar

1/2 cup apricot preserves

3/4 cup flaked coconut

3/4 cup sliced almonds

» In a large bowl, combine the cake mix, 2 eggs, butter and 1 teaspoon vanilla; beat until well blended. Fold in dried apricots. Spread the batter into a greased 15-in. x 10-in. x 1-in. baking pan; set aside.

» In another bowl, beat the cream cheese, confectioners' sugar, preserves and remaining vanilla. Add remaining eggs; beat on low speed just until combined. Gently spread over cake batter. Sprinkle with coconut and almonds.

» Bake at 350° for 25-30 minutes or until golden brown. Cool on a wire rack. Cut into bars. Refrigerate leftovers.

Yield: 2 dozen.

peppermint brownies

I think these are the best brownies around. They've always been well received by friends and family. My brother-in-law likes them so much that I bake them as his gifts for his birthday and holidays.

Tami Samorajski • New Berlin, Wisconsin

1 tablespoon plus 1 cup butter, divided

8 ounces unsweetened chocolate, chopped

4 teaspoons instant coffee granules

1 tablespoon boiling water

5 eggs

3-3/4 cups sugar

2 teaspoons vanilla extract

1/2 teaspoon almond extract

1-2/3 cups all-purpose flour

1/2 teaspoon salt

2 cups coarsely chopped walnuts

44 chocolate-covered peppermint patties

» Line a 13-in. x 9-in. baking pan with foil. Melt 1 tablespoon butter; brush over foil and set aside. In a microwave, melt chocolate and remaining butter; stir until smooth. Cool slightly. Dissolve coffee granules in boiling water.

» In a large bowl, beat eggs and sugar until blended. Beat in the vanilla, almond extract, coffee mixture and chocolate until fluffy. Combine flour and salt; gradually add to chocolate mixture. Stir in walnuts.

» Pour half of the batter into prepared pan. Top with a layer of peppermint patties, filling in the gaps with peppermint pieces. Top with remaining batter.

» Bake at 425° for 23-27 minutes or until top is set. Cool on a wire rack. Using foil, remove brownies from pan. Chill for 6 hours or overnight before cutting.

Yield: 3 dozen.

chocolate strawberry truffle brownies

Some of the strawberry jam I put up every year always makes its way into this treat. I like to bake up a batch as a unique snack for the students I teach.

Teresa Jansen • Advance, Missouri

1-1/4 cups semisweet chocolate chips

1/2 cup butter, cubed

3/4 cup packed brown sugar

2 eggs

1 teaspoon instant coffee granules

2 tablespoons water

3/4 cup all-purpose flour

1/2 teaspoon baking powder

TRUFFLE FILLING:

1 cup (6 ounces) semisweet chocolate chips

1/4 teaspoon instant coffee granules

1 package (8 ounces) cream cheese, softened

1/4 cup sifted confectioners' sugar

1/3 cup strawberry jam or preserves

GLAZE:

1/4 cup semisweet chocolate chips

1 teaspoon shortening

» In a microwave, melt chocolate and butter; stir until smooth. Cool slightly. In a large bowl, beat brown sugar and eggs. Stir in chocolate mixture. Dissolve coffee in water; add to chocolate mixture. Combine flour and baking powder; gradually add to the batter.

» Spread evenly in a greased and floured 9-in. square baking pan. Bake at 350° for 30-35 minutes or until a toothpick inserted near the center comes out clean. Cool.

» Meanwhile, for filling, melt chocolate chips and coffee granules; stir until smooth. Set aside.

» In a small bowl, beat cream cheese until smooth. Add confectioners' sugar and jam; mix well. Beat in melted chocolate until well blended. Spread over brownies.

» For glaze, in a microwave, melt chocolate and shortening; stir until smooth. Drizzle over filling. Chill at least 1-2 hours.

Yield: about 2 dozen.

dark chocolate butterscotch brownies

My daughters and I love homemade brownies. We experimented with many variations and finally came up with this wonderful version. The satiny frosting and butterscotch chips make them irresistible.

Kit Concilus • Meadville, Pennsylvania

4 ounces unsweetened chocolate, chopped

3/4 cup butter, cubed

2 cups sugar

3 egg whites

1-1/2 teaspoons vanilla extract

1 cup all-purpose flour

1 cup 60% cocoa bittersweet chocolate baking chips

1 cup butterscotch chips

GLAZE:

1 cup 60% cocoa bittersweet chocolate baking chips

1/4 cup butter, cubed

» In a microwave, melt unsweetened chocolate and butter; stir until smooth. Cool slightly. In a large bowl, combine sugar and chocolate mixture. Stir in egg whites and vanilla. Gradually add flour to chocolate mixture. Stir in chips.

» Spread into a greased 13-in. x 9-in. baking pan. Bake at 350° for 25-30 minutes or until a toothpick inserted near the center comes out clean (do not overbake). Cool on a wire rack.

» For glaze, in a microwave, melt the chocolate chips and butter; stir until smooth. Immediately spread over the brownies. Cool before cutting.

Yield: about 5 dozen.

rocky road brownies

Anyone who likes rocky road ice cream will love these moist, fudgy brownies loaded with bits of marshmallows, chocolate chips and walnuts. They're great for children's parties.

Rita Lenes • Kent, Washington

3/4 cup butter, cubed

4 ounces unsweetened chocolate, chopped

4 eggs

2 cups sugar

1 teaspoon vanilla extract

1 cup all-purpose flour

2 cups miniature marshmallows

1 cup (6 ounces) semisweet chocolate chips

1 cup chopped walnuts

» In a microwave, melt butter and chocolate, stir until smooth; cool for 10 minutes.

» In a large bowl, beat the eggs, sugar and vanilla until blended. Stir in chocolate mixture. Gradually add the flour until well blended.

» Spread into a greased 13-in. x 9-in. baking pan. Bake at 350° for 25-30 minutes or until a toothpick inserted near the center comes out clean.

» Sprinkle with marshmallows, chocolate chips and walnuts; bake 4 minutes longer. Cool on a wire rack.

Yield: 2 dozen.

brenda's lemon bars

I enjoy baking, and these lemon bars rank among my most-often-requested goodies.

Brenda Hamilton • Nelson, British Columbia

2-1/4 cups all-purpose flour, divided

1/2 cup plus 1 tablespoon confectioners' sugar, divided

1 cup cold butter, cubed

4 eggs

2 cups sugar

2/3 cup lemon juice

1/2 teaspoon baking powder

» In a large bowl, combine 2 cups flour and 1/2 cup confectioners' sugar; cut in butter until crumbly. Press into an ungreased 13-in. x 9-in. baking dish.

» Bake at 350° for 12-15 minutes or until lightly browned. Place on a wire rack to cool slightly.

» Meanwhile, in a small bowl, beat the eggs, sugar, lemon juice, baking powder and remaining flour until frothy. Pour over warm crust.

» Bake for 18-22 minutes or until lightly browned. Cool in pan on a wire rack.

» Dust with remaining confectioners' sugar. Cut into bars. Store in the refrigerator.

Yield: 2 dozen.

Christmas officially arrives at our house when I make this melt-in-your-mouth treat. Red and green maraschino cherries add a jolly finish to each light and creamy morsel.

Kathy Dorman • Snover, Michigan

holiday cheesecake bars

2 cups all-purpose flour

2/3 cup packed brown sugar

2/3 cup cold butter

1 cup chopped walnuts

FILLING:

2 packages (8 ounces each) cream cheese, softened

1/2 cup sugar

2 eggs

1/4 cup 2% milk

2 tablespoons lemon juice

1 teaspoon vanilla extract

Sliced red and green maraschino cherries, optional

» In a large bowl, combine flour and brown sugar; cut in butter until mixture resembles coarse crumbs. Stir in the walnuts. Reserve 1 cup. Press the remaining crumbs onto the bottom of an ungreased 13-in. x 9-in. baking pan. Bake at 350° for 12 minutes.

» Meanwhile, in a large bowl, beat the cream cheese and sugar until light and fluffy. Add eggs; beat on low speed just until combined. Stir in the milk, lemon juice and vanilla. Pour filling over crust. Sprinkle with reserved crumbs.

» Bake 25-30 minutes longer or until edges are lightly browned and filling is almost set. Cool in pan on a wire rack. Cut into squares. Garnish with cherries if desired. Store in refrigerator.

Yield: 2 dozen.

caramel cashew chewies

Caramels, cashews and chocolate chunks add up to make a very tasty snack. Let the kids unwrap all those caramels, counting as they go, to see who unwraps the most.

Amber Kieffer • Aurora, Colorado

3/4 cup butter, softened

3/4 cup packed brown sugar

1 egg

1-1/2 cups all-purpose flour

1 cup old-fashioned oats

1 package (14 ounces) caramels

1/3 cup half-and-half cream

1 cup semisweet chocolate chunks

1 cup salted cashew halves, chopped

» In a large bowl, cream butter and brown sugar until light and fluffy. Beat in egg. Combine flour and oats; gradually add to creamed mixture.

» Press into a 13-in. x 9-in. baking pan coated with cooking spray. Bake at 350° for 15-18 minutes or until golden brown.

» Meanwhile, in a small saucepan, combine caramels and cream. Cook over low heat for 4-5 minutes or until caramels are melted, stirring occasionally. Pour over crust. Sprinkle with chocolate chunks and cashews.

» Bake for 8-10 minutes or until chocolate is melted. Cool on a wire rack before cutting.

Yield: about 3 dozen.

cutting bars & brownies

Generally, bars and brownies should cool completely on a wire rack before being cut. However, crisp bars should be cut while still slightly warm. With a sharp knife, use a gentle sawing motion to cut the bars.

chocolate chip raspberry bars

Chocolate and raspberry are a perfect pairing in these bars featuring a buttery shortbread crust. They are a special treat.

Bev Cudrak • Coaldale, Alberta

1-3/4 cups all-purpose flour

1 cup sugar

1 cup cold butter, cubed

1 egg

1/2 teaspoon almond extract

1 cup seedless raspberry jam

1/2 cup miniature semisweet chocolate chips

» In a large bowl, combine flour and sugar. Cut in butter until mixture resembles coarse crumbs. Stir in egg and extract just until moistened. Set aside 1 cup crumb mixture for topping.

» Press the remaining mixture into a greased 11-in. x 7-in. baking pan. Bake at 350° for 5 minutes. Spread with jam and sprinkle with reserved crumb mixture. Bake 35-40 minutes longer or until golden brown.

» Sprinkle with the semisweet chips. Return to the oven for 30 seconds or until chips are glossy. Cool completely on a wire rack. Cut into bars.

Yield: about 3 dozen.

coconut brownies

1 package fudge brownie mix (13-inch x 9-inch pan size)

1 cup (8 ounces) sour cream

1 cup coconut-pecan frosting

2 eggs

1/4 cup water

1 cup (6 ounces) semisweet chocolate chips

» In a large bowl, combine the brownie mix, sour cream, frosting, eggs and water just until moistened.

» Pour into a 13-in. x 9-in. baking dish coated with cooking spray. Bake at 350° for 30-35 minutes or until center is set (do not overbake). Sprinkle with chocolate chips; let stand for 5 minutes. Spread chips over brownies to frost.

Yield: 2 dozen.

Brownies are an easy way to make something good, and no one seems to tire of them. Served warm with ice cream, these are a favorite!

Barbara Carlucci • Orange Park, Florida

ribbon crispies

These dressed-up rice crispies are a fabulous twist on a longtime favorite. They're perfect for buffet tables and meals eaten on the run. Folks from ages 1 to 101 love them, and they're always appreciated no matter where or when I share them.

Nancy Baker • Boonville, Missouri

1/2 cup butter, cubed

2 jars (7 ounces each) marshmallow creme

11 cups crisp rice cereal

1 to 1-1/2 cups peanut butter

1 to 1-1/2 cups hot fudge ice cream topping, warmed

» In a large saucepan, melt butter over medium-low heat. Stir in the marshmallow creme until smooth. Remove from the heat; stir in cereal until blended.

» Press half of the mixture into a greased 15-in. x 10-in. x 1-in. pan; spread with peanut butter. Carefully spread with hot fudge topping. Press the remaining cereal mixture over fudge layer (pan will be full). Cool for 10 minutes before cutting.

Yield: 2 dozen.

glazed peanut butter bars

Memories of lunchtime at school and my Aunt Shelly's kitchen come to mind when I bite into these sweet, chewy bars. My husband is the biggest fan of these peanut butter and chocolate sensations.

Janis Luedtke • Thornton, Colorado

3/4 cup butter, softened

3/4 cup creamy peanut butter

3/4 cup sugar

3/4 cup packed brown sugar

2 eggs

2 teaspoons water

1-1/2 teaspoons vanilla extract

1-1/2 cups all-purpose flour

1-1/2 cups quick-cooking oats

3/4 teaspoon baking soda

1/2 teaspoon salt

GLAZE:

1-1/4 cups milk chocolate chips

1/2 cup butterscotch chips

1/2 cup creamy peanut butter

» In a large bowl, cream the butter, peanut butter, sugars until light and fluffy. Beat in eggs, water and vanilla. Combine flour, oats, baking soda and salt; gradually add to creamed mixture.

» Spread into a greased 15-in. x 10-in. x 1-in. baking pan. Bake at 325° for 18-22 minutes or until lightly browned.

» For glaze, in a microwave, melt chips and peanut butter; stir until smooth. Pour over warm bars; spread evenly. Cool completely on a wire rack before cutting.

Yield: 4 dozen.

buckeye bars

My mom's passed down the directions for this treat, and now it's a regular in our house. So easy and quick—it makes a wonderful snack any time of the year.

Rachel Dillon • Flemington, New Jersey

1 cup butter, cubed

1-1/2 cups creamy peanut butter, divided

3-3/4 cups confectioners' sugar

5 Nestles Crunch candy bars (1.55 ounces each), chopped

» In a large microwave-safe bowl, combine the butter and 1 cup peanut butter. Microwave, uncovered, on high for 1 minute or until the butter is melted, stirring once. Beat in confectioners' sugar. Spread the bars into a 13-in. x 9-in. pan coated with cooking spray.

» In a microwave, melt candy bars and remaining peanut butter; stir until smooth. Spread over peanut butter layer. Refrigerate until cool.

» Cut into 1-1/2-in. x 1-in. bars. Store in an airtight container in the refrigerator.

Yield: 6-1/2 dozen.

cherry pineapple bars

These goodies are a holiday favorite in our family. I crush the graham crackers by placing them in a plastic zippered bag and using one of my 78 rolling pins!

Barbara McCollum • Waynesburg, Pennsylvania

1-1/2 cups graham cracker crumbs

1/2 cup butter, melted

1 jar (10 ounces) maraschino cherries, drained and patted dry

1 can (8 ounces) crushed pineapple, drained and patted dry

1-1/2 cups white baking chips

1 cup flaked coconut

1 cup chopped walnuts

1 can (14 ounces) sweetened condensed milk

» In a small bowl, combine cracker crumbs and butter. Press into a greased 13-in. x 9-in. baking dish. Sprinkle with the cherries, pineapple, chips, coconut and walnuts; drizzle with condensed milk.

» Bake at 350° for 25 minutes or until edges are golden brown. Cool on a wire rack. Cover and refrigerate overnight. Cut into bars.

Yield: 2 dozen.

blond butterscotch brownies

Toffee and chocolate dot the golden-brown batter of these fudge-like brownies. I do a lot of cooking for the police officers I work with, and they always line up for these.

Jennifer Ann Sopko • Battle Creek, Michigan

2 cups all-purpose flour

2 cups packed brown sugar

2 teaspoons baking powder

1/4 teaspoon salt

1/2 cup butter, melted and cooled

2 eggs

1 teaspoon vanilla extract

1 cup semisweet chocolate chunks

4 Heath candy bars (1.4 ounces each), coarsely chopped

» In a large bowl, combine the flour, brown sugar, baking powder and salt. In another bowl, beat the butter, eggs and vanilla until smooth. Stir into dry ingredients just until combined (batter will be thick).

» Spread into a 13-in. x 9-in. baking pan coated with cooking spray. Sprinkle with chocolate chunks and chopped candy bars; press gently into batter.

» Bake at 350° for 20-25 minutes or until a toothpick inserted near the center comes out clean. Cool in pan on a wire rack. Cut into bars.

Yield: 2 dozen.

coconut graham bars

My mom called these bars "Out-of-This-World Bars." The decadence of this treat goes over well at any get-together.

Patty Van Zyl • Hospers, Iowa

2 cups graham cracker crumbs

1/2 cup sugar

1/2 cup butter, melted

2 cups flaked coconut

1 can (14 ounces) sweetened condensed milk

TOPPING:

1-1/2 cups packed brown sugar

6 tablespoons heavy whipping cream

1/4 cup butter, cubed

3/4 cup semisweet chocolate chips

» In a small bowl, combine graham cracker crumbs, sugar and butter. Press onto the bottom of a greased 13-in. x 9-in. baking pan. Bake at 350° for 8-10 minutes or until lightly browned.

» Combine coconut and milk; spread over warm crust. Bake for 12-15 minutes or until edges are lightly browned. Cool on a wire rack.

» In a large saucepan, combine the brown sugar, cream and butter. Bring to a boil over medium heat, stirring constantly. Boil for 1 minute. Remove from the heat; stir in chocolate chips until melted. Spread over coconut layer. Cool before cutting.

Yield: 4-1/2 dozen.

raspberry patch crumb bars

To give these delectable, fresh raspberry bars even more crunch, add a sprinkling of nuts to the yummy crumb topping. Everyone will want to indulge.

Leanna Thorne • Lakewood, Colorado

3 cups all-purpose flour

1-1/2 cups sugar, divided

1 teaspoon baking powder

1/4 teaspoon salt

1/4 teaspoon ground cinnamon

1 cup shortening

2 eggs, lightly beaten

1 teaspoon almond extract

1 tablespoon cornstarch

4 cups fresh or frozen raspberries

» In a large bowl, combine the flour, 1 cup sugar, baking powder, salt and cinnamon. Cut in shortening until mixture resembles coarse crumbs. Stir in eggs and extract. Press two-thirds of the mixture into a greased 13-in. x 9-in. baking dish.

» In a large bowl, combine cornstarch and remaining sugar; add berries and gently toss. Spoon over crust. Sprinkle with remaining crumb mixture.

» Bake at 375° for 35-45 minutes or until the bars are bubbly and golden brown. Cool on a wire rack. Cut into bars. Store in the refrigerator.

Yield: 3 dozen.

chunky blond brownies

Every bite of these chewy blondies is packed with chunks of white and semisweet chocolate and macadamia nuts. It's a potluck offering that stands out.

Rosemary Dreiske • Lemmon, South Dakota

1/2 cup butter, softened

3/4 cup sugar

3/4 cup packed brown sugar

2 eggs

2 teaspoons vanilla extract

1-1/2 cups all-purpose flour

1 teaspoon baking powder

1/2 teaspoon salt

1 cup white baking chips

1 cup semisweet chocolate chunks

1 jar (3 ounces) macadamia nuts or 3/4 cup blanched almonds, chopped, divided

» In a large bowl, cream butter and sugars until light and fluffy. Beat in eggs and vanilla. Combine the flour, baking powder and salt; add to creamed mixture and mix well. Stir in white chips, chocolate chunks and 1/2 cup nuts.

» Spoon into a greased 13-in. x 9-in. baking pan; spread over the bottom of pan. Sprinkle with remaining nuts. Bake at 350° for 25-30 minutes or until top begins to crack and is golden brown. Cool on a wire rack. Cut into bars.

Yield: 2 dozen.

mocha walnut brownies

These rich, cake-like brownies are generously topped with a scrumptious mocha frosting. They're an excellent dessert to serve to company...or to share when you need a dish to pass. Be sure to hold back a few if you'd like some for the next day.

Jill Bonanno • Prineville, Oregon

4 ounces unsweetened chocolate, chopped

1 cup butter

4 eggs

2 cups sugar

1 teaspoon vanilla extract

1-1/4 cups all-purpose flour

1/2 teaspoon baking powder

1/2 teaspoon salt

1 cup chopped walnuts

MOCHA FROSTING:

4 cups confectioners' sugar

1/2 cup butter, melted

1/3 cup baking cocoa

1/4 cup strong brewed coffee

2 teaspoons vanilla extract

» In a microwave, melt the chocolate and butter; stir until smooth. Cool slightly. In a large bowl, beat eggs and sugar. Stir in vanilla and chocolate mixture. Combine the flour, baking powder and salt; gradually add to chocolate mixture. Stir in walnuts.

» Pour into a greased 13-in. x 9-in. baking pan. Bake at 375° for 30 minutes or until a toothpick inserted near the center comes out clean. Cool on a wire rack.

» In a large bowl, beat frosting ingredients until smooth. Spread over brownies.

Yield: about 2 dozen.

chocolate-drizzled cherry bars

I've been making bars since I was in third grade, but these are special. I bake them for the church Christmas party every year...and I'm always given kudos about them and then asked for the instructions.

Janice Heikkila • Deer Creek, Minnesota

2 cups all-purpose flour

2 cups quick-cooking oats

1-1/2 cups sugar

1-1/4 cups butter, softened

1 can (21 ounces) cherry pie filling

1 teaspoon almond extract

1/4 cup semisweet chocolate chips

3/4 teaspoon shortening

» In a bowl, combine flour, oats, sugar and butter until crumbly. Set aside 1-1/2 cups for topping. Press remaining crumb mixture into an ungreased 13-in. x 9-in. baking dish. Bake at 350° for 15-18 minutes or until edges begin to brown.

» In a small bowl, combine pie filling and extract; carefully spread over crust. Sprinkle with reserved crumb mixture. Bake 20-25 minutes longer or until edges and topping are lightly browned.

» In a microwave, melt the chocolate chips and shortening; stir until smooth. Drizzle over warm bars. Cool bars completely on a wire rack.

Yield: 3 dozen.

chocolate-glazed almond bars

With a moist almond filling and a flaky golden crust, these goodies are sure to be the perfect dessert for a garden get-together.

Robin Hart • North Brunswick, New Jersey

2 cups all-purpose flour

1/2 cup packed brown sugar

1/2 teaspoon salt

3/4 cup cold butter

3 egg whites

1 cup sugar

1 can (12-1/2 ounces) almond cake and pastry filling

2 cups sliced almonds

4 ounces bittersweet chocolate, chopped

» In a large bowl, combine the flour, brown sugar and salt. Cut in butter until mixture resembles coarse crumbs. Pat into a 13-in. x 9-in. baking pan coated with cooking spray. Bake at 350° for 18-22 minutes or until edges are lightly browned.

» Meanwhile, in a bowl, whisk the egg whites, sugar and almond filling until blended. Stir in almonds. Pour over crust. Bake for 20-25 minutes or until set. Cool completely on a wire rack.

» In a microwave, melt chocolate; drizzle over top. Cut into bars. Store in an airtight container in the refrigerator.

Yield: 40 bars.

EDITOR'S NOTE: This recipe was tested with Solo brand cake and pastry filling. Look for it in the baking aisle.

chocolate macaroon brownies

The brownie base makes this recipe different from other macaroon bars. If you don't have a lot of time, just substitute a boxed brownie mix and top it with the filling and frosting.

Emily Engel • Quill Lake, Saskatchewan

BROWNIE BASE:

1-1/2 cups sugar

2/3 cup canola oil

4 eggs, lightly beaten

1 teaspoon vanilla extract

1-1/3 cups all-purpose flour

2/3 cup baking cocoa

1 teaspoon baking powder

1/2 teaspoon salt

COCONUT FILLING:

1 can (14 ounces) sweetened condensed milk

3 cups flaked coconut

1 teaspoon vanilla extract

BUTTER FROSTING:

2 cups confectioners' sugar

1/2 cup baking cocoa

1/2 cup butter, softened

1 teaspoon vanilla extract

1 to 2 tablespoons 2% milk, divided

» In a large bowl, combine sugar and oil until blended. Beat in eggs and vanilla. Combine dry ingredients; gradually add to mixture. Pour into a greased 13-in. x 9-in. baking pan.

» In a small bowl, combine the filling ingredients. Spoon over brownie mixture. Bake at 350° for 30-35 minutes or until a toothpick inserted near the center comes out clean. Cool.

» Meanwhile, for frosting, in a small bowl, beat the sugar, cocoa, butter, vanilla and enough milk to achieve desired spreading consistency. Spread over filling.

Yield: about 2 dozen.

best-loved chocolate bars

Whenever I'm invited to a potluck with family and friends, it's understood that these scrumptious bars will come with me. Our grandchildren request them when they visit. Usually, I wait until they arrive, so we can make the treats together.

Paula Marchesi • Lenhartsville, Pennsylvania

1 package (18-1/4 ounces) chocolate cake mix

1 cup graham cracker crumbs (about 16 squares)

1/2 cup peanut butter

1 egg

3 tablespoons half-and-half cream

1 package (8 ounces) cream cheese, softened

1 jar (11-3/4 ounces) hot fudge ice cream topping

1 package (11-1/2 ounces) milk chocolate chips

1 cup salted peanuts

» In a large bowl, combine the cake mix and cracker crumbs. Cut in peanut butter until mixture resembles coarse crumbs. In a small bowl, whisk egg and cream. Add to crumb mixture just until moistened. Set aside 3/4 cup for topping. Press remaining crumb mixture into a greased 13-in. x 9-in. baking pan.

» In a large bowl, beat cream cheese until fluffy. Beat in ice cream topping until smooth. Spread over the crust. Sprinkle with the chocolate chips, peanuts and reserved crumb mixture.

» Bake at 350° for 25-30 minutes or until set. Cool on a wire rack. Cover; refrigerate for at least 4 hours. Cut into bars. Refrigerate leftovers.

Yield: 2 dozen.

EDITOR'S NOTE: Reduced-fat or generic brands of peanut butter are not recommended for this recipe.

chippy blond brownies

If you love chocolate and butterscotch, you won't be able to resist these chewy brownies. I often include the directions for this dessert inside a baking dish as a wedding present. Everyone, young and old, enjoys these delectable morsels.

Anna Allen • Owings Mills, Maryland

6 tablespoons butter, softened

1 cup packed brown sugar

2 eggs

1 teaspoon vanilla extract

1-1/4 cups all-purpose flour

1 teaspoon baking powder

1/2 teaspoon salt

1 cup (6 ounces) semisweet chocolate chips

1/2 cup chopped pecans

» In a large bowl, cream the butter and brown sugar until light and fluffy. Add the eggs, one at a time, beating well after each addition. Beat in vanilla. Combine the flour, baking powder and salt; gradually add to creamed mixture. Stir in the chocolate chips and pecans.

» Spread into a greased 11-in. x 7-in. baking pan. Bake at 350° for 25-30 minutes or until a toothpick inserted near the center comes out clean. Cool on a wire rack.

Yield: 2 dozen.

chunky pecan bars

Most people can't stop with just one of these additive, rich, luscious bars. They taste just like chocolate pecan pie.

Hazel Baldner • Austin, Minnesota

1-1/2 cups all-purpose flour

1/2 cup packed brown sugar

1/2 cup cold butter, cubed

FILLING:

3 eggs

3/4 cup sugar

3/4 cup dark corn syrup

2 tablespoons butter, melted

1 teaspoon vanilla extract

1-3/4 cups semisweet chocolate chunks

1-1/2 cups coarsely chopped pecans

» In a small bowl, combine the flour and brown sugar; cut in butter until crumbly. Press into a greased 13-in. x 9-in. baking pan. Bake at 350° for 10-15 minutes or until golden brown.

» Meanwhile, in a large bowl, whisk the eggs, sugar, corn syrup, butter and vanilla until blended. Stir in chocolate chunks and pecans. Pour over crust.

» Bake for 20-25 minutes or until bars are set. Cool completely on a wire rack. Cut into bars. Store in an airtight container in the refrigerator.

Yield: about 6 dozen.

cherry almond bars

A sweet lady I used to work for gave me this recipe. It is so easy and so festive-looking—and delicious.

Ruth Ann Stelfox • Raymond, Alberta

2 cups all-purpose flour

1/2 cup packed brown sugar

1 cup cold butter

1 cup golden raisins

1 cup chopped red and/or green maraschino cherries

1 cup sliced almonds

1 can (14 ounces) sweetened condensed milk

» In a large bowl, combine the flour and brown sugar; cut in the butter until crumbly. Press into an ungreased 15-in. x 10-in. x 1-in. baking pan. Bake at 325° for 12-14 minutes or until lightly browned.

» Sprinkle with raisins, cherries and almonds; drizzle with milk. Bake 25-30 minutes longer or until golden brown. Cool on a wire rack. Cut into squares.

Yield: 4 dozen.

meringue coconut brownies

Looking for an ooey-gooey brownie that's fabulous and different? This yummy treat combines a shortbread-like crust and a brown sugar meringue with chocolate, coconut and nuts. Put a few on the side for yourself because they go fast.

Diane Bridge • Clymer, Pennsylvania

3/4 cup butter, softened

1-1/2 cups packed brown sugar, divided

1/2 cup sugar

3 eggs, separated

1 teaspoon vanilla extract

2 cups all-purpose flour

1 teaspoon baking powder

1/4 teaspoon baking soda

1/4 teaspoon salt

2 cups (12 ounces) semisweet chocolate chips

1 cup flaked coconut

3/4 cup chopped walnuts

» In a large bowl, cream butter, 1/2 cup brown sugar and sugar until light and fluffy. Beat in egg yolks and vanilla until well blended. Combine the flour, baking powder, baking soda and salt; gradually add to creamed mixture just until blended (batter will be thick). Spread into a greased 13-in. x 9-in. baking pan. Sprinkle with the chocolate chips, coconut and walnuts.

» In another large bowl, beat egg whites until soft peaks form. Gradually beat in remaining brown sugar, 1 tablespoon at a time. Beat until stiff peaks form. Spread over the top.

» Bake at 350° for 30-35 minutes or until a toothpick inserted near the center comes out clean (do not overbake). Cool on a wire rack. Cut into bars. Store in the refrigerator.

Yield: 3 to 3-1/2 dozen.

mint cookies 'n' cream brownies

I created these brownies for my two sons who love the flavors of mint and chocolate. The creamy mint frosting is a delicious complement to the chocolaty base.

Janell Traubel • Boise, Idaho

1/2 cup butter, softened

1 cup sugar

4 eggs

1-1/2 cups chocolate syrup

1 cup all-purpose flour

6 mint cream-filled chocolate sandwich cookies, chopped

MINT CREAM:
1/2 cup butter, softened

2 cups confectioners' sugar

1 tablespoon 2% milk

1/4 to 1/2 teaspoon mint extract

2 drops green food coloring

Additional mint cream-filled chocolate sandwich cookies, crushed

» In a large bowl, cream butter and sugar until light and fluffy. Add eggs, one at a time, beating well after each addition. Beat in chocolate syrup, then flour, just until blended. Fold in the chopped cookies.

» Pour into a greased 13-in. x 9-in. baking pan. Bake at 350° for 25-30 minutes or until a toothpick inserted near the center comes out clean (do not overbake). Cool brownies completely on a wire rack.

» For mint cream, in a small bowl, cream the butter and confectioners' sugar until light and fluffy. Beat in the milk, extract and food coloring. Frost brownies; sprinkle with crushed cookies. Cut into squares.

Yield: 3-1/2 dozen.

date oat bars

My mother found this recipe many years ago. The citrusy treats taste just as good today as they did back then.

Joyce Eastman • Garden Grove, California

1-3/4 cups chopped dates

1/2 cup water

2 tablespoons brown sugar

1 teaspoon grated orange peel

2 tablespoons orange juice

1 teaspoon lemon juice

CRUST:

1-1/2 cups all-purpose flour

1 teaspoon baking powder

1/2 teaspoon baking soda

1/4 teaspoon salt

1 cup cold butter

1-1/2 cups old-fashioned oats

1 cup packed brown sugar

» In a small saucepan, combine the dates, water, brown sugar and orange peel. Cook and stir over medium heat until mixture comes to a boil, about 4 minutes. Cook and stir 3 minutes

longer or until liquid is absorbed. Remove from the heat. Stir in orange and lemon juices. Cool to room temperature.

» In a large bowl, combine the flour, baking powder, baking soda and salt. Cut in butter until crumbly. Add oats and brown sugar; mix well. Set aside half for the topping. Press remaining crumb mixture into a greased 13-in. x 9-in. baking pan.

» Drop date mixture by small spoonfuls onto crust. Sprinkle with reserved crumb mixture; press down gently. Bake at 325° for 30-35 minutes or until golden brown. Cool on a wire rack. Cut into bars.

Yield: 3 dozen.

I bake for a group of seniors every week, and this is one of the goodies they request most. I always keep the ingredients on hand for last-minute baking emergencies. Give these bars your own twist by replacing the strawberry jam with the fruit jam of your choice.

Karen Mead • Pittsburgh, Pennsylvania

strawberry jam bars

1/2 cup butter, softened

1/2 cup packed brown sugar

1 egg

1 package (18-1/4 ounces) white cake mix

1 cup finely crushed cornflakes

1 cup strawberry jam

» In a large bowl, cream butter and brown sugar until smooth. Add egg; mix well. Gradually add dry cake mix and cornflakes. Set aside 1-1/2 cups for topping. Press remaining dough into a greased 13-in. x 9-in. baking pan.

» Carefully spread jam over crust. Sprinkle with reserved dough; gently press down. Bake at 350° for 30 minutes or until golden brown. Cool completely on a wire rack. Cut into bars.

Yield: 2 dozen.

gooey caramel apple bars

Instead of preparing pies or cakes when feeding a crowd, bake a batch of these caramel apple bars. Since they bake in a large pan, they are very easy to transport to get-togethers.

Taste of Home Test Kitchen

5 cups all-purpose flour

1-1/4 teaspoons sugar

1-1/4 teaspoons salt

1-1/4 cups butter-flavored shortening

3 eggs

1/4 cup cold water

2 tablespoons plus 1-1/2 teaspoons white vinegar

FILLING:
10-1/2 cups sliced peeled tart apples (about 12 medium)

1 cup sugar

1 cup packed brown sugar

1/2 cup all-purpose flour

1-3/4 teaspoons ground cinnamon

1/2 teaspoon salt

1/2 teaspoon ground nutmeg

1/3 cup heavy whipping cream

1/3 cup butter, cubed

1 cup chopped walnuts

1-1/2 teaspoons vanilla extract

» In a large bowl, combine the flour, sugar and salt. Cut in shortening until mixture resembles coarse crumbs. In a small bowl, whisk the eggs, water and vinegar; gradually add to flour mixture, tossing with a fork until dough forms a ball.

» Divide dough in half so that one portion is slightly larger than the other; wrap each in plastic wrap. Refrigerate for 1 hour or until easy to handle.

» Roll out larger portion of dough between two sheets of waxed paper into a 17-in. x 12-in. rectangle. Transfer to an ungreased 15-in. x 10-in. x 1-in. baking pan. Press pastry onto bottom and up sides of pan; trim pastry even with top edges of pan.

» In a large bowl, combine the apples, sugars, flour, cinnamon, salt and nutmeg. Stir in cream.

» In a Dutch oven, melt the butter. Add apple mixture; cook over medium heat for 8-10 minutes or until apples are slightly tender. Stir in walnuts and vanilla. Spoon into crust.

» Roll out remaining pastry; place over filling. Trim and seal edges. Cut slits in top. Bake at 375° for 35-40 minutes or until crust is golden brown and filling is bubbly. Cool on a wire rack.

Yield: 2 dozen.

mock apple pie squares

No one ever guesses these sweet "apple" slices are made with zucchini. In fact, there isn't a bit of apple in them. What I like about this recipe is that it makes a lot using economical ingredients.

Lynn Hamilton • Naperville, Illinois

4 cups all-purpose flour

2 cups sugar

1/2 teaspoon salt

1-1/2 cups cold butter, cubed

FILLING:
8 cups sliced peeled zucchini

2/3 cup lemon juice

1 cup sugar

1 teaspoon ground cinnamon

1/4 teaspoon ground nutmeg

1/2 cup chopped walnuts

1/2 cup golden raisins

» In a large bowl, combine the flour, sugar and salt. Cut in butter until mixture resembles coarse crumbs. Press half of the crumb mixture into a greased 15-in. x 10-in. x 1-in. baking pan. Bake at 375° for 10-12 minutes or until lightly browned. Set remaining crumb mixture aside.

» Meanwhile, in a large saucepan, bring zucchini and lemon juice to a boil. Reduce heat; cover and simmer for 5-6 minutes or until tender. Drain. Stir in the sugar, cinnamon, nutmeg and 1/2 cup reserved crumb mixture. Cook and stir for 2-3 minutes. Stir in walnuts and raisins.

» Spread filling evenly over crust. Sprinkle with remaining crumb mixture. Bake for 25-30 minutes or until golden brown. Cool on a wire rack. Cut into squares.

Yield: about 2-1/2 dozen.

lemon-glazed pecan slices

A tart lemon icing pairs well with these rich bars that resemble pecan pie. Everyone loves them whenever I take them to work or potlucks.

Joan Hallford • North Richland Hills, Texas

1/2 cup cold butter, cubed

1 cup plus 2 tablespoons all-purpose flour, divided

2 eggs

1-1/2 cups packed brown sugar

1 teaspoon vanilla extract

1/2 teaspoon baking powder

1/2 teaspoon salt

1 cup chopped pecans

1/2 cup flaked coconut

1-1/2 cups confectioners' sugar

2 tablespoons lemon juice

» In a bowl, cut butter into 1 cup flour until crumbly. Press into a greased 13-in. x 9-in. baking pan. Bake at 350° for 12 minutes.

» Meanwhile, in a small bowl, beat the eggs, brown sugar and vanilla until blended. Combine the baking powder, salt and remaining flour; gradually add to egg mixture. Stir in pecans and coconut. Spread over warm crust. Bake for 25 minutes or until set. Cool on a wire rack.

» For glaze, combine the confectioners' sugar and lemon juice; spread over bars. Let set before cutting.

Yield: 4 dozen.

double frosted brownies

I grew up on a farm and always liked to help my mother in the kitchen, especially when it came to making confections. When we're planning to serve refreshments at one of our social meetings, this is my the top-pick to bake.

Edith Amburn • Mount Airy, North Carolina

4 eggs

1 cup canola oil

1-1/2 cups sugar

1/2 cup packed brown sugar

1/4 cup water

2 teaspoons vanilla extract

1-1/2 cups all-purpose flour

1/2 cup baking cocoa

1 teaspoon salt

1/2 cup chopped walnuts

FROSTING:
1 can (16 ounces) vanilla frosting

1 tablespoon rum extract

GLAZE:
1 cup (6 ounces) semisweet chocolate chips

1 tablespoon canola oil

» In a large bowl, beat the eggs, oil, sugars, water and vanilla. Combine the flour, cocoa, salt and walnuts; stir into egg mixture until blended.

» Pour into a greased 15-in. x 10-in. x 1-in. baking pan. Bake at 350° for 20-25 minutes or until center is set. Cool on a wire rack. Combine frosting and extract; spread over brownies. Chill for 30 minutes.

» In a microwave, melt chocolate chips and oil; stir until smooth. Drizzle over frosting. Let stand until set before cutting.

Yield: 3 dozen.

oatmeal raisin bars

This dessert has a delicious raisin filling tucked between a golden oat crust and topping. The old-fashioned treats are perfect for potlucks, and fit into most grocery budgets.

Rita Christianson • Glenburn, North Dakota

1 cup sugar

2 tablespoons plus 1-1/2 teaspoons cornstarch

1 teaspoon ground cinnamon

1-1/2 cups (12 ounces) sour cream

3 eggs, lightly beaten

2 cups raisins

CRUMB MIXTURE:
1-3/4 cups all-purpose flour

1-3/4 cups quick-cooking oats

1 cup packed brown sugar

1 teaspoon baking soda

1/2 teaspoon salt

1 cup cold butter, cubed

» In a large saucepan, combine the sugar, cornstarch and cinnamon. Stir in sour cream until smooth. Cook and stir over medium-high heat until thickened and bubbly. Reduce heat; cook and stir 2 minutes longer. Remove from the heat. Stir a small amount of hot filling into eggs; return all to pan, stirring constantly. Bring to a gentle boil; cook and stir 2 minutes longer. Remove from the heat. Gently stir in raisins. Cool to room temperature without stirring.

» Meanwhile, in a large bowl, combine the flour, oats, brown sugar, baking soda and salt. Cut in butter until crumbly.

» Firmly press 3-1/2 cups of crumb mixture into a greased 13-in. x 9-in. baking pan. Spread with raisin filling. Sprinkle with remaining crumb mixture.

» Bake at 350° for 25-30 minutes or until golden brown. Cool on a wire rack. Cut into bars. Refrigerate leftovers.

Yield: about 3 dozen.

» Bake at 350° for 20-25 minutes or until a toothpick inserted near the center comes out clean. Cool on a wire rack.

» For frosting, in a small bowl, beat cream cheese and butter until light and fluffy. Beat in vanilla. Gradually beat in confectioners' sugar. Frost; cut into bars. Store in the refrigerator.

Yield: 3 dozen.

apricot pastry bars

Perfect for a casual gathering or fancier event, this recipe is a crowd-pleaser. These special goodies were among 40 kinds of cookies and bars I made for my niece's wedding reception.

Nancy Foust • Stoneboro, Pennsylvania

4 cups all-purpose flour

1 cup plus 2 tablespoons sugar, divided

3 teaspoons baking powder

1/2 teaspoon salt

1/4 teaspoon baking soda

1 cup shortening

3 eggs, separated

1/4 cup 2% milk

1-1/2 teaspoons vanilla extract

4 cans (12 ounces each) apricot filling

1 cup chopped walnuts

» In a large bowl, combine the flour, 1 cup sugar, baking powder, salt and baking soda. Cut in shortening until mixture resembles coarse crumbs.

» In a small bowl, whisk the egg yolks, 2 egg whites, milk and vanilla; gradually add to crumb mixture, tossing with a fork until dough forms a ball. Divide in half, making one portion slightly larger.

» Roll out larger portion of dough between two large sheets of waxed paper into a 17-in. x 12-in. rectangle. Transfer to an ungreased 15-in. x 10-in. x 1-in. baking pan. Press pastry onto the bottom and up the sides of pan; trim pastry even with top edges. Spread apricot filling over dough; sprinkle with walnuts.

» Roll out remaining pastry to fit top of pan; place over filling. Trim, seal and flute edges. Cut slits in top. Whisk remaining egg white; brush over pastry. Sprinkle with remaining sugar.

» Bake at 350° for 35-40 minutes or until golden brown. Cool on a wire rack.

Yield: about 4 dozen.

carrot cake bars

A friend served these moist, tender cake bars at an outdoor party, and everyone raved about the taste. Often, I'll bake a big panful and freeze some for another day. They're so good!

Agnes Ward • Stratford, Ontario

3 eggs

1-1/4 cups canola oil

2 cups all-purpose flour

2 cups sugar

2 teaspoons ground cinnamon

1 teaspoon baking powder

1/2 teaspoon baking soda

1/4 to 1/2 teaspoon salt

1 jar (6 ounces) carrot baby food

1 container (3-1/2 ounces) applesauce baby food

1 container (3-1/2 ounces) apricot baby food

1/2 cup chopped walnuts, optional

FROSTING:

1 package (8 ounces) cream cheese, softened

1/2 cup butter, softened

1 teaspoon vanilla extract

3-3/4 cups confectioners' sugar

» In a bowl, beat eggs and oil for 2 minutes. Combine flour, sugar, cinnamon, baking powder, baking soda and salt; add to egg mixture. Add baby foods; mix well. Stir in walnuts if desired. Transfer to a greased 15-in. x 10-in. x 1-in. baking pan.

caramel candy bars

You'll love these delectable, buttery bars. They're so rich that a small portion may be enough to satisfy yourself...but don't expect to have many leftovers when you serve them to guests.

Jeannie Klugh • Lancaster, Pennsylvania

1/2 cup butter, softened

1/2 cup packed brown sugar

1-1/3 cups all-purpose flour

CARAMEL LAYER:

1 package (14 ounces) caramels

1/3 cup butter, cubed

1/3 cup evaporated milk

1-2/3 cups confectioners' sugar

1 cup chopped pecans

CHOCOLATE DRIZZLE:

1/4 cup semisweet chocolate chips

1 teaspoon shortening

» In a large bowl, cream butter and brown sugar until light and fluffy. Beat in flour until blended. Press into a greased 13-in. x 9-in. baking dish. Bake at 350° for 12-15 minutes or until golden brown.

» In a small saucepan over medium-low heat, melt caramels and butter with milk until smooth, stirring occasionally. Remove from the heat; stir in confectioners' sugar and pecans. Spread over crust.

» In a microwave, melt chocolate chips and shortening; stir until smooth. Drizzle over caramel layer. Cover and refrigerate for 2 hours or until firm. Cut into bars.

Yield: 2 dozen.

peter peter pumpkin bars

Sweet tooths will polish off this wonderful snack. The delicious orange frosting can be decorated with candy pumpkins.

Barb Schlafer • Appleton, Wisconsin

1/2 cup shortening

1 cup packed brown sugar

2 eggs

2/3 cup canned pumpkin

1 teaspoon vanilla extract

1 cup all-purpose flour

1 teaspoon ground cinnamon

1/2 teaspoon baking powder

1/2 teaspoon baking soda

1/4 teaspoon ground ginger

1/4 teaspoon ground nutmeg

1/2 cup chopped walnuts

ORANGE FROSTING:

3 tablespoons shortening

2-1/4 cups confectioners' sugar

3 tablespoons orange juice

1 tablespoon grated orange peel

Candy pumpkins

» In a large bowl, cream shortening and brown sugar until light and fluffy. Add eggs, one at a time, beating well after each addition. Beat in pumpkin and vanilla. Combine the flour, cinnamon, baking powder, baking soda, ginger and nutmeg; add to creamed mixture and mix well. Stir in nuts.

» Spread into a greased 13-in. x 9-in. baking dish. Bake at 350° for 20-25 minutes or until a toothpick inserted near the center comes out clean. Cool on a wire rack.

» In a large bowl, beat the shortening, confectioners' sugar, orange juice and orange peel until blended. Frost bars; cut into squares. Top with candy pumpkins.

Yield: 2 dozen.

lebkuchen

It is our family's tradition to bake these spice-filled delicacies on Thanksgiving weekend. The recipe came from my great-grandmother.

Esther Kempker • Jefferson City, Missouri

1/2 cup butter, softened

1/2 cup sugar

1/3 cup packed brown sugar

2 eggs

1 cup molasses

1/4 cup buttermilk

4-1/2 cups all-purpose flour

1-1/2 teaspoons baking powder

1 teaspoon baking soda

1 teaspoon ground cinnamon

1/2 teaspoon salt

1/2 teaspoon each ground cloves, allspice and cardamom

1/2 cup ground walnuts

1/2 cup raisins

1/2 cup pitted dates

1/2 cup candied lemon peel

1/3 cup flaked coconut

1/4 cup candied orange peel

3 tablespoons candied pineapple

1/2 teaspoon anise extract

GLAZE:

1 cup sugar

2 tablespoons hot water

1/4 teaspoon vanilla extract

» Line a 15-in. x 10-in. x 1-in. baking pan with foil; grease the foil and set aside. In a large bowl, cream butter and sugars until light and fluffy. Add eggs, one at a time, beating well after each. Beat in molasses and buttermilk. Combine the flour, baking powder, baking soda, cinnamon, salt and spices; gradually add to creamed mixture and mix well. Stir in walnuts.

» In a food processor, combine the raisins, dates, lemon peel, coconut, orange peel and pineapple in batches; cover and process until chopped. Stir into batter. Add anise extract. Press dough into prepared pan.

» Bake at 350° for 25-28 minutes or until lightly browned. Combine glaze ingredients; spread over warm bars. Immediately cut into squares. Cool in pan on a wire rack.

Yield: 3 dozen.

triple-tier brownies

A creamy frosting and crunchy topping make these tasty three-layer brownies a decadent treat. They're a cinch to assemble but are irresistible. Whenever I make them for someone new, they always request a copy of the recipe.

Annmarie Savage • Skowhegan, Maine

1 package fudge brownie mix (13-inch x 9-inch pan size)

1 package (11-1/2 ounces) milk chocolate chips

1 cup peanut butter

3 cups crisp rice cereal

1 can (16 ounces) cream cheese frosting

1 cup salted peanuts, chopped

» Prepare and bake the brownie mix according to package directions, using a greased 13-in. x 9-in. baking pan. Cool on a wire rack.

» In a large saucepan, combine chocolate chips and peanut butter. Cook over low heat for 4-5 minutes or until blended, stirring occasionally. Stir in cereal; set aside.

» Spread frosting over brownies. Sprinkle with peanuts. Spread with peanut butter mixture. Chill for 30 minutes or until set before cutting. Store in the refrigerator.

Yield: about 5 dozen.

walnut bars

Walnuts grow everywhere in California! I grew up on a "walnut acre" and love nuts. When I bake with them, I always think back to harvesttime with my family.

Chante Jones • Alturas, California

1/2 cup butter, softened

1/4 cup sugar

1 egg

1/2 teaspoon vanilla extract

1-1/4 cups all-purpose flour

1/2 teaspoon salt

FILLING:
2 eggs

1-1/2 cups packed brown sugar

2 tablespoons all-purpose flour

1 teaspoon vanilla extract

1/2 teaspoon salt

1/2 teaspoon baking powder

1-1/2 cups chopped walnuts

LEMON GLAZE:
1-1/2 cups confectioners' sugar

2 to 3 tablespoons lemon juice

» In a small bowl, cream butter and sugar until light and fluffy. Beat in egg and vanilla. Combine flour and salt; gradually add to creamed mixture and mix well.

» Press onto the bottom of a greased 13-in. x 9-in. baking pan. Bake at 350° for 20 minutes or until the edges of the bars are lightly browned.

» For filling, in a small bowl, combine the eggs, brown sugar, flour, vanilla, salt and baking powder. Stir in walnuts. Spread over crust.

» Bake for 25 minutes or until filling is golden brown. Cool on a wire rack.

» Combine the confectioners' sugar and enough lemon juice to achieve desired consistency; spread over filling. Let stand until set before cutting.

Yield: 2-1/2 dozen.

can't leave alone bars

A convenient cake mix hurries along the preparation of these tasty bars. I bring these quick-and-easy treats to church meetings, potlucks and housewarming parties. I often make a double batch so we can enjoy some at home.

Kimberly Biel • Java, South Dakota

1 package (18-1/4 ounces) white cake mix

2 eggs

1/3 cup canola oil

1 can (14 ounces) sweetened condensed milk

1 cup (6 ounces) semisweet chocolate chips

1/4 cup butter, cubed

» In a large bowl, combine the cake mix, eggs and oil. Press two-thirds of the mixture into a greased 13-in. x 9-in. baking pan. Set remaining cake mixture aside.

» In a microwave-safe bowl, combine the milk, chocolate chips and butter. Microwave, uncovered, until chips and butter are melted; stir until smooth. Pour over crust.

» Drop teaspoonfuls of remaining cake mixture over top. Bake at 350° for 20-25 minutes or until bars are lightly browned. Cool before cutting.

Yield: 3 dozen.

EDITOR'S NOTE: This recipe was tested in a 1,100-watt microwave.

---

glazed chocolate chip brownies

Shortly after we married, my husband asked if I would bake up a pan of brownies for him to take to work. I said, "Sure—I have the best recipe." He liked to cook, too, and said he had the best recipe. To settle the matter, we each baked a batch and let his coworkers decide. My recipe won!

Dawn Berg • Budd Lake, New Jersey

2/3 cup butter, melted

2 eggs, lightly beaten

1 teaspoon vanilla extract

2 cups sugar

1-1/3 cups all-purpose flour

3/4 cup baking cocoa

1/2 teaspoon baking soda

1/4 teaspoon salt

1/2 cup water

1 cup (6 ounces) semisweet chocolate chips

GLAZE:
3/4 cup semisweet chocolate chips

2 tablespoons butter

1/4 cup 2% milk

1-1/4 cups confectioners' sugar

1 teaspoon vanilla extract

» In a large bowl, combine the butter, eggs and vanilla. Combine the dry ingredients; add to butter mixture. Stir in water and chocolate chips until blended.

» Pour into a greased 13-in. x 9-in. baking pan. Bake at 350° for 30-35 minutes or until brownies pull away from the sides of the pan. Cool on a wire rack.

» In a microwave, melt the chips and butter with milk; stir until smooth. Remove from the heat; whisk in the confectioners' sugar and vanilla until smooth. Cover and refrigerate for at least 20 minutes or until chilled; frost brownies. Cut into bars.

Yield: 4 dozen.

Lemon Chiffon Cake • Chocolate Angel
Food Cake • Apple Harvest Cake •
Orange Sponge Cake • Almond Petits
Fours • Berry Nectarine Buckle
Strawberry Chocolate Shortcake
• Coconut Fudge Cake • Chocolate

cakes

Strawberry Torte • Pecan Pound Cake
• Ginger Peach Upside-Down Cake •
Heavenly Angel Food Cake • Family
Favorite Poke Cake • Streuseled Zucchini
Bundt Cake • Boston Cream Sponge
Cake • Apple-Topped Cake • Toasted
Butter Pecan Cake • Peanut Butter
Banana Cake • Florida Orange Cake •

lemon chiffon cake

This light, airy cake was my dad's top choice. My mom revamped the original recipe to include lemons. I'm not much of a baker, but I find that the dessert is well worth the effort.

Trisha Kammers • Clarkston, Washington

7 eggs, separated

2 cups all-purpose flour

1-1/2 cups sugar

3 teaspoons baking powder

1 teaspoon salt

3/4 cup water

1/2 cup canola oil

4 teaspoons grated lemon peel

2 teaspoons vanilla extract

1/2 teaspoon cream of tartar

LEMON FROSTING:

1/3 cup butter, softened

3 cups confectioners' sugar

4-1/2 teaspoons grated lemon peel

Dash salt

1/4 cup lemon juice

» Place egg whites in a large bowl; let stand at room temperature for 30 minutes.

» In another bowl, combine the flour, sugar, baking powder and salt. Whisk the egg yolks, water, oil, lemon peel and vanilla; add to dry ingredients and beat until well blended. Add cream of tartar to egg whites; beat on medium speed until soft peaks form. Fold into batter.

» Gently spoon into an ungreased 10-in. tube pan. Cut through batter with a knife to remove air pockets. Bake on the lowest oven rack at 325° for 50-55 minutes or until top springs back when lightly touched. Immediately invert pan; cool completely, about 1 hour.

» Run a knife around sides and center tube of pan. Remove cake to a serving plate. In a small bowl, combine frosting ingredients; beat until smooth. Frost top of cake.

Yield: 12-16 servings.

chocolate angel food cake

Low in calories and loaded with the sort of chocolate flavor that everyone craves, this delightful cake offers all of the taste and none of the guilt. It's an all-time favorite of mine.

Mary Relyea • Canastota, New York

1-1/2 cups egg whites (about 10)

1 cup cake flour

2 cups sugar, divided

1/2 cup baking cocoa

1 teaspoon cream of tartar

1 teaspoon vanilla extract

1/4 teaspoon salt

GLAZE:

1/2 cup semisweet chocolate chips

3 tablespoons half-and-half cream

» Place egg whites in a large bowl; let stand at room temperature for 30 minutes. Sift together flour, 1 cup sugar and cocoa twice; set aside.

» Add the cream of tartar, vanilla and salt to the egg whites. Beat on medium speed until soft peaks form. Gradually beat in remaining sugar, about 2 tablespoons at a time, on high until stiff glossy peaks form and sugar is dissolved. Gradually fold in flour mixture, about 1/2 cup at a time.

» Gently spoon into an ungreased 10-in. tube pan. Cut through batter with a knife to remove air pockets. Bake on the lowest oven rack at 350° for 40-50 minutes or until lightly browned and entire top appears dry. Immediately invert the pan; cool completely, about 1 hour.

» Run a knife around side and center tube of pan. Remove cake to a serving plate. For glaze, in a microwave-safe bowl, melt chocolate chips and cream. Stir until smooth. Drizzle over cake.

Yield: 12 servings.

Tender apple slices and subtle essence of orange, vanilla and cinnamon make this old-fashioned cake very popular with my family.

E. Bartuschat • Abington, Massachusetts

apple harvest cake

2-1/4 cups sugar, divided

1 cup canola oil

4 eggs

1/4 cup orange juice

2-1/2 teaspoons vanilla extract

3 cups all-purpose flour

3 teaspoons baking powder

1/2 teaspoon salt

4 medium tart apples, peeled and cubed

2 teaspoons ground cinnamon

Whipped cream and additional cinnamon, optional

» In a large bowl, beat 2 cups sugar, oil, eggs, orange juice and vanilla until well blended. Combine the flour, baking powder and salt; gradually beat into sugar mixture until blended. Stir in apples.

» Spread half of the batter into a greased 13-in. x 9-in. baking dish. Combine cinnamon and remaining sugar; sprinkle over batter. Carefully spread remaining batter over the top.

» Bake at 350° for 40-50 minutes or until a toothpick inserted near the center comes out clean. Cool on a wire rack. Garnish with whipped cream and additional cinnamon if desired.

Yield: 12-15 servings.

» Gently spoon into an ungreased 10-in. tube pan. Cut through batter with a knife to remove air pockets. Bake on the lowest oven rack at 325° for 45-55 minutes or until cake springs back when lightly touched. Immediately invert pan; cool completely, about 1 hour.

» Run a knife around sides and center tube of pan. Remove cake to a serving plate. For glaze, melt butter in a small saucepan; remove from the heat. Add confectioners' sugar, water and vanilla; stir until smooth. Pour over cake, allowing it to drizzle down sides.

Yield: 12 servings.

orange sponge cake

This was the cake that my dad used to request for his birthday every year. For a wedding present, my Aunt Marilyn included this recipe in a family cookbook for me.

Amy Sauser • Omaha, Nebraska

6 eggs, separated

1-1/3 cups cake flour

1-1/2 cups sugar, divided

1/4 teaspoon salt

1/2 cup orange juice

3 teaspoons grated orange peel

3/4 teaspoon cream of tartar

GLAZE:
1/3 cup butter, cubed

2 cups confectioners' sugar

3 to 5 teaspoons water

1-1/2 teaspoons vanilla extract

» Place egg whites in a large bowl; let stand at room temperature for 30 minutes. Sift the flour, 1/3 cup sugar and salt together twice; set aside.

» In another bowl, beat egg yolks on high speed for 5 minutes or until thick and lemon-colored. Gradually beat in 2/3 cup sugar. Add orange juice and peel; beat 3 minutes longer. Gradually add flour mixture and mix well.

» Add cream of tartar to egg whites; beat on medium speed until soft peaks form. Gradually beat in remaining sugar, 1 tablespoon at a time, on high until stiff peaks form. Fold into batter.

almond petits fours

Dainty, bite-sized cakes are often the highlight of a ladies' luncheon. Serve them on a platter with a small tongs so guests can easily help themselves to these lovely creations.

Taste of Home Test Kitchen

1 can (8 ounces) almond paste

3/4 cup butter, softened

3/4 cup sugar

4 eggs

1 cup cake flour

1/4 cup seedless raspberry spreadable fruit

GLAZE:
4-1/2 cups sugar

2-1/4 cups water

1/4 teaspoon cream of tartar

1-1/2 teaspoons clear vanilla extract

1/4 teaspoon almond extract

6 cups confectioners' sugar

Assorted food coloring

» Line a 15-in. x 10-in. x 1-in. baking pan with parchment paper; coat the paper with cooking spray and set aside.

» In a large bowl, cream the almond paste, butter and sugar until light and fluffy. Add eggs, one at a time, beating well after each addition. Beat in flour. Spread evenly into prepared pan.

» Bake at 325° for 12-15 minutes or until a toothpick inserted near the center comes out clean. Cool for 10 minutes before removing from pan to a wire rack to cool completely.

» Cut cake in half widthwise. Spread jam over one half; top with remaining half. Cut into assorted 1-1/2-in. shapes.

» In a large saucepan, combine the sugar, water and cream of tartar. Cook over medium-high heat, without stirring, until a candy thermometer reads 226°. Remove from the heat; cool at room temperature to 100°. Stir in extracts. Using a portable mixer, beat in confectioners' sugar until smooth. Tint some of glaze with food coloring.

» Gently dip petits fours, one at a time, into warm glaze. Remove with a fork; allow excess glaze to drip off. (If glaze becomes too thick, stir in 1 teaspoon hot water at a time to thin.) Place petits fours on wire racks over waxed paper; let dry completely.

Yield: 2-1/2 dozen.

EDITOR'S NOTE: We recommend that you test your candy thermometer before each use by bringing water to a boil; the thermometer should read 212°. Adjust your recipe temperature up or down based on your test.

berry nectarine buckle

I found this recipe in a magazine quite a long time ago, but modified it over the years. We enjoy its combination of blueberries, raspberries, blackberries and nectarines, particularly when the cake is served warm with low-fat frozen yogurt.

Lisa Sjursen-Darling • Scottsville, New York

1/3 cup all-purpose flour

1/3 cup packed brown sugar

1 teaspoon ground cinnamon

3 tablespoons cold butter

BATTER:
6 tablespoons butter, softened

3/4 cup plus 1 tablespoon sugar, divided

2 eggs

1-1/2 teaspoons vanilla extract

2-1/4 cups all-purpose flour

2-1/2 teaspoons baking powder

1/2 teaspoon salt

1/2 cup fat-free milk

1 cup fresh blueberries

1 pound medium nectarines, peeled, sliced and patted dry or 1 package (16 ounces) frozen unsweetened sliced peaches, thawed and patted dry

1/2 cup fresh raspberries

1/2 cup fresh blackberries

» For topping, in a small bowl, combine the flour, brown sugar and cinnamon; cut in butter until crumbly. Set aside.

» In a large bowl, cream the butter and 3/4 cup sugar until light and fluffy. Add eggs, one at a time, beating well after each addition. Beat in vanilla. Combine the flour, baking powder and salt; add to creamed mixture alternately with milk, beating well after each addition. Set aside 3/4 cup batter. Fold blueberries into remaining batter.

» Spoon into a 13-in. x 9-in. baking dish coated with cooking spray. Arrange nectarines on top; sprinkle with remaining sugar. Drop reserved batter by teaspoonfuls over nectarines. Sprinkle with raspberries, blackberries and reserved topping.

» Bake at 350° for 35-40 minutes or until a toothpick inserted near the center comes out clean. Serve warm.

Yield: 20 servings.

nutty chocolate cake

I got the idea for this incredibly easy yet spectacular dessert from a magazine. It is absolutely gorgeous on a buffet table.

Linda DuVal • Colorado Springs, Colorado

1 package (18-1/4 ounces) chocolate cake mix

1 can (8 ounces) almond paste

1/2 cup butter, softened

1/2 cup heavy whipping cream

2 cups (12 ounces) semisweet chocolate chips

1 cup (8 ounces) sour cream

Dash salt

1/2 cup sliced almonds, toasted

» Prepare and bake cakes according to package directions, using two greased 9-in. round baking pans. Cool for 10 minutes before removing from pans to wire racks to cool completely.

» For filling, in a small bowl, beat almond paste and butter until smooth. Gradually beat in cream until fluffy. Cut each cake horizontally in half; spread filling over bottom layers. Replace top layers.

» In a large microwave-safe bowl, melt chocolate chips; stir until smooth. Stir in sour cream and salt. Spread over the top of each cake. Sprinkle with almonds. Refrigerate leftovers.

Yield: 2 cakes (8 servings each).

pecan pound cake

A crispy crust, rich, buttery taste and crunchy pecans make this pound cake a real standout. It's a delicious breakfast or snack. If you have a small group, don't worry...this cake freezes very well.

Joan Ferguson • Elkhorn, Nebraska

2 cups butter, softened

2 cups sugar

9 eggs

1 tablespoon lemon juice

3 teaspoons vanilla extract

1 teaspoon grated lemon peel

3 cups all-purpose flour

1 teaspoon baking powder

1/4 teaspoon salt

4 cups chopped pecans

1-1/2 cups golden raisins

Confectioners' sugar, optional

» In a large bowl, cream butter and sugar until light and fluffy. Add eggs, one at a time, beating well after each addition. Beat in the lemon juice, vanilla and lemon peel. Combine the flour, baking powder and salt; gradually add to creamed mixture just until combined. Fold in pecans and raisins.

» Pour into a greased and floured 10-in. fluted tube pan. Bake at 350° for 1-1/4 to 1-1/2 hours or until a toothpick inserted near the center comes out clean. Cool for 10 minutes; remove from pan to a wire rack to cool completely. Dust with confectioners' sugar if desired.

Yield: 12-16 servings.

triple-layer lemon cake

A smooth and silky citrus filling separates the three layers of my lemon cake. It's a homemade standby recipe that my friends never tire of. Serve it at a special spring or summer gathering.

Connie Jurjevich • Atmore, Alabama

2 cups sugar

3/4 cup canola oil

4 eggs, separated

1 teaspoon vanilla extract

3 cups all-purpose flour

3 teaspoons baking powder

1/4 teaspoon salt

1 cup 2% milk

FILLING:
3/4 cup sugar

2 tablespoons cornstarch

1/8 teaspoon salt

1/2 cup water

1 egg, lightly beaten

1/3 cup lemon juice

1-1/2 teaspoons grated lemon peel

1 tablespoon butter, softened

FROSTING:
1 cup butter, softened

6 cups confectioners' sugar

2 tablespoons lemon juice

1 teaspoon grated lemon peel

4 to 6 tablespoons heavy whipping cream

» In a large bowl, beat sugar and oil. Beat in egg yolks and vanilla. Combine dry ingredients; add to sugar mixture alternately with milk, beating well after each addition. In a large bowl, beat egg whites until stiff peaks form; fold into batter.

» Pour into three greased and waxed paper-lined 9-in. round baking pans. Bake at 350° for 20-25 minutes or until a toothpick inserted near the center comes out clean. Cool for 10 minutes before removing to wire racks to cool completely.

» For filling, in a large saucepan, combine the sugar, cornstarch and salt. Stir in water until smooth. Cook and stir over medium-high heat until thickened and bubbly. Reduce heat; cook and stir 2 minutes longer. Remove from the heat. Stir a small amount of hot filling into egg; return to all the pan, stirring constantly. Bring to a gentle boil; cook and stir 2 minutes longer. Remove

from the heat. Gently stir in lemon juice, peel and butter. Cool to room temperature without stirring. Cover and refrigerate.

» In a large bowl, combine the butter, confectioners' sugar, lemon juice, peel and enough cream to achieve desired spreading consistency. Spread filling between cake layers. Frost top and sides of cake. Store in the refrigerator.

Yield: 12-14 servings.

strawberry chocolate shortcake

I like to make this scrumptious, tiered treat for Valentine's Day parties. It's simple to prepare but looks so elegant and striking.

Suzanne McKinley • Lyons, Georgia

3-1/2 cups biscuit/baking mix

2/3 cup plus 2 teaspoons sugar, divided

1/2 cup baking cocoa

1 cup 2% milk

1/3 cup butter, melted

1 egg white

2-1/2 pints fresh strawberries

2 cups heavy whipping cream

3 tablespoons confectioners' sugar

1 cup chocolate syrup

» In a large bowl, combine the biscuit mix, 2/3 cup sugar and cocoa. Stir in milk and butter; mix well. Drop by 1/3 cupfuls at least 2 in. apart onto a greased baking sheet. Beat egg white until foamy; brush over shortcakes. Sprinkle with remaining sugar. Bake at 400° for 15-18 minutes. Cool on wire racks.

» Set aside 10 whole strawberries; slice remaining strawberries. In a large bowl, beat cream and confectioners' sugar until soft peaks form.

» Just before serving, split shortcakes horizontally. Spoon half of the whipped cream and all of the sliced berries between cake layers. Spoon remaining whipped cream on top. Drizzle with chocolate syrup; top with a whole berry.

Yield: 10 servings.

old-fashioned carrot cake

A pleasingly moist cake, this treat is the one I requested that my mom make each year for my birthday. It's dotted with sweet carrots and a hint of cinnamon. The fluffy, buttery frosting is scrumptious with chopped walnuts stirred in. One piece of this cake is never enough!

Kim Orr • West Grove, Pennsylvania

4 eggs

2 cups sugar

1 cup canola oil

2 cups all-purpose flour

2 to 3 teaspoons ground cinnamon

3/4 teaspoon baking soda

1/2 teaspoon baking powder

1/4 teaspoon salt

1/4 teaspoon ground nutmeg

2 cups grated carrots

FROSTING:

1/2 cup butter, softened

1 package (3 ounces) cream cheese, softened

1 teaspoon vanilla extract

3-3/4 cups confectioners' sugar

2 to 3 tablespoons 2% milk

1 cup chopped walnuts

Orange and green food coloring, optional

» In a large bowl, combine the eggs, sugar and oil. Combine the flour, cinnamon, baking soda, baking powder, salt and nutmeg; beat into egg mixture. Stir in carrots.

» Pour into two greased and floured 9-in. round baking pans. Bake at 350° for 35-40 minutes or until a toothpick inserted near the center comes out clean. Cool for 10 minutes before removing from pans to wire racks to cool completely.

» For frosting, in another large bowl, cream butter and cream cheese until fluffy. Beat in vanilla. Gradually beat in confectioners' sugar. Add enough milk to achieve desired spreading consistency. Reserve 1/2 cup frosting for decorating if desired. Stir walnuts into remaining frosting.

» Spread frosting between layers and over top and sides of cake. If decorating the cake, tint 1/4 cup reserved frosting orange and 1/4 cup green. Cut a small hole in the corner of pastry or plastic bag; insert #7 round pastry tip. Fill the bag with orange frosting. Pipe twelve carrots on top of cake, so that each slice will have a carrot. Using #67 leaf pastry tip and the green frosting, pipe a leaf at the top of each carrot.

» Store cake in the refrigerator.

Yield: 12 servings.

family-favorite poke cake

You'll need only a handful of ingredients, including Milky Way candy bars and ice cream topping, for this yummy version of popular poke cake. It's so easy, kids may want to whip it together themselves.

Taste of Home Test Kitchen

1 package (18-1/4 ounces) yellow cake mix

10 fun-size Milky Way candy bars, divided

1 can (14 ounces) sweetened condensed milk

1 jar (12 ounces) Milky Way ice cream topping

1 carton (12 ounces) frozen whipped topping, thawed

» Prepare and bake cake according to package directions, using a greased 13-in. x 9-in. baking pan. Chop six candy bars. Remove cake from the oven; immediately sprinkle with chopped candy bars. Cool on a wire rack for 10 minutes.

» Using the end of a wooden spoon handle, poke 20 holes in warm cake. Pour milk over cake; cool for 10 minutes. Pour ice cream topping over cake; cool completely.

» Spread whipped topping over cake. Chop remaining candy bars; sprinkle over cake. Cover and store in the refrigerator.

Yield: 12-15 servings.

» In a microwave, melt chocolate and butter; stir until smooth. Cool. Transfer to a large bowl; beating sugar until blended. Add the eggs, one at a time, beating well after each addition. Beat in vanilla. Combine the flour, baking soda and salt; gradually add to chocolate mixture alternately with water, beating well after each addition.

» Pour into two greased and floured 9-in. round baking pans. Bake at 350° for 28-33 minutes or until a toothpick inserted near the center comes out clean. Cool for 10 minutes before removing from pans to wire racks.

» In a large bowl, combine filling ingredients; set aside. For glaze, in a microwave-safe bowl, melt chocolate and butter; stir until smooth. Stir in confectioners' sugar, water and vanilla until smooth. Cool slightly.

» Place one cake layer on a serving plate. Spread with half of the whipped topping; drizzle with half of the glaze. Top with half of the filling. Repeat layers. Store in the refrigerator.

Yield: 10-12 servings.

chocolate strawberry torte

The gorgeous torte combines two great ingredients—chocolate and strawberries. It's one of my favorites.

Paula Magnus • Republic, Washington

5 ounces semisweet chocolate, chopped

3/4 cup butter, cubed

1-1/2 cups sugar

3 eggs

2 teaspoons vanilla extract

2-1/2 cups all-purpose flour

1 teaspoon baking soda

1/4 teaspoon salt

1-1/2 cups water

STRAWBERRY FILLING:
4 cups sliced fresh strawberries

2 tablespoons sugar

1 teaspoon vanilla extract

GLAZE:
3 ounces semisweet chocolate, chopped

1 tablespoon butter

1 cup confectioners' sugar

3 tablespoons water

1/2 teaspoon vanilla extract

1 carton (8 ounces) frozen whipped topping, thawed

pineapple upside-down cake

Here's a classic dessert that's been updated with packaged items for convenience. It has the same fabulous flavor as any from-scratch cake.

Karen Ann Bland • Gove, Kansas

1/4 cup butter, melted

1 can (20 ounces) sliced pineapple

10 pecan halves

1 jar (12 ounces) apricot preserves

1 package (18-1/4 ounces) yellow cake mix

» Pour butter into a well-greased 13-in. x 9-in. baking dish. Drain pineapple, reserving 1/4 cup juice. Arrange pineapple slices in prepared pan; place a pecan half in the center of each slice. Combine the apricot preserves and reserved pineapple juice; spoon over pineapple slices.

» Prepare cake batter according to package directions; pour over pineapple.

» Bake at 350° for 45-50 minutes or until a toothpick inserted near the center comes out clean. Immediately invert onto a large serving platter. Cool slightly; serve warm.

Yield: 12-15 servings.

coconut fudge cake

A big piece of this delectable cake is a chocolate and coconut devotee's dream. You should see my husband, children and grandkids smile when I serve it.

Johnnie McLeod • Bastrop, Louisiana

1 tablespoon shortening

1 package (8 ounces) cream cheese, softened

2-1/4 cups sugar, divided

3 eggs

2 teaspoons vanilla extract, divided

1 cup (6 ounces) semisweet chocolate chips

1/2 cup flaked coconut

1 cup buttermilk

1 cup canola oil

1 cup cold brewed coffee

3 cups all-purpose flour

3/4 cup baking cocoa

2 teaspoons baking powder

1-1/2 teaspoons baking soda

1-1/2 teaspoons salt

1/2 cup chopped pecans

CHOCOLATE GLAZE:

1 cup confectioners' sugar

3 tablespoons baking cocoa

2 to 3 tablespoons hot water

2 tablespoons butter, melted

2 teaspoons vanilla extract

» Grease a 10-in. fluted tube pan with shortening and lightly coat with flour; set aside. In a small bowl, beat the cream cheese, 1/4 cup sugar, 1 egg and 1 teaspoon vanilla until smooth. Fold in chocolate chips and coconut; set aside.

» In a large bowl, combine the buttermilk, oil, coffee, and remaining eggs and vanilla. Combine the flour, cocoa, baking powder, baking soda, salt and remaining sugar; add to buttermilk mixture, beating just until combined. Fold in pecans.

» Pour half of the batter into prepared pan. Spoon reserved cream cheese mixture over batter to within 1/2 in. of edges; top with remaining batter.

» Bake at 350° for 60-70 minutes or until a toothpick inserted near the center comes out clean. Cool for 20-25 minutes before removing from pan to a wire rack to cool completely.

» In a small bowl, combine glaze ingredients until smooth. Drizzle over cake.

Yield: 12-16 servings.

lemon sheet cake

Lemon pie filling lends a splash of citrus flavor to convenient cake mix, and a rich cream cheese frosting gives it sweetness. My family likes this cake cold, so I cut it into squares and freeze it before serving.

Alyce Dubisar • North Bend, Oregon

1 package (18-1/4 ounces) lemon cake mix

4 eggs

1 can (15-3/4 ounces) lemon pie filling

1 package (3 ounces) cream cheese, softened

1/2 cup butter, softened

2 cups confectioners' sugar

1-1/2 teaspoons vanilla extract

» In a large bowl, beat the cake mix and eggs until well blended. Fold in pie filling.

» Spread into a greased 15-in. x 10-in. x 1-in. baking pan. Bake at 350° for 18-20 minutes or until a toothpick inserted near the center comes out clean. Cool on a wire rack.

» In a bowl, beat cream cheese, butter and confectioners' sugar until smooth. Stir in vanilla. Spread over cake. Store in refrigerator.

Yield: 30-35 servings.

holiday fruitcake

I experimented in the kitchen and came up with this delicious recipe myself. I think it has just the right mix of nuts and fruit.

Allene Spence • Delbarton, West Virginia

3 cups whole red and green candied cherries

3 cups diced candied pineapple

1 package (1 pound) shelled walnuts

1 package (10 ounces) golden raisins

1 cup shortening

1 cup sugar

5 eggs

4 tablespoons vanilla extract

3 cups all-purpose flour

3 teaspoons baking powder

1 teaspoon salt

» In a large bowl, combine the cherries, pineapple, walnuts and raisins; set aside. In another large bowl, cream shortening and sugar until light and fluffy. Beat in eggs and vanilla. Combine the flour, baking powder and salt; add to creamed mixture and mix well. Pour over fruit mixture and stir to coat.

» Transfer to a greased and floured 10-in. tube pan. Bake at 300° for 2 hours or until a toothpick inserted near the center comes out clean. Cool for 10 minutes before removing from pan to a wire rack to cool completely.

» Wrap tightly and store in a cool place. Slice with a serrated knife; bring to room temperature before serving.

Yield: 16 servings.

cinnamon-sugar rhubarb cake

A real crowd-pleaser, this tender, snack-like cake is chock-full of rhubarb and sprinkled with a sweet cinnamon-sugar topping. Everyone will be asking for the recipe...or seconds!

Marlys Haber • White, South Dakota

1/2 cup shortening

1 cup packed brown sugar

1 cup sugar, divided

1 egg

1 teaspoon vanilla extract

2 cups all-purpose flour

1 teaspoon baking soda

1/2 teaspoon salt

1 cup buttermilk

2 cups diced fresh or frozen rhubarb

1 teaspoon ground cinnamon

» In a large bowl, cream the shortening, brown sugar and 1/2 cup sugar until light and fluffy. Add egg and vanilla; beat for 2 minutes. Combine the flour, baking soda and salt; add to creamed mixture alternately with buttermilk, beating well after each addition. Stir in rhubarb.

» Pour into a greased 13-in. x 9-in. baking dish. Combine the cinnamon and remaining sugar; sprinkle over batter. Bake at 350° for 40-45 minutes or until a toothpick inserted near the center comes out clean. Serve warm.

Yield: 12-16 servings.

EDITOR'S NOTE: If using frozen rhubarb, measure rhubarb while still frozen, then thaw completely. Drain in a colander, but do not press liquid out.

ginger peach upside-down cake

I made this cake often when our children were young. It takes only five ingredients but looks so festive and tastes so good!

June Tubb • Viroqua, Wisconsin

1/4 cup butter, melted

1/2 cup packed brown sugar

1 can (15-1/4 ounces) sliced peaches, drained and patted dry

1/4 cup red candied cherries, halved

1 package (14-1/2 ounces) gingerbread cake/cookie mix

» In a small bowl, combine butter and brown sugar. Spoon into an ungreased 10-in. fluted tube pan. Alternately arrange peaches and cherries in pan.

» Prepare gingerbread batter according to package directions for cake; carefully pour over fruit.

» Bake at 350° for 35-40 minutes or until a toothpick inserted near the center comes out clean. Cool for 5 minutes before inverting onto a serving plate. Cool completely before cutting.

Yield: 12 servings.

heavenly angel food cake

This light, moist cake is one of my top picks for a dessert. It's just delightful and is special enough for most any occasion.

Fayrene De Koker • Vancouver, Washington

1-1/2 cups egg whites (about 12)

1-1/4 cups confectioners' sugar

1 cup all-purpose flour

1-1/2 teaspoons cream of tartar

1-1/2 teaspoons vanilla extract

1/2 teaspoon almond extract

1/4 teaspoon salt

1 cup sugar

» Place egg whites in a bowl; let stand at room temperature for 30 minutes. Sift confectioners' sugar and flour together twice; set aside.

» Add the cream of tartar, extracts and salt to egg whites; beat on medium speed until soft peaks form. Gradually add sugar, about 2 tablespoons at a time, beating on high until stiff glossy peaks form and sugar is dissolved. Gradually fold in flour mixture, about 1/2 cup at a time.

» Gently spoon into an ungreased 10-in. tube pan. Cut through the batter with a knife to remove air pockets. Bake on the lowest oven rack at 350° for 40-45 minutes or until lightly browned and entire top appears dry. Immediately invert pan; cool completely, about 1 hour.

» Run a knife around side and center tube of pan. Remove cake to a serving plate.

Yield: 20 servings.

pumpkin sheet cake

The cream cheese frosting wonderfully complements this spice cake.

Sandra McKenzie • Braham, Minnesota

1-1/2 cups sugar

1 can (15 ounces) solid-pack pumpkin

1 cup canola oil

4 eggs

2 cups all-purpose flour

2 teaspoons baking powder

2 teaspoons ground cinnamon

1 teaspoon baking soda

1/4 teaspoon salt

1/4 teaspoon ground cloves

CREAM CHEESE FROSTING:
2 packages (3 ounces each) cream cheese, softened

1/2 cup butter, softened

2 teaspoons vanilla extract

4-1/2 cups confectioners' sugar

24 candy pumpkins

» In a large bowl, beat the sugar, pumpkin, oil and eggs. Combine the flour, baking powder, cinnamon, baking soda, salt and cloves; gradually add to pumpkin mixture and mix well.

» Pour into a greased 15-in. x 10-in. x 1-in. baking pan. Bake at 350° for 20-25 minutes or until a toothpick inserted near the center comes out clean. Cool on a wire rack.

» For frosting, in a small bowl, beat the cream cheese, butter and vanilla until smooth. Gradually beat in confectioners' sugar. Spread over cake; garnish with candy pumpkins. Cover and refrigerate until serving.

Yield: 24 servings.

» Pour into two greased and floured 9-in. round baking pans. Bake at 350° for 25-30 minutes or until a toothpick inserted near the center comes out clean. Cool for 10 minutes before removing from pans to wire racks.

» For frosting, combine the brown sugar, egg whites, water and cream of tartar in a small heavy saucepan over low heat. With a hand mixer, beat on low speed for 1 minute. Continue beating on low over low heat until frosting reaches 160°, about 20 minutes.

» Pour into a large bowl; add vanilla. Beat on high until stiff peaks form, about 7 minutes. Spread between layers and over top and sides of cake. Refrigerate leftovers.

Yield: 12-16 servings.

sour cream spice cake

The dense, old-fashioned dessert is rich in spices. The fluffy, sweet frosting is a delectable contrast to the cake.

Edna Hoffman • Hebron, Indiana

1/2 cup butter, softened

1-1/2 cups packed brown sugar

3 eggs, separated

1 teaspoon vanilla extract

1-3/4 cups cake flour

1-1/2 teaspoons ground allspice

1 teaspoon baking soda

1 teaspoon ground cinnamon

1 teaspoon ground cloves

1/2 teaspoon salt

1 cup (8 ounces) sour cream

FROSTING:

1 cup packed brown sugar

2 egg whites

1/3 cup water

1/4 teaspoon cream of tartar

1-1/2 teaspoons vanilla extract

» In a large bowl, cream butter and brown sugar until light and fluffy. Beat in egg yolks and vanilla. Combine the dry ingredients; add to creamed mixture alternately with sour cream, beating well after each addition. In a small bowl, beat egg whites until stiff; gently fold into batter.

italian cream cheese cake

Buttermilk makes every bite of this awesome treat moist and flavorful. I rely on this recipe year-round.

Joyce Lutz • Centerview, Missouri

1/2 cup butter, softened

1/2 cup shortening

2 cups sugar

5 eggs, separated

1 teaspoon vanilla extract

2 cups all-purpose flour

1 teaspoon baking soda

1 cup buttermilk

1-1/2 cups flaked coconut

1 cup chopped pecans

CREAM CHEESE FROSTING:

2 packages (one 8 ounces, one 3 ounces) cream
   cheese, softened

3/4 cup butter, softened

6 cups confectioners' sugar

1-1/2 teaspoons vanilla extract

3/4 cup chopped pecans

» In a large bowl, cream the butter, shortening and sugar until light and fluffy. Beat in egg yolks and vanilla. Combine flour and baking soda; add to creamed mixture alternately with buttermilk. Beat just until combined. Stir in coconut and pecans.

» In a bowl, beat egg whites until stiff peaks form. Fold a fourth of the egg whites into batter, then fold in remaining whites. Pour into three greased and floured 9-in. round baking pans.

» Bake at 350° for 20-25 minutes or until a toothpick inserted near the center comes out clean. Cool for 10 minutes before removing from pans to wire racks to cool completely.

» In a large bowl, beat cream cheese and butter until smooth. Beat in confectioners' sugar and vanilla until fluffy. Stir in pecans. Spread frosting between layers and over top and sides of cake. Store in the refrigerator.

Yield: 12 servings.

streuseled zucchini bundt cake

After managing to lose 40 pounds, I like to keep a number of lighter recipes on hand. This cake is a favorite morning snack. It even won a blue ribbon at our county fair.

Regina Stock • Topeka, Kansas

2 cups shredded zucchini, patted dry

1-1/3 cups fat-free plain yogurt

3/4 cup sugar

2 egg whites

1/3 cup canola oil

1 egg

4 teaspoons vanilla extract, divided

3 cups all-purpose flour

1-1/2 teaspoons baking powder

1 teaspoon baking soda

1/2 teaspoon salt

1 tablespoon dry bread crumbs

1/3 cup packed brown sugar

1/3 cup chopped walnuts

1/3 cup raisins

1 tablespoon ground cinnamon

1/2 teaspoon ground allspice

3/4 cup confectioners' sugar

2 to 3 teaspoons fat-free milk

» In a large bowl, beat the zucchini, yogurt, sugar, egg whites, oil, egg and 3 teaspoons vanilla until well blended. In a small bowl, combine the flour, baking powder, baking soda and salt; gradually beat into zucchini mixture until blended.

» Coat a 10-in. fluted tube pan with cooking spray; sprinkle with bread crumbs. Pour a third of the batter into pan. Combine the brown sugar, walnuts, raisins and spices; sprinkle half over batter. Top with another third of the batter. Sprinkle with remaining brown sugar mixture; top with remaining batter.

» Bake at 350° for 55-65 minutes or until a toothpick inserted near the center comes out clean. Cool for 10 minutes before removing from pan to a wire rack to cool completely.

» In a small bowl, combine the confectioners' sugar, remaining vanilla and enough milk to achieve desired consistency; drizzle over cake.

Yield: 14 servings.

chocolate bliss marble cake

This cake is served at all of our family parties. It's low in fat but still delicious. Just one piece satisfies your craving for something sweet.

Josephine Piro • Easton, Pennsylvania

5 egg whites

1/4 cup baking cocoa

1/4 cup hot water

1 cup sugar, divided

1 cup fat-free milk

3 tablespoons canola oil

1 teaspoon vanilla extract

3/4 teaspoon almond extract

2-1/2 cups all-purpose flour

3 teaspoons baking powder

1/2 teaspoon salt

1-1/2 cups reduced-fat whipped topping

4 ounces semisweet chocolate

1-1/2 cups fresh raspberries

» Let the egg whites stand at room temperature for 30 minutes. Dissolve cocoa in water; let stand until cool.

» In a large bowl, beat 3/4 cup sugar, milk, oil and extracts until well blended. Combine the flour, baking powder and salt; gradually beat into sugar mixture until blended.

» In another bowl with clean beaters, beat egg whites on medium speed until soft peaks form. Beat in remaining sugar, 1 tablespoon at a time, on high until stiff peaks form. Gradually fold into batter. Remove 2 cups of the batter; stir in reserved cocoa mixture.

» Coat a 10-in. fluted tube pan with cooking spray. Alternately spoon the plain and chocolate batters into pan. Cut through batter with a knife to swirl.

» Bake at 350° for 30-35 minutes or until a toothpick inserted near the center comes out clean. Cool for 10 minutes before removing from pan to a wire rack to cool completely.

» For topping, in a microwave, melt the whipped topping and chocolate; stir until smooth.

» Place cake on a serving plate. Drizzle with topping. Arrange raspberries in center of cake.

Yield: 16 servings.

peanut butter banana cake

I've had this well-worn recipe for as long as I've been married. The cake is one of my scrumptious staples for potluck suppers and other get-togethers.

Lee Deneau • Lansing, Michigan

1/2 cup butter, softened

1-1/2 cups sugar

2 eggs

1 cup mashed ripe bananas (2 to 3 medium)

1 teaspoon vanilla extract

2 cups all-purpose flour

2 teaspoons baking powder

1 teaspoon baking soda

1/2 cup 2% milk

FROSTING:

1/3 cup creamy peanut butter

1/3 cup 2% milk

1-1/2 teaspoons vanilla extract

3 cups confectioners' sugar

» In a large bowl, cream the butter and sugar until light and fluffy. Add eggs, one at a time, beating well after each addition. Beat in bananas and vanilla. Combine the flour, baking powder and baking soda; add to creamed mixture alternately with milk, beating well after each addition.

» Transfer to a greased 13-in. x 9-in. baking pan. Bake at 350° for 30-35 minutes or until a toothpick inserted near the center comes out clean. Cool on a wire rack.

» For frosting, in a small bowl, beat the peanut butter, milk and vanilla until blended; gradually beat in the confectioners' sugar until smooth. Spread over cake.

Yield: 12-15 servings.

A friend brought this pretty pink cake to work for a birthday party. You can use any flavor of yogurt, but so far, I don't know anyone who's tried any other than black cherry because it's so delectable.

Judy Lentz • Emmetsburg, Iowa

black cherry cake

1 package (18-1/4 ounces) white cake mix

1-1/4 cups water

4 egg whites

1/3 cup canola oil

1-1/2 cups (12 ounces) fat-free sugar-free black cherry yogurt, divided

1 carton (8 ounces) frozen fat-free whipped topping, thawed

» In a large bowl, combine the cake mix, water, egg whites and oil; beat on low speed for 30 seconds. Beat on medium for 2 minutes. Fold in one carton of yogurt.

» Pour into a 13-in. x 9-in. baking dish coated with cooking spray. Bake at 350° for 30-35 minutes or until a toothpick inserted near the center comes out clean. Cool on a wire rack.

» Place the remaining yogurt in a small bowl; fold in whipped topping. Spread over cake. Store in the refrigerator.

Yield: 15 servings.

blueberry sour cream torte

For a pleasant taste of summer, consider my berry specialty. Cinnamon and nutmeg lend a hint of spice to the tasty filling, but lemon peel offers a refreshing bit of citrus.

Corinne Jagocki • Palm Coast, Florida

3/4 cup butter, softened

1/4 cup sugar

2 egg yolks

2 cups all-purpose flour

1 teaspoon baking powder

1/2 teaspoon salt

FILLING:
4 cups fresh or frozen blueberries

1 cup sugar, divided

1/4 cup quick-cooking tapioca

1/2 teaspoon ground cinnamon

1/2 teaspoon grated lemon peel

1/8 teaspoon ground nutmeg

2 egg yolks

2 cups (16 ounces) sour cream

1 teaspoon vanilla extract

» In a large bowl, cream butter and sugar until light and fluffy. Beat in egg yolks. Combine the flour, baking powder and salt; gradually add to the creamed mixture and mix well.

» Press onto the bottom and 1 in. up the sides of a greased 9-in. springform pan. Place pan on a baking sheet. Bake at 400° for 10-12 minutes or until lightly browned. Cool on a wire rack.

» In a large saucepan, gently toss the blueberries, 1/2 cup sugar, tapioca, cinnamon, lemon peel and nutmeg. Let stand for 15 minutes. Cook, uncovered, over medium heat until mixture comes to a boil. Cook and stir for 2 minutes. Remove from the heat; pour into crust.

» In a large bowl, beat the egg yolks, sour cream, vanilla and remaining sugar. Spoon over blueberry mixture. Return pan to baking sheet.

» Bake at 350° for 35-40 minutes or until center is set. Cool on a wire rack for 10 minutes. Carefully run a knife around edge of pan to loosen; cool 1 hour longer. Refrigerate for at least 4 hours before serving. Refrigerate leftovers.

Yield: 10-12 servings.

orange layer cake

I make this cake every year for Christmas. With its creamy nut frosting and tangy orange flavor, it's one my family is always happy to have.

Virginia Ford • El Sobrante, California

1/2 cup shortening

1-1/2 cups sugar

2 eggs

1 tablespoon grated orange peel

2-1/4 cups all-purpose flour

2 teaspoons baking powder

1 teaspoon salt

1/4 teaspoon baking soda

3/4 cup water

1/4 cup orange juice

FILLING/FROSTING:
2 tablespoons plus 1-1/2 teaspoons all-purpose flour

1/2 cup 2% milk

1/2 cup shortening

1/2 cup sugar

1/4 teaspoon salt

1/2 teaspoon vanilla extract

1/2 cup chopped walnuts

1 cup confectioners' sugar

» In a large bowl, cream shortening and sugar until light and fluffy. Add eggs, one at a time, beating well after each addition. Beat in orange peel. Combine the flour, baking powder, salt and baking soda; gradually add to creamed mixture alternately with the water and orange juice, beating well after each addition.

» Pour into two greased and floured 9-in. round baking pans. Bake at 350° for 20-25 minutes or until a toothpick inserted near the center comes out clean. Cool for 10 minutes before removing from pans to wire racks to cool completely.

» In a small saucepan, stir flour and milk until smooth. Bring to a boil; cook and stir for 1 minute or until thickened. Remove from the heat; cool to lukewarm.

» In a small bowl, cream the shortening, sugar and salt until light and fluffy. Beat in vanilla. Add cooled milk mixture; beat on high speed for 5 minutes or until fluffy. Remove about 2/3 cup; fold in nuts. Spread between cake layers.

» Gradually add confectioners' sugar to remaining filling; beat until fluffy. Frost top and sides of cake.

Yield: 12 servings.

hummingbird cake

This impressive cake is my dad's favorite, so I always make it for his birthday. It also makes a great Easter dessert.

Nancy Zimmerman • Cape May Courthouse, New Jersey

2 cups mashed ripe bananas

1-1/2 cups canola oil

3 eggs

1 can (8 ounces) unsweetened crushed pineapple, undrained

1-1/2 teaspoons vanilla extract

3 cups all-purpose flour

2 cups sugar

1 teaspoon salt

1 teaspoon baking soda

1 teaspoon ground cinnamon

1 cup chopped walnuts

PINEAPPLE FROSTING:
1/4 cup shortening

2 tablespoons butter, softened

1 teaspoon grated lemon peel

1/4 teaspoon salt

6 cups confectioners' sugar

1/2 cup unsweetened pineapple juice

2 teaspoons half-and-half cream

Chopped walnuts, optional

» In a large bowl, beat the bananas, oil, eggs, pineapple and vanilla until well blended. In another bowl, combine the flour, sugar, salt, baking soda and cinnamon; gradually beat into banana mixture until blended. Stir in walnuts.

» Pour into three greased and floured 9-in. round baking pans. Bake at 350° for 25-30 minutes or until a toothpick inserted near the center comes out clean. Cool for 10 minutes before removing from pans to wire racks to cool completely.

» For frosting, in a large bowl, beat the shortening, butter, lemon peel and salt until fluffy. Add confectioners' sugar alternately with pineapple juice. Beat in cream. Spread between layers and over top and sides of cake. Sprinkle with walnuts if desired.

Yield: 12-14 servings.

greasing a cake pan

To grease the bottom and sides of a baking pan, either spray with cooking spray or use shortening. When using shortening, place a dab of it on a white paper towel and rub the shortening over the inside of the pan.

chocolate cookie cake

This is a showstopper and tastes as good as it looks. It's a quicker version of a favorite scratch cake. Using a boxed mix saves time when my schedule is hectic.

Renee Zimmer • Gig Harbor, Washington

1 package (18-1/4 ounces) white cake mix

16 cream-filled chocolate sandwich cookies, coarsely crushed

1 package (3 ounces) cream cheese, softened

2 tablespoons 2% milk

2 cups heavy whipping cream

3/4 cup confectioners' sugar

Additional cream-filled chocolate sandwich cookies

» Prepare cake batter according to package directions; stir in crushed cookies. Spoon into a greased and floured 10-in. fluted tube pan.

» Bake at 350° for 33-38 minutes or until a toothpick inserted near the center comes out clean. Cool for 10 minutes before removing from pan to a wire rack to cool completely.

» In a small bowl, beat the cream cheese and milk until smooth. Beat in cream until mixture begins to thicken. Gradually add confectioners' sugar; beat until stiff peaks form. Frost cake. Garnish with additional cookies. Refrigerate leftovers.

Yield: 12 servings.

coconut pineapple cake

This dessert is incredibly tender and dense, which makes it ideal for chilling and cutting up ahead of time to serve as bars at social events. We're always being asked for this recipe.

Krista Smith Kliebenstein • Westminster, Colorado

2 eggs

2 cups sugar

1 teaspoon vanilla extract

2 cups all-purpose flour

1/2 teaspoon baking soda

1/2 teaspoon baking powder

1/2 teaspoon salt

1 can (20 ounces) crushed pineapple, undrained

1/2 cup chopped walnuts

FROSTING:

1 package (8 ounces) cream cheese, softened

1/2 cup butter, softened

2 cups confectioners' sugar

1/2 cup flaked coconut

» In a large bowl, beat the eggs, sugar and vanilla until fluffy. Combine the flour, baking soda, baking powder and salt; add to egg mixture alternately with pineapple. Stir in walnuts.

» Pour into a greased 13-in. x 9-in. baking pan. Bake at 350° for 35-40 minutes or until a toothpick inserted near the center comes out clean. Cool on a wire rack.

» In a bowl, beat the cream cheese, butter and confectioners' sugar until smooth. Frost cake. Sprinkle with coconut. Store in the refrigerator.

Yield: 12 servings.

florida orange cake

This is a perfect showcase for Florida oranges, with juice in the cake and marmalade in the frosting. Everyone always comments on how luscious it is.

Terry Bray • Auburndale, Florida

1 package (18-1/4 ounces) yellow cake mix

1 cup orange juice

3 eggs

1/3 cup water

1/3 cup canola oil

FROSTING:

1 package (8 ounces) cream cheese, softened

1/4 cup butter, softened

1 tablespoon orange marmalade

3 cups confectioners' sugar

» In a large bowl, combine the cake mix, orange juice, eggs, water and oil; beat on low speed for 30 seconds. Beat on medium for 2 minutes.

» Pour into a greased 13-in. x 9-in. baking pan. Bake at 350° for 30-35 minutes or until a toothpick inserted near the center comes out clean. Cool on a wire rack.

» For frosting, in a small bowl, beat cream cheese and butter until smooth. Beat in orange marmalade and confectioners' sugar. Spread over cake. Store in the refrigerator.

Yield: 12-16 servings.

frosting too thin or thick?

If your frosting is not the right consistency for spreading, it's easily fixed. If it is too thick, add milk a teaspoon at a time until it's spreadable. If it's too thin, beat in some sifted confectioners' sugar until it is spreadable.

lemon pound cake

If you and your family like lemon, you'll be delighted with this impressive-looking cake. Every bite is sweet and tart at the same time.

Traci Wynne • Denver, Pennsylvania

1-1/4 cups butter, softened

1 package (8 ounces) cream cheese, softened

3 cups sugar

6 eggs

3 tablespoons lemon juice

2 teaspoons vanilla extract

1 teaspoon lemon extract

1/2 teaspoon orange extract

2-3/4 cups all-purpose flour

1/8 teaspoon salt

GLAZE:

1 cup confectioners' sugar

1 tablespoon butter, melted

2 tablespoons lemon juice

1 teaspoon grated lemon peel

» In a large bowl, cream the butter, cream cheese and sugar until light and fluffy, about 5 minutes. Add eggs, one at a time, beating well after each addition. Stir in lemon juice and extracts. Combine flour and salt; add to creamed mixture just until combined.

» Pour into a greased and floured 10-in. tube pan. Bake at 325° for 65-70 minutes or until a toothpick inserted near the center comes out clean. Cool for 10 minutes before removing from pan to a wire rack to cool completely.

» In a small bowl, whisk the glaze ingredients; drizzle over cake.

Yield: 12-16 servings.

delightful banana cake

Nuts and chocolate chips add a fun touch to this cake that feeds a crowd. And there's so much delicious browned-butter drizzle, it adds a perfect touch to this lovely dessert.

Vicki Raatz • Waterloo, Wisconsin

2 eggs, separated

1/4 cup plus 1 tablespoon butter, softened, divided

1-1/2 cups sugar, divided

1 cup mashed ripe bananas (2 to 3 medium)

1/3 cup reduced-fat sour cream

1/4 cup unsweetened applesauce

1 teaspoon vanilla extract

2 cups all-purpose flour

2-1/2 teaspoons baking powder

1/2 teaspoon salt

1/4 teaspoon baking soda

1/2 cup semisweet chocolate chips

1 tablespoon water

1/2 cup chopped walnuts or chopped pecans

DRIZZLE:

2 tablespoons butter

1 cup confectioners' sugar

1/2 teaspoon vanilla extract

1 to 2 tablespoons fat-free milk

» Place egg whites in a small bowl; let stand at room temperature for 30 minutes.

» In a large bowl, beat 1/4 cup butter and 1 cup sugar until crumbly, about 2 minutes. Add egg yolks; mix well. In a small bowl, beat the bananas, sour cream, applesauce and vanilla until blended. Combine the flour, baking powder, salt and baking soda; add to the butter mixture alternately with the banana mixture. In a microwave, melt chocolate chips and remaining butter; stir until smooth. Cool slightly; stir in water.

» Beat the egg whites on medium speed until soft peaks form. Gradually beat in remaining sugar, 1 tablespoon at a time, on high until stiff glossy peaks form and sugar is dissolved. Fold into batter. Fold in walnuts.

» Coat a 10-in. fluted tube pan with cooking spray and sprinkle with flour; add a third of the cake batter. Drizzle with half of the chocolate mixture. Repeat layers; top with remaining batter.

» Bake at 350° for 40-45 minutes or until a toothpick inserted near the center comes out clean. Cool for 10 minutes before removing from pan to a wire rack to cool completely.

» For drizzle, in a small heavy saucepan, melt butter until lightly browned. Remove from the heat; stir in the confectioners' sugar, vanilla and enough milk to achieve desired consistency. Drizzle over cake.

Yield: 16 servings.

golden pound cake

This moist Bundt cake is quick to put together with a lemon cake mix, vanilla pudding mix and a can of Mountain Dew. I sometimes substitute orange cake mix and a can of orange Crush soda.

Vicki Boyd • Mechanicsville, Virginia

1 package (18-1/4 ounces) lemon cake mix

1 package (3.4 ounces) instant vanilla pudding mix

4 eggs

3/4 cup canola oil

1 can (12 ounces) Mountain Dew

Confectioners' sugar, optional

» In a large bowl, combine the cake mix, pudding mix, eggs, oil and soda; beat on low speed for 30 seconds. Beat on medium for 2 minutes.

» Pour into a greased and floured 10-in. fluted tube pan. Bake at 350° for 45-50 minutes or until a toothpick inserted near the center comes out clean. Cool for 10 minutes before removing from pan to a wire rack to cool completely. Dust with confectioners' sugar if desired.

Yield: 12 servings.

poppy seed chiffon cake

This terrific cake recipe was given to me by my grandchild. I hope you enjoy it as much as we do.

Barbara Sonsteby • Mesa, Arizona

7 eggs, separated

1/2 cup poppy seeds

1 cup hot water

2 cups all-purpose flour

1-1/2 cups sugar

3 teaspoons baking powder

1 teaspoon salt

1/4 teaspoon baking soda

1 cup canola oil

2 teaspoons vanilla extract

1/2 teaspoon cream of tartar

» Let eggs stand at room temperature for 30 minutes. In a small bowl, soak poppy seeds in hot water for 15 minutes.

» In a large bowl, combine the flour, sugar, baking powder, salt and baking soda. In a small bowl, whisk the egg yolks, oil, vanilla and poppy seeds with water. Add to dry ingredients; beat until well blended.

» In another large bowl, beat egg whites and cream of tartar until stiff peaks form. Fold into batter.

» Pour into an ungreased 10-in. tube pan. Cut through batter with a knife to remove air pockets. Bake on the lowest oven rack at 350° for 50-55 minutes or until cake springs back when lightly touched. Immediately invert pan; cool completely, about 1 hour.

» Run a knife around side and center tube of pan. Remove cake to a serving plate.

Yield: 12-16 servings.

apple-topped cake

Complete with apples, nuts and cinnamon, this is ideal with cups of coffee. Baking it in a springform pan helps ensure incredible results.

David Heppner • Brandon, Florida

3 tablespoons butter, softened

3/4 cup sugar

1 egg

1 egg white

1 cup vanilla yogurt

1/3 cup unsweetened applesauce

2 tablespoons canola oil

2 teaspoons vanilla extract

2 cups all-purpose flour

1 teaspoon baking powder

1/2 teaspoon baking soda

1/2 teaspoon salt

1-1/2 cups chopped peeled apples

2 tablespoons chopped walnuts

1 tablespoon brown sugar

1/2 teaspoon ground cinnamon

1/8 teaspoon ground allspice

» In a large bowl, beat butter and sugar until crumbly, about 2 minutes. Add the egg, egg white, yogurt, applesauce, oil and vanilla; beat until smooth. Combine the dry ingredients; add to butter mixture, beating just until moistened.

» Pour into a 9-in. springform pan coated with cooking spray. Sprinkle with apples and walnuts. Combine the brown sugar, cinnamon and allspice; sprinkle over top.

» Bake at 375° for 47-52 minutes or until a toothpick inserted near the center comes out clean. Cool on a wire rack. Run a knife around edge of pan to loosen. Remove sides of pan. Refrigerate leftovers.

Yield: 10 servings.

strawberry marble cake

Perfect for special occasions, this strawberry swirl cake makes a pretty presentation at the end of a meal. I also serve it with afternoon tea, and it's a quick sell at any bake sale.

Margery Richmond • Fort Collins, Colorado

1-1/2 cups egg whites (about 10)

1 package (10 ounces) frozen unsweetened strawberries, thawed and drained

1-1/2 cups sugar, divided

1-1/4 cups cake flour

1-1/2 teaspoons cream of tartar

1/2 teaspoon salt

1 teaspoon vanilla extract

1 teaspoon almond extract

Red food coloring, optional

Whipped topping and sliced fresh strawberries, optional

» Let egg whites stand at room temperature for 30 minutes. In a food processor, puree strawberries; strain puree and discard seeds. Set aside.

» Sift together 3/4 cup sugar and the flour twice; set aside. Add cream of tartar and salt to egg whites; beat on medium speed until soft peaks form. Gradually beat in remaining sugar, 2 tablespoons at a time, on high until stiff glossy peaks form and sugar is dissolved. Gradually fold in flour mixture, about 1/2 cup at a time.

» Transfer half of the batter to another bowl; fold in extracts. Fold 1/4 cup strawberry puree into remaining batter; add food coloring if desired.

» Gently spoon batters, alternating colors, into an ungreased 10-in. tube pan. Cut through with a knife to swirl. Bake on the lowest oven rack at 350° for 45-50 minutes or until lightly browned and top appears dry. Immediately invert pan; cool completely, about 1 hour.

» Run a knife around side and center tube of pan. Serve cake with remaining puree; garnish with whipped topping and fresh strawberries if desired.

Yield: 12 servings.

boston cream sponge cake

I'm not a big fan of rich desserts, so I frequently make this fluffy cake. The homemade custard and chocolate frosting make it delicious.

Jan Badovinac • Harrison, Arkansas

5 eggs

1 cup sugar

1/2 teaspoon salt

1 teaspoon vanilla extract

1-1/4 cups all-purpose flour

CUSTARD:

3/4 cup sugar

2 tablespoons cornstarch

1-1/2 cups 2% milk

6 egg yolks, lightly beaten

1 teaspoon vanilla extract

1/2 cup butter, softened

CHOCOLATE FROSTING:

2 tablespoons butter, softened

1 ounce unsweetened chocolate, melted and cooled

1 cup confectioners' sugar

3 tablespoons heavy whipping cream

1 teaspoon vanilla extract

» In a large bowl, beat eggs until lemon-colored. Gradually add sugar and salt, beating until thick and lemon-colored. Beat in vanilla. Fold in flour, 2 tablespoons at a time. Pour into two greased and floured 9-in. round baking pans.

» Bake at 350° for 17-20 minutes or until cake springs back when lightly touched. Cool for 10 minutes before removing from pans to wire racks to cool completely.

» For custard, combine sugar and cornstarch in a saucepan. Gradually stir in milk until smooth. Bring to a boil; cook and stir for 2 minutes. Remove from the heat. Stir a small amount of hot mixture into egg yolks; return all to the pan. Bring to a gentle boil, stirring constantly. Remove from the heat; stir in vanilla. Cool completely.

» In a large bowl, cream butter until light and fluffy. Gradually beat in custard.

» Cut each cake horizontally into two layers. Place bottom layer on a serving plate; top with a third of the filling. Repeat layers twice. Top with remaining cake layer.

» In a small bowl, combine frosting ingredients. Spread over top of cake. Refrigerate.

Yield: 12-16 servings.

I love to bake and have won several ribbons at the county fair. When we're asked to take a dish to a potluck, I often help my mom make it. This scrumptious cake is fun to serve because everyone likes it!

Abigail Crawford • Lake Butler, Florida

chocolate chip cake

1 package (18-1/4 ounces) yellow cake mix

1 package (3.4 ounces) instant vanilla pudding mix

1 cup 2% milk

1 cup canola oil

4 eggs

1 cup miniature semisweet chocolate chips

5 tablespoons grated German sweet chocolate, divided

2 tablespoons confectioners' sugar

» In a bowl, combine cake and pudding mixes, milk, oil and eggs. Beat on low speed for 30 seconds. Beat on medium for 2 minutes. Stir in chocolate chips and 3 tablespoons grated chocolate. Pour into a greased and floured 10-in. fluted tube pan.

» Bake at 350° for 55-65 minutes or until a toothpick inserted near the center comes out clean. Cool for 10 minutes before removing from pan to a wire rack to cool completely. Combine confectioners' sugar and remaining grated chocolate; sprinkle over cake.

Yield: 12 servings.

» In a large bowl, cream sugar and remaining butter until light and fluffy. Add eggs, one at a time, beating well after each addition. Beat in vanilla. Combine the flour, baking powder and salt; add to creamed mixture alternately with milk. Beat just until combined. Fold in 2 cups reserved pecans.

» Spread evenly into three greased and waxed paper-lined 9-in. round baking pans. Bake at 350° for 25-30 minutes or until a toothpick inserted near the center comes out clean. Cool for 10 minutes; remove from pans to wire racks to cool completely.

» For frosting, in a large bowl, beat the cream cheese, butter, confectioners' sugar and vanilla until smooth. Beat in enough milk to achieve spreading consistency. Spread frosting between layers and over top and sides of cake. Sprinkle with remaining pecans. Store in the refrigerator.

Yield: 12-16 servings.

toasted butter pecan cake

If you like butter pecan ice cream, you'll love this cake. Loads of nuts are folded into the batter, and more are sprinkled over the rich, sensational frosting.

Phyllis Edwards • Fort Valley, Georgia

1 cup plus 2 tablespoons butter, softened, divided

2-2/3 cups chopped pecans

2 cups sugar

4 eggs

2 teaspoons vanilla extract

3 cups all-purpose flour

2 teaspoons baking powder

1/2 teaspoon salt

1 cup 2% milk

FROSTING:

2 packages (one 8 ounces, one 3 ounces) cream cheese, softened

2/3 cup butter, softened

6-1/2 cups confectioners' sugar

1-1/2 teaspoons vanilla extract

1 to 2 tablespoons 2% milk

» In a small heavy skillet, melt 2 tablespoons butter. Add pecans; cook over medium heat until toasted, about 4 minutes. Set aside to cool.

upside-down strawberry shortcake

For a tasty twist at dessert time, this unique spring shortcake has a bountiful berry layer on the bottom. The tempting cake is a sweet our family has savored for years.

Debra Falkiner • St. Charles, Missouri

1 cup miniature marshmallows

2 packages (10 ounces each) frozen sweetened sliced strawberries

1 package (3 ounces) strawberry gelatin

1/2 cup shortening

1-1/2 cups sugar

3 eggs

1 teaspoon vanilla extract

2-1/4 cups all-purpose flour

3 teaspoons baking powder

1/2 teaspoon salt

1 cup 2% milk

Fresh strawberries and whipped cream

» Sprinkle marshmallows evenly into a greased 13-in. x 9-in. baking dish; set aside. In a small bowl, combine strawberries and gelatin powder; set aside.

» In a bowl, cream shortening and sugar until light and fluffy. Add eggs, one at a time, beating well after each addition. Beat in vanilla. Combine flour, baking powder and salt; add to creamed mixture alternately with milk, beating well after each addition.

» Pour batter over the marshmallows. Spoon strawberry mixture evenly over batter. Bake at 350° for 45-50 minutes or until a toothpick inserted near the center comes out clean. Cool on a wire rack. Cut into squares. Garnish with strawberries and whipped cream.

Yield: 12-16 servings.

mocha nut torte

My husband doesn't like chocolate cake, but this spectacular three-layer torte is one he looks forward to having. I've been using this recipe for special occasions for a long time.

Megan Shepherdson • Winnipeg, Manitoba

7 eggs, separated

1 cup sugar, divided

1 teaspoon vanilla extract

1-1/4 cups ground walnuts

1-1/4 cups ground pecans

1/4 cup dry bread crumbs

1 teaspoon baking powder

3/4 teaspoon salt, divided

FILLING:
1 cup heavy whipping cream

1/2 cup confectioners' sugar

1 teaspoon vanilla extract

MOCHA FROSTING:
1/4 cup butter, cubed

4 ounces unsweetened chocolate, chopped

1/2 cup brewed coffee

2 teaspoons vanilla extract

3 to 3-1/4 cups confectioners' sugar

Pecan halves, optional

» Line three 9-in. round baking pans with waxed paper; set aside. Place egg whites in a large bowl; let stand at room temperature for 30 minutes.

» Meanwhile, in another bowl, beat egg yolks until slightly thickened. Gradually add 1/2 cup sugar, beating until thick and lemon-colored. Beat in vanilla. Combine nuts, crumbs, baking powder and 1/2 teaspoon salt; stir into yolk mixture until combined.

» Add remaining salt to egg whites; beat on medium speed until soft peaks form. Gradually beat in remaining sugar, about 2 tablespoons at a time, on high until stiff glossy peaks form and sugar is dissolved. Gradually fold into batter just until blended. Divide among prepared pans.

» Bake at 375° for 20-25 minutes or until tops spring back when lightly touched. Invert pans; cool for 20 minutes. Remove from pans to wire racks; cool completely. Remove waxed paper.

» In a small bowl, beat cream until it begins to thicken. Add confectioners' sugar and vanilla; beat until stiff peaks form. Cover and refrigerate until assembling.

» In a large saucepan, melt butter and chocolate over low heat. Remove from the heat. Stir in coffee, vanilla and enough confectioners' sugar to achieve frosting consistency. Spread filling between layers. Frost top and sides of cake. Garnish with pecans if desired.

Yield: 12 servings.

truffle torte

The biggest sweet tooths are satisfied with just a small slice of this rich, decadent torte. A white-chocolate pattern on top and chopped pecans around the side give it an elegant finish.

Mary Choate • Spring Hill, Florida

3/4 cup butter, cubed

8 ounces semisweet chocolate, chopped

6 eggs

3/4 cup sugar

1 teaspoon vanilla extract

3/4 cup ground pecans

1/4 cup all-purpose flour

GANACHE:
4 ounces semisweet chocolate chips, chopped

1/2 cup heavy whipping cream

2 tablespoons butter

GARNISH:
2 ounces white baking chocolate

3/4 cup finely chopped pecans

Pecan halves, optional

» Line the bottom of a greased 9-in. springform pan with waxed paper; grease the paper and set aside.

» In a microwave, melt butter and chocolate; stir until smooth. Cool. In a large bowl, beat eggs until frothy; gradually add sugar, beating for 4-5 minutes or until mixture triples in volume. Gradually beat in chocolate mixture and vanilla. Combine pecans and flour; fold into batter. Pour into prepared pan.

» Bake at 350° for 30-35 minutes or until cake springs back when lightly touched. Cool on a wire rack for 15 minutes. Run a knife around edge of pan; remove sides of pan. Invert cake onto wire rack; carefully remove pan bottom and waxed paper. Cool completely.

» Place chocolate chips in a small bowl. In a small saucepan, bring cream just to a boil. Pour over chocolate; whisk until smooth. Stir in butter.

» Transfer to a small bowl; cover and refrigerate until mixture reaches spreading consistency, stirring occasionally. Place cake on a serving plate. Pour ganache over cake and quickly spread to edges.

» In a microwave, melt white chocolate; stir until smooth. Transfer to a heavy-duty resealable plastic bag; cut a small hole in a corner of bag.

» Pipe thin horizontal lines 1 in. apart over ganache. Use a sharp knife to draw right angles across the piped lines. Press pecans onto side of torte. Top with pecan halves if desired. Cover and refrigerate for 30 minutes or until set.

Yield: 18 servings.

white chocolate christmas torte

Talk about a scene-stealer! This raspberry-filled cake, an exceptional dessert for any meal, is an especially lovely ending for a holiday feast.

Carol Gillespie • Chambersburg, Pennsylvania

1-1/2 cups butter, cubed

3/4 cup water

4 ounces white baking chocolate, chopped

1-1/2 cups buttermilk

4 eggs, lightly beaten

1 teaspoon vanilla extract

1/4 teaspoon rum extract

3-1/2 cups all-purpose flour, divided

1 cup chopped pecans, toasted

2-1/4 cups sugar

1-1/2 teaspoons baking soda

WHITE CHOCOLATE CREAM FROSTING:
4 ounces white baking chocolate, chopped

2 packages (one 8 ounces, one 3 ounces) cream cheese, softened

1/2 cup butter, softened

1 teaspoon vanilla extract

1/4 teaspoon rum extract

6 cups confectioners' sugar

1 cup seedless raspberry jam, divided

» In a large saucepan, combine butter, water and white chocolate; cook and stir over low heat until melted. Remove from the heat; stir in the buttermilk, eggs and extracts.

» In a small bowl, combine 1/2 cup flour and pecans. In a large bowl, combine the sugar, baking soda and remaining flour. Gradually beat in butter mixture. Stir in pecan mixture.

» Pour into three greased and floured 9-in. round baking pans. Bake at 350° for 25-30 minutes or until a toothpick inserted near the center comes out clean. Cool for 10 minutes before removing from pans to wire racks to cool completely.

» For frosting, in a microwave, melt white chocolate; stir until smooth. Cool for 10 minutes, stirring occasionally.

» In a large bowl, beat cream cheese and butter. Gradually beat in melted chocolate and extracts. Gradually beat in confectioners' sugar until smooth.

» To assemble, spread 2 tablespoons of jam over one cake layer; spread with 1/2 cup frosting. Repeat layers twice. Spread remaining frosting over top and sides of torte. Warm remaining jam; drizzle over dessert plates. Top with a slice of torte.

Yield: 12-15 servings.

coconut-topped oatmeal cake

This old-fashioned confection has mass appeal and was passed down from my husband's grandmother.

Tamra Duncan • Decatur, Arkansas

1-1/2 cups boiling water

1 cup quick-cooking oats

1/2 cup butter, softened

1 cup sugar

1 cup packed brown sugar

2 eggs

1-1/2 cups all-purpose flour

1 teaspoon baking soda

1 teaspoon ground cinnamon

1/2 teaspoon salt

TOPPING:

1 cup packed brown sugar

1/2 cup butter

1/2 cup 2% milk

1 cup flaked coconut

1/2 cup chopped pecans

1 teaspoon vanilla extract

» In a small bowl, pour boiling water over oats; let stand for 5 minutes. In a large bowl, cream butter and sugars until light and fluffy. Add eggs, one at a time, beating well after each addition. Combine the flour, baking soda, cinnamon and salt; add to the creamed mixture alternately with the oat mixture, beating well after each addition.

» Transfer to a greased 13-in. x 9-in. baking pan. Bake at 350° for 30-35 minutes or until a toothpick inserted near the center comes out clean.

» Meanwhile, in a small saucepan, bring the brown sugar, butter and milk to a boil over medium heat. Remove from the heat; stir in the coconut, pecans and vanilla. Pour over warm cake. Cool completely.

Yield: 12-16 servings.

» In a small bowl, fold whipped topping into 1/3 cup butterscotch topping. Place one cake layer on a serving plate. Spread with half of the filling; top with half of the chopped pears. Drizzle with 2 tablespoons butterscotch topping. Repeat layers.

» Arrange pecan halves on top of cake. Drizzle with remaining butterscotch topping. Refrigerate until serving.

Yield: 10 servings.

lovely cherry layer cake

This eye-catching confection is a variation of an Italian recipe that's been in my family for years. The cannoli filling tucked between the cake layers is incredibly rich and delectable.

Jennifer Ciccia • Hamburg, New York

1 package (18-1/4 ounces) white cake mix

CANNOLI FILLING:

2 packages (8 ounces each) cream cheese, softened

1 carton (15 ounces) ricotta cheese

1 cup confectioners' sugar

1 teaspoon vanilla extract

1/2 teaspoon almond extract

1 jar (16 ounces) maraschino cherries

1 cup miniature chocolate chips

FROSTING:

1 cup shortening

1 cup butter, softened

7-1/2 cups confectioners' sugar

3 teaspoons vanilla extract

4 to 5 tablespoons water

Pink and green gel food coloring

» Prepare and bake cake according to package directions, using two greased and floured 9-in. round baking pans. Cool for 10 minutes; remove from pans to wire racks to cool completely.

» In a large bowl, beat cream cheese and ricotta until fluffy. Add confectioners' sugar and extracts; beat until smooth.

» Drain the cherries well, reserving 1 teaspoon cherry juice. Chop cherries. Stir chopped cherries, chocolate chips and reserved cherry juice into the ricotta mixture. Refrigerate for 1 hour or until spreadable.

» In another large bowl, cream shortening and butter until light and fluffy. Gradually add confectioners' sugar and vanilla; beat until smooth. Add enough water to achieve a spreadable consistency. Tint 3/4 cup frosting pink. Tint 1/4 cup frosting green. Set aside 1-1/2 cups white frosting.

pecan pear torte

This delicious pear-flavored cake is topped with butterscotch whipped cream and will be a showstopper when you present it at any get-together you attend.

Jeanne Holt • Saint Paul, Minnesota

1 can (15 ounces) pear halves

1 package (18-1/4 ounces) butter recipe golden cake mix

1/2 cup butter, softened

3 eggs

1 teaspoon vanilla extract

1/2 cup chopped pecans, toasted

TOPPING:

1 carton (8 ounces) frozen whipped topping, thawed

2/3 cup butterscotch ice cream topping, divided

2 cups chopped peeled ripe pears

1/3 cup pecan halves, toasted

» Drain pears, reserving liquid. Puree pears in a blender; add enough reserved liquid to measure 1 cup.

» In a large bowl, combine the cake mix, butter, eggs, vanilla, chopped pecans and pear puree; beat on low speed for 30 seconds. Beat on medium for 2 minutes. Pour into two greased and floured 9-in. round baking pans.

» Bake at 375° for 20-25 minutes or until a toothpick inserted near the center comes out clean. Cool for 10 minutes before removing from pans to wire racks to cool completely.

» Cut each cake horizontally into two layers. Place one layer on a serving plate; spread with a third of the filling. Repeat layers twice. Top with remaining cake layer. Spread remaining white frosting over the top and sides of cake.

» To decorate, cut a small hole in the corner of pastry or plastic bag; insert tip #5. Fill the bag with reserved white frosting; pipe vines on cake. Change to shell tip #21; pipe shell border along bottom and top edges. Use petal tip #103 and pink frosting to pipe the rosebuds. Use leaf tip #67 and green frosting to pipe the leaves. Store in the refrigerator.

Yield: 14 servings.

EDITOR'S NOTE: Use of a coupler ring will allow you to easily change pastry tips for different designs.

german chocolate-cream cheesecake

My daughter requests this as her birthday cake, and I take it to potlucks, church dinners or any time the dessert is my responsibility.
Kathy Johnson • Lake City, South Dakota

1 package (18-1/4 ounces) German Chocolate cake mix

2 packages (8 ounces each) cream cheese, softened

1-1/2 cups sugar

4 eggs, lightly beaten

FROSTING:

1 cup sugar

1 cup evaporated milk

1/2 cup butter, cubed

3 egg yolks, lightly beaten

1 teaspoon vanilla extract

1-1/2 cups flaked coconut

1 cup chopped pecans

» Prepare cake batter according to package directions; set aside. In a small bowl, beat cream cheese and sugar until smooth. Add eggs; beat on low speed just until combined.

» Pour half of the cake batter into a greased 13-in. x 9-in. baking dish. Gently pour cream cheese mixture over batter. Gently spoon remaining batter over top; spread to edge of pan.

» Bake at 325° for 70-75 minutes or until a toothpick inserted near the center comes out clean. Cool in the pan on a wire rack for 1 hour.

» For frosting, in a heavy saucepan, combine the sugar, milk, butter and egg yolks. Cook and stir over medium-low heat until thickened and a thermometer reads 160° or is thick enough to coat the back of a metal spoon.

» Remove from the heat. Stir in vanilla; fold in coconut and pecans. Cool until frosting reaches spreading consistency. Frost cooled cake. Refrigerate leftovers.

Yield: 16 servings.

pumpkin pound cake

Instead of traditional pumpkin pie, I bake this scrumptious cake for Thanksgiving. As it bakes, the comforting, spicy aroma fills the house. It's a perfect ending to a large meal.

Virginia Loew • Leesburg, Florida

2-1/2 cups sugar

1 cup canola oil

3 eggs

3 cups all-purpose flour

2 teaspoons baking soda

1 teaspoon ground cinnamon

1 teaspoon ground nutmeg

1/2 teaspoon salt

1/4 teaspoon ground cloves

1 can (15 ounces) solid-pack pumpkin

Confectioners' sugar

» In a bowl, combine sugar and oil until blended. Add eggs, one at a time, beating well after each addition. Combine flour, baking soda, cinnamon, nutmeg, salt and cloves; add to egg mixture alternately with pumpkin, beating well after each addition.

» Transfer to a greased 10-in. fluted tube pan. Bake at 350° for 60-65 minutes or until toothpick inserted near the center comes out clean. Cool for 10 minutes before inverting onto a wire rack. Remove pan and cool completely. Dust with confectioners' sugar.

Yield: 12-16 servings.

buttermilk torte

When I was growing up, my family lived on a farm, and we were always very busy with chores. This luscious dessert was one of our top picks because it was so easy to make.

Carol Ledvina • Mishicot, Wisconsin

3/4 cup butter-flavored shortening

1-3/4 cups sugar, divided

2 eggs, separated

1 teaspoon vanilla extract

2-1/2 cups all-purpose flour

1 teaspoon baking soda

1 teaspoon ground cinnamon

1/2 teaspoon salt

1-1/4 cups buttermilk

1/4 teaspoon cream of tartar

1/2 cup semisweet chocolate chips

1/2 cup flaked coconut

» Grease the bottom only of a 10-in. springform pan; set aside. In a large bowl, cream shortening and 1-1/2 cups sugar until light and fluffy. Beat in egg yolks and vanilla. Combine the flour, baking soda, cinnamon and salt; add to the creamed mixture alternately with buttermilk, beating well after each addition. Transfer to prepared pan.

» Bake at 325° for 50-55 minutes or until a toothpick inserted near the center comes out clean. Remove from the oven; increase heat to 375°.

» In a small bowl, beat the egg whites and cream of tartar on medium speed until soft peaks form. Gradually add remaining sugar, 1 tablespoon at time, beating on high until stiff glossy peaks form.

» Spread evenly over warm cake, sealing edges to sides of pan. Sprinkle chips and coconut over the top. Bake for 15 minutes or until coconut and meringue are golden brown. Run a knife around edge of pan; remove sides. Cool completely on a wire rack. Refrigerate leftovers.

Yield: 12 servings.

cherry-swirl chiffon cake

This impressive-looking cake always elicits oohs and aahs when it makes an appearance on a buffet. For a change, use peppermint extract in place of cherry extract if you desire.

Edna Hoffman • Hebron, Indiana

8 egg whites

2-1/4 cups cake flour

1-1/2 cups sugar

3 teaspoons baking powder

1 teaspoon salt

5 egg yolks

3/4 cup water

1/2 cup canola oil

2 teaspoons cherry extract

1/2 teaspoon cream of tartar

6 drops red food coloring

FROSTING:
2/3 cup sugar

2 egg whites

1/3 cup light corn syrup

2 tablespoons plus 2 teaspoons water

1/4 teaspoon cream of tartar

1 teaspoon vanilla extract

1/2 teaspoon cherry extract

12 drops red food coloring

Crushed cherry hard candies, optional

» Place egg whites in a large bowl; let stand at room temperature for 30 minutes. Meanwhile, in another bowl, combine the flour, sugar, baking powder and salt. Whisk the egg yolks, water, oil and extract; add to dry ingredients. Beat until well blended.

» Add cream of tartar to egg whites; beat on medium speed until stiff peaks form. Fold into batter. Remove a third of the batter to a small bowl; tint pink with red food coloring. Alternately spoon plain and pink batters into an ungreased 10-in. tube pan. Cut through batter with a knife to swirl.

» Bake on the lowest oven rack at 325° for 60-70 minutes or until cake springs back when lightly touched. Immediately invert pan; cool completely, about 1 hour.

» For frosting, in a small heavy saucepan, combine the sugar, egg whites, corn syrup, water and cream of tartar over low heat. With a hand mixer, beat on low speed for 1 minute. Continue beating on low over low heat until frosting reaches 160°, about 8-10 minutes. Pour into the bowl of a heavy-duty stand mixer; add extracts. Beat on high until frosting forms stiff peaks, about 7 minutes.

» Run a knife around side and center tube of pan. Remove cake to a serving plate. Frost top and sides of cake. Add drops of food coloring to frosting at base of cake; with a spatula, blend color up toward top of cake. Sprinkle with candies if desired.

Yield: 12 servings.

testing for doneness

Angel food, sponge and chiffon cakes that are baked in tube pans are done when the top springs back when lightly touched with your fingers. Also check the cracks on the top of the cakes. They should look and feel dry.

lemon angel cake roll

Tart and delicious, this pretty cake roll will tickle any lemon lover's fancy. Its feathery, angel food texture is complemented with a lovely, tangy lemon filling.

Taste of Home Test Kitchen

9 egg whites

1-1/2 teaspoons vanilla extract

3/4 teaspoon cream of tartar

1 cup plus 2 tablespoons sugar

3/4 cup cake flour

1 tablespoon confectioners' sugar

FILLING:

1 cup sugar

3 tablespoons cornstarch

1 cup water

1 egg, lightly beaten

1/4 cup lemon juice

1 tablespoon grated lemon peel

Yellow food coloring, optional

Additional confectioners' sugar

» Place the egg whites in a bowl; let stand at room temperature for 30 minutes. Meanwhile, line a 15-in. x 10-in. x 1-in. baking pan with waxed paper; lightly coat paper with cooking spray and set aside.

» Add vanilla and cream of tartar to egg whites; beat on medium speed until soft peaks form. Gradually beat in sugar, 2 tablespoons at a time, on high until stiff glossy peaks form and sugar is dissolved. Fold in flour, about 1/4 cup at a time.

» Carefully spread batter into prepared pan. Bake at 350° for 15-20 minutes or until cake springs back when lightly touched. Cool for 5 minutes.

» Turn cake onto a kitchen towel dusted with 1 tablespoon confectioners' sugar. Gently peel off waxed paper. Roll up cake in the towel jelly-roll style, starting with a short side. Cool completely on a wire rack.

» In a large saucepan, combine sugar and cornstarch; stir in water until smooth. Cook and stir over medium-high heat until thickened and bubbly. Reduce heat; cook and stir 2 minutes longer. Remove from the heat. Stir a small amount of hot mixture into egg; return all to the pan, stirring constantly. Bring to a gentle boil; cook and stir 2 minutes longer.

» Remove from the heat. Gently stir in lemon juice, peel and food coloring if desired. Cool to room temperature without stirring.

» Unroll cake; spread filling to within 1/2 in. of edges. Roll up again. Place seam side down on a serving plate; sprinkle with additional confectioners' sugar.

Yield: 10 servings.

chocolate party cake

This moist cake is so delicious with its luscious coffee-flavored icing. Friends usually ask for the recipe.

Gloria Warczak • Cedarburg, Wisconsin

1 package (18-1/4 ounces) devil's food cake mix

1 package (3.4 ounces) cook-and-serve chocolate pudding mix

1 envelope whipped topping mix (Dream Whip)

1 cup water

1/4 cup canola oil

4 eggs

MOCHA RUM ICING:

2 tablespoons butter, softened

2 cups confectioners' sugar

1/3 cup baking cocoa

2 tablespoons refrigerated nondairy creamer

1/2 teaspoon rum extract

2 to 3 tablespoons brewed coffee

Chopped pecans, optional

» In a large bowl, combine the first six ingredients; beat on low speed for 30 seconds. Beat on medium for 4 minutes. Pour into a greased and floured 10-in. fluted tube pan.

» Bake at 350° for 35-40 minutes or until a toothpick inserted near the center comes out clean. Cool for 10 minutes before removing from pan to a wire rack to cool completely.

» For icing, in a small bowl, beat the butter, confectioners' sugar, cocoa, creamer, extract and enough coffee to achieve desired drizzling consistency. Drizzle over cake. Garnish with pecans if desired.

Yield: 12 servings.

pineapple carrot cake

I entered this old-fashioned, tender cake in a Colorado Outfitters Association dessert contest, and it took first place!

Cheri Eby • Gunnison, Colorado

1 can (8 ounces) unsweetened crushed pineapple

2 cups shredded carrots

4 eggs

1 cup sugar

1 cup packed brown sugar

1 cup canola oil

2 cups all-purpose flour

2 teaspoons baking soda

2 teaspoons ground cinnamon

1/4 teaspoon salt

3/4 cup chopped walnuts

FROSTING:

2 packages (8 ounces each) cream cheese, softened

1/4 cup butter, softened

2 teaspoons vanilla extract

1-1/2 cups confectioners' sugar

» Drain the pineapple, reserving 2 tablespoons juice (discard remaining juice or save for another use). In a large bowl, beat the carrots, eggs, sugars, oil, pineapple and reserved juice until well blended. In a small bowl, combine the flour, baking soda, cinnamon and salt; gradually beat into pineapple mixture until blended. Stir in walnuts.

» Transfer to a greased 13-in. x 9-in. baking dish. Bake at 350° for 35-40 minutes or until a toothpick inserted near the center comes out clean. Cool on a wire rack.

» For frosting, in a large bowl, beat cream cheese and butter until smooth. Beat in vanilla. Gradually beat in confectioners' sugar until smooth. Spread over cake.

Yield: 12 servings.

orange chocolate torte

This eye-catching dessert takes the cake at any gathering. Chocolate truffles on top make a fantastic finishing touch.

Georgiana Hagman • Louisville, Kentucky

2 cups (12 ounces) semisweet chocolate chips

6 tablespoons butter, cubed

4 egg yolks

6 tablespoons confectioners' sugar

1/4 cup chocolate sprinkles or ground pecans

CAKE:
1 cup butter, softened

2-1/2 cups sugar

4 eggs

1-1/2 teaspoons orange extract

2-1/4 cups all-purpose flour

1 cup baking cocoa

2 teaspoons baking powder

1/2 teaspoon baking soda

1/2 teaspoon salt

2 cups water

FROSTING:
1 cup butter, cubed

1 cup (6 ounces) semisweet chocolate chips

1/3 cup plus 7 to 8 tablespoons milk, divided

1 teaspoon orange extract

2-3/4 cups sifted confectioners' sugar

Chocolate sprinkles

» In a large heavy saucepan, stir chocolate chips and butter until melted. In a small bowl, beat egg yolks until lemon-colored. Gradually stir in warm chocolate mixture; return all to the pan. Cook and stir over medium heat until mixture reaches 160°.

» Remove from the heat. Stir in confectioners' sugar until blended. Place 1/2 cup in a small bowl; pour remaining chocolate mixture into a small bowl for filling. Cover each bowl with a paper towel. Let stand for up to 1 hour or until soft-set.

» For truffles, roll the 1/2-cup portion into 12 balls. Roll in sprinkles or pecans. Cover and refrigerate until serving.

» In a large bowl, cream butter and sugar until light and fluffy. Add eggs, one at a time, beating well after each addition. Beat in extract. Combine the flour, cocoa, baking powder, baking soda and salt; gradually add to creamed mixture alternately with water.

» Pour into three greased and floured 9-in. round baking pans. Bake at 350° for 25-30 minutes or until a toothpick inserted near the center comes out clean. Cool for 10 minutes; remove from pans to wire racks to cool completely.

» For frosting, in a microwave-safe bowl, combine the butter, chocolate chips and 1/3 cup milk; microwave until melted; stir until smooth. Whisk in the extract until smooth. Gradually whisk in the confectioners' sugar.

» Transfer to a large bowl. Place in a large bowl of ice water. With a hand mixer, beat on medium speed until stiff peaks form, about 7 minutes; set aside.

» For the filling, gradually add enough of the remaining milk to the reserved chocolate mixture, beating until filling achieves spreading consistency.

» Place one cake layer on a serving plate; spread with half of the filling. Repeat layers. Spread 2-2/3 cups frosting over top and sides of cake. Using a #195 star tip, pipe the remaining frosting into 12 rosettes on top of cake. Place a truffle on each rosette. Press chocolate sprinkles onto sides of cake. Store in the refrigerator.

Yield: 12 servings.

» In a large bowl, combine the flour, sugar, baking powder and salt. In another bowl, whisk the water, oil, egg yolks and melted chocolate. Add to dry ingredients; beat until well blended. In another bowl, beat egg whites and cream of tartar until stiff peaks form; fold into batter.

» Pour into prepared pans. Bake at 350° for 15-20 minutes or until a toothpick inserted near the center comes out clean. Cool for 10 minutes before removing from pans to wire racks to cool completely. Carefully remove waxed paper.

» In a large saucepan, combine filling ingredients. Cook and stir over medium heat until mixture comes to a boil. Chill for 2 hours or until filling reaches spreading consistency, stirring occasionally. Beat with a mixer until fluffy.

» Cut each cake horizontally into two layers. Place bottom layer on a serving plate; top with a fifth of the filling. Repeat layers.

» For frosting, in a large bowl, beat the cream, confectioners' sugar and cocoa until stiff peaks form. Spread over top and sides of cake. Garnish with chocolate curls.

Yield: 12 servings.

chocolate chiffon torte

This classic recipe is one I made often when we lived on the farm, and I had lots of cream to use up.

Iola Egle • Bella Vista, Arkansas

6 eggs, separated

2 cups cake flour

1-1/2 cups sugar

3 teaspoons baking powder

1/2 teaspoon salt

1/2 cup water

1/2 cup canola oil

2 ounces semisweet chocolate, melted and cooled

1/2 teaspoon cream of tartar

FILLING:
1-1/2 cups heavy whipping cream

1-1/4 cups semisweet chocolate chips

1/4 cup butter, cubed

FROSTING:
1 cup heavy whipping cream

1/2 cup confectioners' sugar

1 tablespoon baking cocoa

Chocolate curls

» Let eggs stand at room temperature for 30 minutes. Line three 9-in. round baking pans with waxed paper and grease the paper; set aside.

shortcake for 50

Folks are always delighted to see these individual shortcakes on the buffet table. They're surprisingly easy to make.

Clara Honeyager • Mukwonago, Wisconsin

10-1/2 cups all-purpose flour

4-1/4 cups sugar, divided

1/2 cup plus 1 tablespoon baking powder

4 teaspoons salt

1 cup cold butter, cubed

3 cups heavy whipping cream

1-1/2 cups water

8 quarts fresh strawberries, sliced

Whipped cream or ice cream

» In a large bowl, combine flour, 2-1/4 cups sugar, baking powder and salt; cut in butter until crumbly. Stir in cream and water just until moistened.

» Drop by 1/4 cupfuls 2 in. apart onto ungreased baking sheets. Bake at 450° for 15 minutes or until golden brown. Cool on wire racks. Combine berries and remaining sugar.

» To serve, split shortcakes horizontally; spoon about 1/3 cup berries and whipped cream on bottom halves. Replace tops; top with another 1/3 cup of berries and additional cream.

Yield: 50 servings.

classic red velvet cake

This ruby-red cake with its lovely cream cheese frosting has become my signature dessert. I can't go to any family function without it. The cake has a buttery taste.

Katie Sloan • Charlotte, North Carolina

1/2 cup shortening

1-1/2 cups sugar

2 eggs

1 bottle (1 ounce) red food coloring

3 teaspoons white vinegar

1 teaspoon butter flavoring

1 teaspoon vanilla extract

2-1/2 cups cake flour

1/4 cup baking cocoa

1 teaspoon baking soda

1 teaspoon salt

1 cup buttermilk

FROSTING:

1 package (8 ounces) cream cheese, softened

1/2 cup butter, softened

3-3/4 cups confectioners' sugar

3 teaspoons vanilla extract

» In a large bowl, cream shortening and sugar until light fluffy. Add eggs, one at a time, beating well after each addition. Beat in the food coloring, vinegar, butter flavoring and vanilla. Combine the flour, cocoa, baking soda and salt; add to creamed mixture alternately with buttermilk, beating well after each addition.

» Pour into three greased and floured 9-in. round baking pans. Bake at 350° for 20-25 minutes or until a toothpick inserted near the center comes out clean. Cool for 10 minutes before removing from pans to wire racks to cool completely.

» In a large bowl, combine frosting ingredients; beat until smooth and creamy. Spread frosting between layers and over top and sides of cake.

Yield: 12 servings.

cappuccino torte

Get-togethers are a time to spend with good friends...they are also a chance to enjoy every bite of rich desserts like this!

Marcia Orlando • Boyertown, Pennsylvania

1-1/4 cups graham cracker crumbs

1/4 cup sugar

1/3 cup butter, melted

GANACHE:
2-1/2 cups semisweet chocolate chips

2 cups heavy whipping cream

1/2 cup butter, cubed

2 tablespoons corn syrup

CAPPUCCINO BUTTERCREAM:
1 tablespoon instant coffee granules

1 tablespoon hot water

1-1/2 cups packed brown sugar

1/2 cup water

6 egg yolks

1-1/2 cups cold butter

4 ounces unsweetened chocolate, melted and cooled

COFFEE WHIPPED CREAM:
1-1/4 cups heavy whipping cream, divided

2 teaspoons instant coffee granules

2 tablespoons confectioners' sugar

1/2 teaspoon vanilla extract

Chocolate curls, optional

» In a large bowl, combine the crumbs, sugar and butter; press onto the bottom of an ungreased 9-in. springform pan. Chill.

» For ganache, place chocolate chips in a large bowl. In a small saucepan, bring cream just to a boil. Pour over chocolate; whisk until smooth. Add butter and corn syrup; stir until smooth. Cool slightly, stirring occasionally. Pour over crust. Chill until firm, about 2 hours.

» For buttercream, dissolve the coffee granules in hot water; set aside. In a large heavy saucepan over medium-high heat, bring brown sugar and water to a boil. Cook and stir until sugar is dissolved. Remove from the heat. Add a small amount of hot mixture to egg yolks; return all to pan, stirring constantly. Cook and stir for 2-5 minutes or until mixture is thickened. Remove from heat; stir in dissolved coffee. Cool to room temperature.

» In a bowl, beat butter until fluffy. Gradually beat in cooked sugar mixture. Beat on high for 2 minutes or until fluffy and light

caramel-colored. Beat in cooled chocolate until blended. Spread over ganache layer. Refrigerate for 4 hours or overnight.

» Several hours before serving, prepare coffee whipped cream. In a small bowl, combine 1 tablespoon cream and coffee; stir until coffee is dissolved. Beat in remaining cream until it begins to thicken. Gradually add confectioners' sugar and vanilla; beat until stiff peaks form.

» Carefully run a knife around edge of springform pan to loosen; remove sides. Frost top of torte with whipped cream; garnish with chocolate curls if desired. Refrigerate until serving.

Yield: 16 servings.

creaming cakes

For good height on cake layers, let butter soften at room temperature. If softening in a microwave, heat a few seconds at a time... don't melt the butter. Cream softened butter or shortening with sugar until light and fluffy. This should take about 5 minutes.

in vanilla. Combine the flour, baking powder and baking soda; add to creamed mixture alternately with buttermilk, beating well after each addition (batter will be thick).

» Pour into a greased and floured 10-in. fluted tube pan. Bake at 350° for 45-50 minutes or until a toothpick inserted near the center comes out clean. Cool for 10 minutes before removing from pan to a wire rack to cool completely.

» For icing, in a small saucepan, combine the butter, brown sugar and cream. Bring to a boil over medium heat, stirring constantly. Remove from the heat; cool for 5-10 minutes. Gradually beat in confectioners' sugar until smooth. Drizzle over cake.

Yield: 12-16 servings.

special-occasion chocolate cake

This won Grand Champion at the 2000 Alaska State Fair, and you will see why once you taste it. This decadent chocolate cake boasts a silky ganache filling and fudgy buttercream frosting.

Cindi Paulson • Anchorage, Alaska

1 cup baking cocoa

2 cups boiling water

1 cup butter, softened

2-1/4 cups sugar

4 eggs

1-1/2 teaspoons vanilla extract

2-3/4 cups all-purpose flour

2 teaspoons baking soda

1/2 teaspoon baking powder

1/2 teaspoon salt

GANACHE:
10 ounces semisweet chocolate, chopped

1 cup heavy whipping cream

2 tablespoons sugar

FROSTING:
1 cup butter, softened

4 cups confectioners' sugar

1/2 cup baking cocoa

1/4 cup 2% milk

2 teaspoons vanilla extract

GARNISH:
3/4 cup sliced almonds, toasted

buttermilk cake with caramel icing

This cake is so moist and tender, it melts in your mouth! It's been a staple for my family for years and goes over extremely well at church potluck meals.

Anna Jean Allen • West Liberty, Kentucky

1 cup butter, softened

2-1/3 cups sugar

3 eggs

1-1/2 teaspoons vanilla extract

3 cups all-purpose flour

1 teaspoon baking powder

1/2 teaspoon baking soda

1 cup buttermilk

ICING:
1/4 cup butter, cubed

1/2 cup packed brown sugar

1/3 cup heavy whipping cream

1 cup confectioners' sugar

» In a large bowl, cream butter and sugar until light and fluffy. Add eggs, one at a time, beating well after each addition. Beat

» In a small bowl, combine cocoa and water; set aside. In a large bowl, cream butter and sugar until light and fluffy. Add eggs, one at a time, beating well after each addition. Beat in vanilla. Combine the flour, baking soda, baking powder and salt; add to creamed mixture alternately with cocoa mixture, beating well after each addition.

» Pour into three greased and floured 9-in. round baking pans. Bake at 350° for 25-30 minutes or until a toothpick inserted near the center comes out clean. Cool for 10 minutes before removing from pans to wire racks to cool completely.

» For ganache, place chocolate in a small bowl. In a small saucepan, bring cream and sugar to a boil. Pour over chocolate; whisk gently until smooth. Refrigerate for 35-45 minutes or until ganache begins to thicken, stirring occasionally.

» For frosting, in a bowl, beat butter until fluffy. Add confectioners' sugar, cocoa, milk and vanilla; beat until smooth.

» Place one cake layer on a serving plate; spread with 1 cup frosting. Top with second layer and 1 cup ganache; sprinkle with 1/2 cup almonds. Top with third layer; frost top and sides of cake. Warm ganache until pourable; pour over cake, allowing some to drape down the sides. Sprinkle with remaining almonds. Refrigerate until serving.

Yield: 12 servings.

holiday walnut torte

This is one of my grandma's best-loved recipes—delicate layers of nut-filled cake put together with apricot glaze and cream cheese frosting. It's heavenly!

Eileen Korecko • Hot Springs Village, Arkansas

3 eggs

1-1/2 cups sugar

3 teaspoons vanilla extract

1-3/4 cups all-purpose flour

1 cup ground walnuts

2 teaspoons baking powder

1/2 teaspoon salt

1-1/2 cups heavy whipping cream

GLAZE:

2/3 cup apricot preserves

1 tablespoon sugar

FROSTING:

1/2 cup butter, softened

1 package (3 ounces) cream cheese, softened

2 cups confectioners' sugar

1 teaspoon vanilla extract

3/4 cup ground walnuts, divided

» In a large bowl, beat the eggs, sugar and vanilla on high speed for 5 minutes or until thick and lemon-colored. Combine the flour, walnuts, baking powder and salt; beat into egg mixture. Beat cream until stiff peaks form; fold into batter.

» Pour into two greased and floured 9-in. round baking pans. Bake at 350° for 25-30 minutes or until a toothpick inserted near the center comes out clean. Cool for 10 minutes before removing from pans to wire racks to cool completely.

» In a small saucepan over medium heat, cook and stir preserves and sugar until sugar is dissolved. Set aside 1/2 cup. Brush remaining glaze over cake tops.

» In a large bowl, beat butter and cream cheese until fluffy. Add confectioners' sugar and vanilla; beat until smooth. Spread 1/2 cup frosting over one cake; top with second cake and 3/4 cup frosting. Sprinkle 1/2 cup walnuts over the top.

» Spread reserved glaze over sides of cake; press remaining walnuts onto sides. Pipe remaining frosting around top edge of cake. Store in the refrigerator.

Yield: 10-12 servings.

chippy macaroon angel cake

This homemade angel cake, filled with coconut and chocolate chips, is as light as a cloud. It's so pretty with the sweetened whipped cream frosting piped around it.

Joyce Platfoot • Wapakoneta, Ohio

1-1/2 cups egg whites (about 10)

1-1/2 cups confectioners' sugar

1 cup cake flour

1-1/2 teaspoons cream of tartar

1 teaspoon almond extract

1 teaspoon vanilla extract

1/4 teaspoon salt

1 cup sugar

1 cup (6 ounces) miniature semisweet chocolate chips

1/2 cup flaked coconut

TOPPING:
1 cup heavy whipping cream

2 tablespoons confectioners' sugar

1/2 cup flaked coconut, toasted

» Place egg whites in a large bowl; let stand at room temperature for 30 minutes. Sift confectioners' sugar and flour together twice; set aside.

» Add the cream of tartar, extracts and salt to egg whites; beat on medium speed until soft peaks form. Gradually add sugar, 1 tablespoon at a time, beating on high until glossy peaks form and sugar is dissolved. Gradually fold in flour mixture, about 1/2 cup at a time. Fold in chocolate chips and coconut.

» Gently spoon into an ungreased 10-in. tube pan. Cut through batter with a knife to remove air pockets. Bake on the lowest oven rack at 325° for 50-55 minutes or until top springs back when lightly touched and cracks feel dry. Immediately invert baking pan; cool completely.

» For topping, in a large bowl, beat cream until it begins to thicken. Add the confectioners' sugar; beat until stiff peaks form. Serve with cake; sprinkle with the coconut. Refrigerate any leftover topping.

Yield: 12-16 servings.

meringue torte

My grandmother, who came here from Sweden when she was 21, used to make this cake for our birthdays, and it is still a family favorite.

Ruth Grover • Portland, Connecticut

3/4 cup butter, softened

3/4 cup sugar

6 egg yolks

1 teaspoon vanilla extract

1-1/2 cups all-purpose flour

1-1/2 teaspoons baking powder

6 tablespoons 2% milk

MERINGUE:
6 egg whites

1-1/2 cups sugar

1/2 teaspoon vanilla extract

1/2 cup plus 3 tablespoons finely chopped walnuts, divided

FILLING:
2 cups heavy whipping cream

1/4 cup confectioners' sugar

2 cups fresh raspberries

» In a large bowl, cream butter and sugar until light and fluffy. Add egg yolks, one at a time, beating well after each addition. Beat in vanilla. Combine flour and baking powder; add to creamed mixture alternately with milk, beating well after each addition. Pour into three parchment paper-lined 9-in. round baking pans; set aside.

» In a large bowl, beat egg whites on medium speed until foamy. Gradually beat in sugar, 1 tablespoon at a time, on high until stiff glossy peaks form and sugar is dissolved. Add vanilla. Fold in 1/2 cup walnuts. Spread meringue evenly over cake batter; sprinkle with remaining walnuts.

» Bake at 325° for 30-35 minutes or until meringue is lightly browned. Cool on wire racks for 10 minutes (meringue will crack). Loosen edges of cakes from pans with a knife. Using two large spatulas, carefully remove one cake to a serving plate, meringue side up. Carefully remove remaining cakes, meringue side up, to wire racks.

» In a large bowl, beat cream until it begins to thicken. Gradually add confectioners' sugar; beat until stiff peaks form. Carefully spread half of the filling over cake on serving plate; top with half of the raspberries. Repeat layers. Top with remaining cake. Store in the refrigerator.

Yield: 16-18 servings.

six-layer coconut cake

I found this recipe when going through my grandmother's old files. It is simply the best.

Angela Leinenbach • Mechanicsville, Virginia

1 cup butter, softened

3 cups sugar

3 teaspoons vanilla extract

4 cups cake flour

1 teaspoon baking soda

1/2 teaspoon baking powder

1/2 teaspoon salt

2 cups buttermilk

6 egg whites

FILLING:
1/2 cup sugar

2 tablespoons cornstarch

1 cup orange juice

4 eggs, lightly beaten

1/4 cup butter

2 tablespoons grated orange peel

1 teaspoon orange extract

FROSTING:
1 cup sugar

2 egg whites

1/2 cup water

1/4 teaspoon salt

1/8 teaspoon cream of tartar

1/4 teaspoon vanilla extract

2 cups flaked coconut

» In a large bowl, cream butter and sugar until light and fluffy. Add vanilla. Combine the flour, baking soda, baking powder and salt; add to creamed mixture alternately with buttermilk. In another large bowl and with clean beaters, beat egg whites on high speed until stiff peaks form; gently fold into batter.

» Pour into three greased and floured 9-in. round baking pans. Bake at 350° for 25-30 minutes or until a toothpick comes out clean. Cool for 10 minutes; Remove from pans to wire racks to cool completely.

» In a saucepan, combine sugar and cornstarch. Gradually stir in orange juice until smooth. Cook and stir over medium-high heat until thickened and bubbly. Reduce heat; cook and stir 2 minutes longer. Remove from the heat. Stir a small amount of hot filling into eggs; return all to pan, stirring constantly. Bring to a gentle boil; cook and stir 2 minutes longer. Remove from the heat. Gently stir in the butter, orange peel and extract. Cool to room temperature without stirring. Cover and refrigerate.

» For frosting, in a large heavy saucepan, combine the sugar, egg whites, water, salt and cream of tartar over low heat or double boiler over simmering water. With a portable mixer, beat on low speed for 1 minute. Continue beating on low over low heat until frosting reaches 160°, about 12 minutes. Pour into the bowl of a heavy-duty stand mixer; add vanilla. Beat on high until frosting forms stiff peaks, about 7 minutes.

» Split each cake into two horizontal layers. Place bottom layer on a serving plate; spread with 1/3 cup filling. Repeat four more times. Top with the remaining cake layer. Spread the frosting over top and sides of cake. Sprinkle with the coconut. Store in the refrigerator.

Yield: 12-14 servings.

marble chiffon cake

This high cake won a blue ribbon for best chiffon cake at our county fair. The delicately flavored orange cake has ribbons of chocolate swirled throughout.

Sharon Evans • Rockwell, Iowa

7 eggs, separated

1/3 cup baking cocoa

1/4 cup boiling water

3 tablespoons plus 1-1/2 cups sugar, divided

2 tablespoons plus 1/2 cup canola oil, divided

2-1/4 cups all-purpose flour

1 tablespoon baking powder

1 teaspoon salt

3/4 cup water

1/2 teaspoon cream of tartar

2 teaspoons grated orange peel

ORANGE GLAZE:

2 cups confectioners' sugar

1/3 cup butter, melted

3 to 4 tablespoons orange juice

1/2 teaspoon grated orange peel

» Let eggs stand at room temperature for 30 minutes. In a bowl, whisk the cocoa, boiling water, 3 tablespoons sugar and 2 tablespoons oil; cool and set aside.

» In a large bowl, combine the flour, baking powder, salt and remaining sugar. In another bowl, whisk the egg yolks, water and remaining oil. Add to dry ingredients; beat until well blended. In another bowl, beat egg whites and cream of tartar until stiff peaks form; fold into batter.

» Remove 2 cups of batter; stir into cocoa mixture. To the remaining batter, add orange peel. Alternately spoon the batters into an ungreased 10-in. tube pan. Swirl with a knife.

» Bake on the lowest oven rack at 325° for 70-75 minutes or until cake springs back when lightly touched. Immediately invert pan; cool completely, about 1 hour.

» Run a knife around side and center tube of pan. Remove cake to a serving plate.

» For glaze, in a small bowl, combine the confectioners' sugar, butter and enough orange juice to reach desired drizzling consistency. Add orange peel; Drizzle over cake.

Yield: 12 -14 servings.

company chocolate cake

Chocoholics will love this brownie-like treat. Its sweet chocolate sauce is a pleasant change from frosting. Served with a scoop of vanilla ice cream, this snack will go over big with everyone at the table.

Susan Hansen • Auburn, Alabama

2 cups cake flour

2 cups sugar

1 teaspoon baking soda

1/4 teaspoon salt

1/4 cup baking cocoa

1 cup water

1 cup butter, cubed

2 eggs

1/2 cup buttermilk

1 teaspoon vanilla extract

CHOCOLATE SAUCE:
1-3/4 cups sugar

2 tablespoons baking cocoa

2/3 cup 2% milk

2 tablespoons butter

1 teaspoon vanilla extract

Vanilla ice cream

Maraschino cherries, optional

» In a large bowl, combine the flour, sugar, baking soda and salt; set aside. In a small saucepan, combine cocoa and water until smooth; add butter. Bring to a boil over medium heat, stirring constantly; add to dry ingredients and stir well. Combine the eggs, buttermilk and vanilla; stir into chocolate mixture.

» Pour into a greased 13-in. x 9-in. baking pan. Bake at 350° for 30-35 minutes or until a toothpick inserted near the center comes out clean. Cool on a wire rack.

» For chocolate sauce, in a small saucepan, combine the sugar, cocoa, milk and butter. Bring to a boil; boil for 1 minute. Remove from the heat; stir in vanilla. Serve warm with cake and ice cream. Garnish with cherries if desired.

Yield: 20 servings.

triple-layer banana cake

A year-round family dessert, the recipe for this moist layer cake was passed on to me by my mother. My grandchildren can't keep their fingers out of the icing, which tastes just like peanut butter fudge.

Patty Roberts • Athens, Ohio

3/4 cup butter, softened

2 cups sugar

3 eggs

1-1/2 cups mashed ripe bananas (about 3 medium)

1-1/2 teaspoons vanilla extract

3 cups all-purpose flour

1-1/2 teaspoons baking powder

1-1/2 teaspoons baking soda

3/4 teaspoon salt

1 cup buttermilk

FROSTING:
6 tablespoons peanut butter

3 tablespoons butter, softened

5-1/4 cups confectioners' sugar

8 to 10 tablespoons 2% milk

Peanut halves, optional

» In a large bowl, cream butter and sugar until light and fluffy. Add eggs, one at a time, beating well after each addition. Beat in bananas and vanilla. Combine the flour, baking powder, baking soda and salt; add to creamed mixture alternately with buttermilk, beating well after each addition.

» Pour into three greased and floured 9-in. round baking pans. Bake at 350° for 25-30 minutes or until a toothpick inserted near the center comes out clean. Cool for 10 minutes before removing from pans to wire racks to cool completely.

» For frosting, in a large bowl, beat the peanut butter and butter until smooth. Beat in confectioners' sugar and enough milk to achieve spreading consistency. Frost between layers and over top and sides of cake. Garnish with peanuts if desired.

Yield: 14 servings.

Patriotic Cupcakes • Peanut Butter Cupcakes • Surprise Cupcakes • Lemon Sparkle Cupcakes • Chocolate Cookie Cupcakes • Banana Nut Cupcakes • Spice Cupcakes • Raspberry Peach Cupcakes • Cream Chocolate Cupcakes

cupcakes

• Pineapple Upside-Down Cupcakes Coconut Pecan Cupcakes • German Chocolate Cupcakes • Clown Cupcakes Yellow Cupcakes • Shoofly Cupakes Toffee Mocha Cupcakes • Blueberry Angel Cupcakes • Pink Velvet Cupcakes • Cherry Gingerbread Cupcakes • Chip Lover's Cupcakes • Pumpkin Cupcakes

peanut butter cupcakes

Peanut butter lovers can double their pleasure with these little cakes. I use the popular ingredient in the cupcakes as well as their creamy homemade frosting.

Ruth Hutson • Westfield, Indiana

1/3 cup butter, softened

1/2 cup peanut butter

1-1/4 cups packed brown sugar

1 egg

1 teaspoon vanilla extract

2 cups all-purpose flour

1/2 teaspoon salt

1/2 teaspoon baking powder

1/2 teaspoon baking soda

1/4 teaspoon ground cinnamon

3/4 cup 2% milk

FROSTING:

1/3 cup peanut butter

2 cups confectioners' sugar

2 teaspoons honey

1 teaspoon vanilla extract

3 to 4 tablespoons 2% milk

Chocolate-coated sunflower seeds, optional

» In a large bowl, cream the butter, peanut butter and brown sugar until light and fluffy. Beat in egg and vanilla. Combine the dry ingredients; add to creamed mixture alternately with milk, beating well after each addition.

» Fill paper-lined muffin cups two-thirds full. Bake at 350° for 18-22 minutes or until a toothpick inserted near the center comes out clean. Cool for 10 minutes before removing from pans to wire racks to cool completely.

» For frosting, in a small bowl, cream peanut butter and sugar until light and fluffy. Beat in honey and vanilla. Beat in enough milk to achieve a spreading consistency. Frost cupcakes. Sprinkle with sunflower seeds if desired.

Yield: about 1-1/2 dozen.

EDITOR'S NOTE: Reduced-fat or generic brands of peanut butter are not recommended for this recipe.

surprise cupcakes

My mother taught me this simple way to fill cupcakes with fruit jelly. Take these tender treats to your next get-together and watch faces light up after just one bite.

Edith Holliday • Flushing, Michigan

1 cup shortening

2 cups sugar

2 eggs

2 teaspoons vanilla extract

3-1/2 cups all-purpose flour

5 teaspoons baking powder

1 teaspoon salt

1-1/2 cups 2% milk

3/4 cup strawberry or grape jelly

Frosting of your choice

Colored sprinkles, optional

» In a large bowl, cream shortening and sugar until light and fluffy. Add eggs, one at a time, beating well after each addition. Beat in vanilla. Combine the flour, baking powder and salt; add to creamed mixture alternately with milk, beating well after each addition.

» Fill 36 paper-lined muffin cups half full. Spoon 1 teaspoon jelly in the center of each.

» Bake at 375° for 15-20 minutes or until a toothpick inserted 1 in. from the edge comes out clean. Cool for 5 minutes; remove from pans to wire racks to cool completely. Frost cupcakes; decorate with sprinkles if desired.

Yield: 3 dozen.

A basic cake mix is turned into a special treat with everybody's favorite chocolate sandwich cookie. And since there's cookie in every bite, kids will love these delicious cupcakes!

Mary Wiebe • Altona, Manitoba

chocolate cookie cupcakes

1 package (18-1/4 ounces) white cake mix

1-1/4 cups water

1/4 cup canola oil

3 egg whites

1 cup coarsely crushed cream-filled chocolate sandwich cookies (about 9 cookies)

1 can (16 ounces) vanilla frosting

Additional crushed cream-filled chocolate sandwich cookies

» In a large bowl, combine the cake mix, water, oil and egg whites; beat on low speed for 30 seconds. Beat on high for 2 minutes. Gently fold in cookie crumbs. Fill paper-lined muffin cups two-thirds full.

» Bake at 350° for 18-22 minutes or until a toothpick inserted near the center comes out clean. Cool for 10 minutes before removing from pans to wire racks to cool completely. Frost cupcakes; sprinkle with additional cookie crumbs.

Yield: 2 dozen.

banana nut cupcakes

These moist cupcakes taste like little loaves of banana bread. I keep ripe bananas in the freezer, so I can whip up these bites whenever I need them for a bake sale or party. I like to top them with a rich cream cheese frosting.

Vicki Abrahamson • Silverdale, Washington

1/3 cup butter-flavored shortening

2/3 cup sugar

2 eggs

1 cup mashed ripe bananas (about 3 medium)

2 tablespoons 2% milk

1 tablespoon vanilla extract

1-1/3 cups all-purpose flour

2 teaspoons baking powder

1/2 teaspoon baking soda

1/4 teaspoon salt

1/4 cup chopped nuts

» In a large bowl, cream shortening and sugar until light and fluffy. Beat in the eggs. Stir in the bananas, milk and vanilla. Combine the flour, baking powder, baking soda and salt; gradually add to creamed mixture and mix well. Stir in nuts.

» Fill paper-lined muffin cups two-thirds full. Bake at 350° for 18-20 minutes or until a toothpick inserted near the center comes out clean. Cool for 5 minutes before removing from pans to wire racks.

Yield: 15 cupcakes.

german chocolate cupcakes

These treats disappear quickly when I take them to the school where I teach. Pecans, coconut and brown sugar dress up the topping nicely.

Lettice Charmasson • San Diego, California

1 package (18-1/4 ounces) German chocolate cake mix

1 cup water

3 eggs

1/2 cup canola oil

3 tablespoons chopped pecans

3 tablespoons flaked coconut

3 tablespoons brown sugar

» In a large bowl, combine cake mix, water, eggs and oil. Beat on low speed for 30 seconds. Beat on medium for 2 minutes.

» Fill paper-lined muffin cups three-fourths full. Combine pecans, coconut and brown sugar; sprinkle over batter. Bake at 400° for 15-20 minutes or until a toothpick inserted near the center comes out clean. Cool for 10 minutes before removing from pans to wire racks to cool completely.

Yield: about 2 dozen.

raspberry peach cupcakes

A cake mix is the base for this snack. They have an appealing combination of fresh fruit and white chocolate. The luscious lemon buttercream frosting adds a citrus tang to the sweet treats.

Arlene Butler • Ogden, Utah

1 cup white baking chips

6 tablespoons butter, cubed

1 package (18-1/4 ounces) white cake mix

1 cup 2% milk

3 eggs

1 teaspoon vanilla extract

1 cup fresh raspberries

1/2 cup chopped peeled fresh peaches or frozen unsweetened peach slices, thawed and chopped

LEMON FROSTING:
1/2 cup butter, softened

3 cups confectioners' sugar

2 tablespoons lemon juice

Fresh raspberries and peach pieces, optional

» In a microwave, melt chips and butter; stir until smooth.

» In a large bowl, combine the cake mix, milk, eggs, vanilla and melted chips; beat on low speed for 30 seconds. Beat on medium for 2 minutes. Fold in raspberries and peaches.

» Fill paper-lined muffin cups three-fourths full. Bake at 350° for 15-20 minutes or until a toothpick inserted near the center comes out clean. Cool for 10 minutes before removing from pans to wire racks to cool completely.

» For frosting, in a small bowl, beat the butter, confectioners' sugar and lemon juice until smooth. Frost cupcakes. Top with fruit if desired.

Yield: 2 dozen.

pouring batter without a mess

Place the cupcake batter into a large resealable plastic bag. Press out the air and seal the bag. Snip off one bottom corner with scissors, then squeeze out the batter into muffin cups.

patriotic cupcakes

Serve a dessert that's sure to be the star of your Fourth of July menu. One year, I divided the batter from regular cupcakes into portions and used food coloring to make red, white and blue treats. Use different food coloring for various holidays.

Jodi Rugg • Aurora, Illinois

1 package (18-1/4 ounces) white cake mix

1/2 teaspoon blue food coloring

1/2 teaspoon red food coloring

1 can (16 ounces) vanilla frosting

Red, white and blue sprinkles

» Prepare cake batter according to package directions.

» In a small bowl, combine 1-1/3 cups batter and the blue food coloring. In another bowl, combine 1-1/3 cups batter and the red food coloring. Leave remaining batter plain.

» Fill paper-lined muffin cups with 2 tablespoons red batter, 2 tablespoons plain batter and 2 tablespoons blue batter. Bake at 350° for 20-24 minutes or until a toothpick inserted near the center comes out clean. Cool for 10 minutes before removing from pans to wire racks to cool completely. Frost with vanilla frosting; decorate with sprinkles.

Yield: 1-1/2 dozen.

» Fill paper-lined muffin cups two-thirds full. Bake at 350° for 20-25 minutes or until a toothpick inserted near the center comes out clean. Cool for 10 minutes before removing from pans to a wire rack to cool completely.

» For frosting, in a small bowl, beat the cream cheese and butter until fluffy. Add confectioners' sugar; beat until smooth. Frost the cupcakes.

strawberry cupcake cones

This is a delightful, fun way to serve a cupcake. I share these with the neighborhood kids, and they love the ice cream cone look and ease of eating. Adults who try them say snacking on them makes them feel young again.

Barb Kietzer • Niles, Michigan

2 cups all-purpose flour

1/2 cup sugar

2 teaspoons baking powder

1/2 teaspoon baking soda

1/2 teaspoon salt

2 eggs

3/4 cup (6 ounces) strawberry yogurt

1/2 cup canola oil

1 cup chopped fresh strawberries

15 ice cream cake cones (about 3 inches tall)

1 cup (6 ounces) semisweet chocolate chips

1 tablespoon shortening

Colored sprinkles

» In a large bowl, combine the first five ingredients. In another bowl, beat the eggs, yogurt, oil and strawberries; stir into dry ingredients just until moistened.

» Place the ice cream cones in muffin cups; spoon about 3 tablespoon batter into each cone. Bake at 375° for 19-21 minutes or until a toothpick inserted near the center comes out clean. Cool completely.

» In a microwave, melt chocolate chips and shortening; stir until smooth. Dip muffin tops in chocolate; allow excess to drip off. Decorate with sprinkles.

pumpkin cupcakes

A unique mix of pineapple and pumpkin creates moist cupcakes with mouthwatering flavor and texture. A fluffy frosting caps these treats.

Mary Relyea • Canastota, New York

2/3 cup shortening

2 eggs

3/4 cup maple syrup

1/2 cup 2% milk

1-1/2 cups all-purpose flour

1-1/4 teaspoons baking powder

1/2 teaspoon salt

1/2 teaspoon baking soda

1/2 teaspoon ground ginger

1/2 teaspoon ground allspice

1 cup canned pumpkin

1 can (8 ounces) crushed pineapple, drained

1 package (8 ounces) cream cheese, softened

1/4 cup butter, softened

1-1/2 cups confectioners' sugar

» In a large bowl, beat shortening until light and fluffy. Add eggs, one at a time, beating well after each addition (mixture will appear curdled). Beat in syrup and milk. Combine the flour, baking powder, salt, baking soda, ginger and allspice; add to shortening mixture and beat just until moistened. Stir in pumpkin and pineapple.

For frosting, in a small bowl, beat butter until light and fluffy. Beat in the confectioners' sugar, vanilla, cinnamon, nutmeg and enough milk to achieve a spreading consistency. Frost the cupcakes.

Yield: 2 dozen.

clown cupcakes

Throwing a children's party can be a real circus if you serve these colorful clown delights. Set up a decorating table and let the kids make funny faces with their favorite candies.

Taste of Home Test Kitchen

1 package (18-1/4 ounces) yellow cake mix

3 cans (16 ounces each) vanilla frosting, divided

Yellow, red and blue paste food coloring

24 ice cream sugar cones

Assorted candies: M&M's miniature baking bits, red shoestring licorice and cherry sour ball candies

» Prepare and bake cake batter according to package directions for cupcakes. Cool completely on wire racks. Divide two cans of frosting among three bowls; tint with yellow, red and blue food coloring.

» For clown hats, use a serrated knife or kitchen scissors to cut 2 in. from the open end of each cone. Frost cones with tinted frosting; decorate with baking bits. Place on waxed paper for 30 minutes or until frosting is set.

» Frost cupcakes with remaining vanilla frosting. Leaving room for the hat on each cupcake, make a clown face and hair with candies. Pipe a matching ruffle on each. Carefully position a hat on each cupcake.

Yield: 2 dozen.

raisin-zucchini spice cupcakes

We were out of flour one night when I wanted to make zucchini muffins, so I used a package of spice cake mix instead. They were a huge hit with the kids and my husband.

Tracy Scherer • Climax, Michigan

1 package (18-1/4 ounces) spice cake mix

1-1/3 cups water

1/4 cup canola oil

3 eggs

2 cups shredded zucchini

1/2 cup raisins

CINNAMON FROSTING:
1/4 cup butter, softened

1-3/4 cups confectioners' sugar

1 teaspoon vanilla extract

1/2 teaspoon ground cinnamon

1/8 teaspoon ground nutmeg

1 to 2 tablespoons 2% milk

» In a large bowl, combine the cake mix, water, oil and eggs; beat on low speed for 30 seconds. Beat on medium for 2 minutes. Stir in zucchini and raisins.

» Fill paper-lined muffin cups two-thirds full. Bake at 350° for 18-22 minutes or until a toothpick inserted near the center comes out clean. Cool for 10 minutes before removing to wire racks to cool completely.

mini pineapple upside-down cakes

These individual pineapple upside-down cakes are an eye-catching addition to my dessert buffet table. A cake mix really cuts down the prep time.

Cindy Colley • Othello, Washington

2/3 cup packed brown sugar

1/3 cup butter, melted

1 can (20 ounces) pineapple tidbits

12 maraschino cherries, halved

1 package (18-1/4 ounces) yellow cake mix

3 eggs

1/3 cup canola oil

» In a small bowl, combine the brown sugar and butter until blended. Spoon into 24 greased muffin cups. Drain pineapple, reserving the juice. Place a cherry half cut side down in each muffin cup; arrange pineapple around cherries.

» In a large bowl, combine the cake mix, eggs, oil and reserved pineapple juice. Beat on low speed for 30 seconds. Beat on medium for 2 minutes. Spoon over pineapple, filling each cup three-fourths full.

» Bake at 350° for 18-22 minutes or until a toothpick inserted near the center comes out clean. Immediately invert onto wire racks to cool.

Yield: 2 dozen.

shoofly cupcakes

These old-fashioned molasses cupcakes were my grandmother's specialty. To keep them from disappearing too quickly, she used to store them out of sight. We always figured out her hiding places!

Beth Adams • Jacksonville, Florida

4 cups all-purpose flour

2 cups packed brown sugar

1/4 teaspoon salt

1 cup cold butter, cubed

2 teaspoons baking soda

2 cups boiling water

1 cup molasses

» In a large bowl, combine the flour, brown sugar and salt. Cut in butter until crumbly. Set aside 1 cup for topping. Add baking soda to remaining crumb mixture. Stir in water and molasses.

» Fill paper-lined muffin cups two-thirds full. Sprinkle with reserved crumb mixture. Bake at 350° for 20-25 minutes or until a toothpick inserted near the center comes out clean. Cool for 10 minutes before removing from pans to wire racks to cool.

Yield: 2 dozen.

EDITOR'S NOTE: This recipe does not use eggs.

These cute bite-size treats are packed with banana flavor, chocolate chips and topped off with a creamy frosting. They make a great, fast snack when the kids come home from school or a even a sweet addition to appetizer buffets.

Beverly Coyde • Gasport, New York

banana-chip mini cupcakes

1 package (14 ounces) banana quick bread and muffin mix

3/4 cup water

1/3 cup sour cream

1 egg

1 cup miniature semisweet chocolate chips, divided

1 tablespoon shortening

» In a large bowl, combine the muffin mix, water, sour cream and egg; stir just until moistened. Fold in 1/2 cup chocolate chips.

» Fill greased or paper-lined miniature muffin cups two-thirds full. Bake at 375° for 12-15 minutes or until a toothpick inserted near the center comes out clean. Cool for 5 minutes before removing from pans to wire racks to cool completely.

» For the frosting, in a small microwave-safe bowl, melt the shortening and remaining chocolate chips; stir until smooth. Frost the cupcakes.

Yield: 3-1/2 dozen.

» Fill paper-lined muffin cups two-thirds full. Bake at 350° for 18-20 minutes or until a toothpick inserted near the center comes out clean. Cool for 10 minutes before removing from pans to wire racks to cool completely.

» For frosting, in a large microwave-safe bowl, melt the butter and chocolate; stir until smooth. Cool for 10 minutes. With a portable mixer, beat in the confectioners' sugar, sour cream and vanilla on low until smooth. Frost the cupcakes. Store in the refrigerator.

Yield: 2 dozen.

yellow cupcakes

Nothing is better than homemade cupcakes. They are so delicious and fluffy. Choose whatever frosting you want to top these treats.

Taste of Home Test Kitchen

2/3 cup butter, softened

1-3/4 cups sugar

2 eggs

1-1/2 teaspoons vanilla extract

2-1/2 cups all-purpose flour

2-1/2 teaspoons baking powder

1/2 teaspoon salt

1-1/4 cups 2% milk

Frosting of your choice

» In a large bowl, cream butter and sugar until light and fluffy. Add eggs, one at a time, beating well after each addition. Beat in vanilla. Combine the flour, baking powder and salt; add to the creamed mixture alternately with milk, beating well after each addition.

» Fill paper-lined muffin cups three-fourths full. Bake at 350° for 15-20 minutes or until a toothpick inserted near the center comes out clean. Cool for 10 minutes before removing from pans to wire racks to cool completely. Frost cupcakes.

Yield: 22-24 cupcakes.

sour cream chocolate cupcakes

The sour cream is definitely the ingredient that gives these moist, chocolaty cupcakes their wonderful texture.

Alicsa Mayer • Alta Vista, Kansas

1/4 cup butter, cubed

4 ounces unsweetened chocolate, chopped

2 eggs

2 cups sugar

1 cup water

3/4 cup sour cream

1 teaspoon vanilla extract

2 cups all-purpose flour

1 teaspoon baking soda

FROSTING:
1/2 cup butter, cubed

4 ounces unsweetened chocolate, chopped

4 cups confectioners' sugar

1/2 cup sour cream

2 teaspoons vanilla extract

» In a microwave, melt butter and chocolate; stir until smooth. Cool for 10 minutes. In a large bowl, beat the eggs, sugar, water, sour cream and vanilla. Combine flour and baking soda; add to the egg mixture and mix well. Add chocolate mixture; beat on high speed for 2-3 minutes.

easy peel cupcake liners

Spray cupcake liners with cooking spray before you fill them with batter. Then when the liners are peeled off, the cupcakes will be less like to tear or crumble.

» Bake at 350° for 20-22 minutes or until a toothpick inserted in cake comes out clean. Cool for 10 minutes before removing from pans to wire racks to cool completely.

» For frosting, in a large bowl, cream the butter, shortening and confectioners' sugar until smooth. Beat in 3 tablespoons milk and vanilla until creamy. Set aside 1 cup frosting; frost cupcakes with remaining frosting.

» Stir baking cocoa and remaining milk into reserved frosting. Cut a small hole in a corner of a pastry or plastic bag; insert star tip. Fill bag with chocolate frosting. Pipe a rosette on top of each cupcake; garnish with a cookie.

Yield: 1-1/2 dozen.

lemon sparkle cupcakes

Bursting with lemony zing, these cup cakes don't require frosting. In fact, my family prefers the crunchy sugar-and-spice topping.

Janice Porter • Platte, South Dakota

2/3 cup shortening

1 cup sugar

3 eggs

1-2/3 cups all-purpose flour

2-1/2 teaspoons baking powder

1/2 teaspoon salt

2/3 cup 2% milk

1 tablespoon grated lemon peel

TOPPING:
1/4 cup sugar

1 tablespoon grated lemon peel

1/8 teaspoon ground nutmeg

» In a large bowl, cream shortening and sugar until light and fluffy. Add eggs, one at a time, beating well after each addition. Combine the flour, baking powder and salt; add to the creamed mixture alternately with milk, beating well after each addition. Stir in lemon peel.

» Fill paper-lined muffin cups two-thirds full. Combine topping ingredients; sprinkle a rounded 1/2 teaspoonful of the topping over each cupcake.

» Bake at 350° for 20-24 minutes or until a toothpick inserted near the center comes out clean. Cool for 10 minutes before removing from pans to wire racks to cool completely.

Yield: about 1-1/4 dozen.

chip lover's cupcakes

Making chocolate chip cookies is a challenge with three teenagers who are always grabbing a sample of the dough. Their love of cookie dough inspired the recipe for this dessert that adults will enjoy, too.

Donna Scully • Middletown, Delaware

1 package (18-1/4 ounces) white cake mix

1/4 cup butter, softened

1/4 cup packed brown sugar

2 tablespoons sugar

1/3 cup all-purpose flour

1/4 cup confectioners' sugar

1/4 cup miniature semisweet chocolate chips

BUTTERCREAM FROSTING:

1/2 cup butter, softened

1/2 cup shortening

4-1/2 cups confectioners' sugar

4 tablespoons 2% milk, divided

1-1/2 teaspoons vanilla extract

1/4 cup baking cocoa

18 miniature chocolate chip cookies

» Prepare cake batter according to package directions; set aside. For filling, in a small bowl, cream butter and sugars until light and fluffy. Gradually beat in flour and confectioners' sugar until blended. Fold in chocolate chips.

» Fill paper-lined muffin cups half full with cake batter. Drop filling by tablespoonfuls into the center of each; cover with the remaining batter.

cherry gingerbread cupcakes

A sweet frosting with a hint of lemon complements these little spice cakes, each with a maraschino cherry in the center. They're one of my dad's favorite desserts and a sure way of getting him to come over for a cup of coffee.

Laura McAllister • Morganton, North Carolina

1/2 cup shortening

1 cup sugar

2 eggs

1 cup molasses

3 cups all-purpose flour

1 teaspoon baking soda

1 teaspoon ground ginger

1 teaspoon ground cinnamon

1 cup buttermilk

1/2 cup chopped walnuts

24 maraschino cherries, well drained

LEMON CREAM CHEESE FROSTING:
4 ounces cream cheese, softened

1/4 cup butter, softened

1 teaspoon vanilla extract

1 teaspoon grated lemon peel

1-3/4 to 2 cups confectioners' sugar

» In a large bowl, cream shortening and sugar until light and fluffy. Beat in eggs and molasses. Combine the flour, baking soda, ginger and cinnamon; gradually add to creamed mixture alternately with buttermilk, beating well after each addition. Stir in walnuts.

» Fill paper-lined muffin cups two-thirds full; place a cherry in the center of each. Bake at 375° for 20-24 minutes or until a toothpick inserted near the center comes out clean. Cool for 10 minutes; remove from pans to wire racks to cool completely.

» For frosting, in a small bowl, beat cream cheese and butter until smooth; add vanilla and lemon peel. Gradually beat in confectioners' sugar. Frost cupcakes.

Yield: 2 dozen.

coconut pecan cupcakes

Pecan lovers have lots to cheer about with these flavorful cupcakes. I created the recipe for my best friend, Ann, who said she loved Italian cream cake but didn't want a whole cake. These sensations have a wonderful aroma and a fabulous flavor.

Tina Harrison • Prairieville, Louisiana

5 eggs, separated

1/2 cup butter, softened

1/2 cup shortening

2 cups sugar

3/4 teaspoon vanilla extract

1/4 teaspoon almond extract

1-1/2 cups all-purpose flour

1/4 cup cornstarch

1/2 teaspoon baking soda

1/2 teaspoon salt

1 cup buttermilk

2 cups flaked coconut

1 cup finely chopped pecans

FROSTING:
1 package (8 ounces) cream cheese, softened

1/4 cup butter, softened

1/2 teaspoon vanilla extract

1/4 teaspoon almond extract

3-3/4 cups confectioners' sugar

3/4 cup chopped pecans

» Let eggs stand at room temperature for 30 minutes. In a large bowl, cream the butter, shortening and sugar until light and fluffy. Add egg yolks, one at a time, beating well after each addition. Stir in extracts. Combine the flour, cornstarch, baking soda and salt; add to the creamed mixture alternately with buttermilk, beating well after each addition.

» In a small bowl, beat egg whites on high speed until stiff peaks form. Fold into batter. Stir in coconut and pecans.

» Fill paper-lined muffin cups three-fourths full. Bake at 350° for 20-25 minutes or until a toothpick inserted near the center comes out clean. Cool for 10 minutes; remove from pans to wire racks to cool completely.

» In a large bowl, combine frosting ingredients until smooth; frost cupcakes. Store in the refrigerator.

Yield: 2 dozen.

toffee mocha cupcakes

Chocolate, toffee and espresso make a mouthwatering combination. The yummy sweets are perfect for any party or gathering. Make plenty—they'll go fast!

Brenda Melancon • Gonzales, Louisiana

2 tablespoons instant espresso granules

1 cup boiling water

1/2 cup butter-flavored shortening

1-1/4 cups sugar

2 eggs

1-3/4 cups all-purpose flour

1/4 cup baking cocoa

1-1/2 teaspoons baking powder

1/2 teaspoon baking soda

1/2 teaspoon salt

1 cup milk chocolate toffee bits

FROSTING:
1 can (16 ounces) vanilla frosting

2 teaspoons instant espresso granules

1/3 cup miniature semisweet chocolate chips

1/4 cup milk chocolate toffee bits

» Dissolve espresso granules in boiling water; cool.

» In a large bowl, cream shortening and sugar until light and fluffy. Add eggs, one at a time, beating well after each addition. Combine the flour, cocoa, baking powder, baking soda and salt; add to creamed mixture alternately with espresso mixture and mix well. Fold in toffee bits.

» Fill paper-lined muffin cups three-fourths full. Bake at 350° for 20-22 minutes or until a toothpick inserted near the center comes out clean. Cool for 10 minutes before removing from pans to wire racks.

» In a large bowl, combine frosting and espresso granules. Frost cupcakes; sprinkle with chocolate chips and toffee bits.

Yield: 16 cupcakes.

» Fill paper-lined muffin cups two-thirds full. Bake at 350° for 23-27 minutes or until a toothpick inserted near the center comes out clean. Cool for 10 minutes before removing from pans to wire racks to cool completely.

» Meanwhile, place the white chips in a small bowl. In a small saucepan, bring cream just to a boil. Pour over chips; whisk until smooth. Stir in butter. Transfer to a large bowl. Chill for 30 minutes, stirring once.

» Beat on high for 2-3 minutes or until soft peaks form and frosting is light and fluffy. Cut a small hole in the corner of a pastry or plastic bag; insert #30 star tip. Fill bag with frosting; frost cupcakes. Sprinkle with coarse sugar and edible glitter. Store in the refrigerator.

Yield: 2 dozen.

EDITOR'S NOTE: Edible glitter is available from Wilton Industries. Call 1-800/794-5866 or visit *www.wilton.com*.

pink velvet cupcakes

Pretty in pink, these cupcakes were a big success at my daughter's princess-themed birthday party. They would be perfect for gatherings throughout the year, too!

Paulette Smith • Winston Salem, North Carolina

1 cup butter, softened

1-1/4 cups sugar

1/8 teaspoon pink paste food coloring

3 eggs

1 teaspoon vanilla extract

2-1/2 cups all-purpose flour

1-1/2 teaspoons baking powder

1/4 teaspoon baking soda

1/4 teaspoon salt

1 cup buttermilk

WHITE CHOCOLATE GANACHE:
2 cups white baking chips

1/2 cup heavy whipping cream

1 tablespoon butter

Pink coarse sugar and edible glitter

» In a large bowl, cream the butter, sugar and food coloring until light and fluffy. Add eggs, one at a time, beating well after each addition. Beat in vanilla. Combine the flour, baking powder, baking soda and salt; add to creamed mixture alternately with buttermilk, beating well after each addition.

blueberry angel cupcakes

Like angel food cake, these yummy cupcakes don't last long at my house. They're so light and airy they nearly melt in your mouth.

Kathy Kittell • Lenexa, Kansas

11 egg whites

1 cup plus 2 tablespoons cake flour

1-1/2 cups sugar, divided

1-1/4 teaspoons cream of tartar

1 teaspoon vanilla extract

1/2 teaspoon salt

1-1/2 cups fresh or frozen blueberries

1 teaspoon grated lemon peel

GLAZE:
1 cup confectioners' sugar

3 tablespoons lemon juice

» Place egg whites in a large bowl; let stand at room temperature for 30 minutes. Sift together flour and 1/2 cup sugar three times; set aside.

» Add cream of tartar, vanilla and salt to egg whites; beat on medium speed until soft peaks form. Gradually add remaining sugar, about 2 tablespoons at a time, beating on high until stiff glossy peaks form and sugar is dissolved. Gradually fold in flour mixture, about 1/2 cup at a time. Fold in blueberries and lemon peel.

» Fill paper-lined muffin cups three-fourths full. Bake at 375° for 14-17 minutes or until cupcakes spring back when lightly touched. Immediately remove the cupcakes from pans to wire racks to cool completely.

» In a small bowl, whisk confectioners' sugar and lemon juice until smooth. Brush over cupcakes. Let stand until set.

Yield: 2-1/2 dozen.

EDITOR'S NOTE: If using frozen blueberries, use without thawing to avoid discoloring the batter.

peanut-filled devil's food cupcakes

This recipe features a luscious peanut butter filling surrounded with devil's food and then iced with a velvety layer of ganache. These treats are just to die for!

Mary Lou Timpson • Colorado City, Arizona

1/2 cup plus 2 tablespoons butter, softened

1-1/2 cups sugar

3 eggs

1 teaspoon vanilla extract

1-1/4 cups cake flour

1/2 cup baking cocoa

1 teaspoon baking soda

1/2 teaspoon salt

1/4 teaspoon baking powder

1/2 cup buttermilk

1/2 cup strong brewed coffee

FILLING:
1 cup creamy peanut butter

1/2 cup butter, softened

1-1/4 cups confectioners' sugar

GANACHE:
4 ounces semisweet chocolate, chopped

1/2 cup heavy whipping cream

1/2 cup dry roasted peanuts

» In a large bowl, beat butter and sugar until crumbly, about 2 minutes. Add eggs, one at a time, beating well after each addition. Beat in vanilla. Combine the flour, cocoa, baking soda, salt and baking powder; add to creamed mixture alternately with buttermilk and coffee just until combined.

» Filled paper-lined muffin cups half full. Bake at 325° for 15-20 minutes or until a toothpick inserted near the center comes out clean. Cool for 10 minutes before removing from pans to wire racks to cool completely.

» For filling, in a small bowl, beat peanut butter and butter until fluffy. Gradually add confectioners' sugar; beat until smooth. Cut a small hole in the corner of a pastry or plastic bag; insert a small tip. Add filling. Push the tip through the bottom of paper liner to fill each cupcake.

» For ganache, place chocolate in a small bowl. In a saucepan, bring cream just to a boil. Pour over chocolate; whisk until smooth. Cool 10 minutes or until mixture is slightly thickened.

» Place a heaping tablespoonful of ganache on top of each cupcake; spread toward the edges. Sprinkle with peanuts. Chill for 20 minutes or until set. Refrigerate leftovers.

Yield: 2 dozen.

Jam-Topped Strawberry Cheesecakes Ladyfinger Cheesecake • Blueberry Swirl Cheesecake • Peanut Butter Cup Cheesecake • Frosted Chocolate Chip Cheesecake • Americana Peanut Cheesecake • Banana Cheesecake •

cheesecakes

White Chocolate Raspberry Cheesecake • Layered Hazelnut Cheesecake • Black Forest Cheesecake • Traditional Cheesecake • Mallow Cranberry Cheesecake • Tiramisu Cheesecake Dessert • Candybar Cheesecake • Cannoli Cheesecake • Pumpkin Cheesecake • Holiday Cheesecake

chocolate-dipped strawberry cheesecake

This light, creamy and airy dessert is perfect for entertaining. The cheesecake has a unique flavor from the chocolate crust. It always brings compliments and adds a touch of elegance to your table.

Kathy Berger • Dry Ridge, Kentucky

1-3/4 cups chocolate graham cracker crumbs (about 9 whole crackers)

1/4 cup butter, melted

1 pound fresh or frozen strawberries, thawed

2 envelopes unflavored gelatin

1/2 cup cold water

2 packages (8 ounces each) fat-free cream cheese, cubed

1 cup (8 ounces) fat-free cottage cheese

Sugar substitute equivalent to 3/4 cup sugar

1 carton (8 ounces) frozen reduced-fat whipped topping, thawed, divided

13 medium fresh strawberries

4 ounces semisweet chocolate, chopped

» In a small bowl, combine cracker crumbs and butter. Press onto the bottom and 1 in. up the sides of a 9-in. springform pan coated with cooking spray. Place on a baking sheet. Bake at 350° for 10 minutes or until set. Cool on a wire rack.

» Hull strawberries if necessary; puree in a food processor. Remove and set aside. In a small saucepan, sprinkle gelatin over cold water; let stand for 1 minute. Heat over low heat, stirring until gelatin is completely dissolved. Transfer to the food processor; add the cream cheese, cottage cheese and sugar substitute. Cover and process until smooth.

» Add the strawberry puree; cover and process until blended. Transfer to a large bowl; fold in 2 cups whipped topping. Pour into crust. Cover and refrigerate for 2-3 hours or until set.

» For garnish, wash strawberries and gently pat with paper towels until completely dry. Cut tops off berries. In a microwave, melt chocolate; stir until smooth. Dip each berry tip until half of the berry is coated, allowing excess to drip off. Place with tips pointing up on a waxed paper-lined baking sheet; refrigerate for at least 30 minutes.

» Carefully run a knife around edge of springform pan to loosen; remove sides of pan. Arrange berries, chocolate tips up, around edge of cheesecake and place one in the center. Garnish with remaining whipped topping.

Yield: 12 servings.

EDITOR'S NOTE: This recipe was tested with Splenda No Calorie Sweetener.

jam-topped mini cheesecakes

Presto! We turned cheesecake into finger food in just 15 minutes. For fun, experiment with a variety of jams and preserves—like strawberry and apricot.

Taste of Home Test Kitchen

1 cup graham cracker crumbs

3 tablespoons butter, melted

1 package (8 ounces) cream cheese, softened

1/3 cup sugar

1 egg, lightly beaten

1 teaspoon vanilla extract

Assorted jams, warmed

» In a small bowl, combine graham cracker crumbs and butter. Press gently onto the bottom of 12 paper-lined muffin cups. In another small bowl, beat the cream cheese, sugar and vanilla until smooth. Add egg; beat on low until just combined. Spoon over crusts.

» Bake at 350° for 15-16 minutes or until center is set. Cool for 10 minutes before removing from pan to a wire rack to cool completely. Refrigerate for at least 1 hour.

» Remove the paper liners; top each cheesecake with 1 teaspoon of jam.

Yield: 1 dozen.

My mom got this recipe from a friend, and after we tried it, we promised we'd never make cheesecake any other way.

Marcia Savery • New Bedford, Massachusetts

ladyfinger cheesecake

4-1/2 cups sliced fresh strawberries (about 2 pounds)

2 tablespoons plus 2 cups sugar, divided

3 packages (3 ounces each) ladyfingers, split

4 packages (8 ounces each) cream cheese, softened

2 cups heavy whipping cream

» In a large bowl, combine strawberries and 2 tablespoons sugar. Cover; refrigerate for at least 1 hour. Meanwhile, arrange 25 split ladyfingers around the edges of a lightly greased 10-in. springform pan. Place 25 more on the bottom; set aside.

» In a large bowl, beat cream cheese and remaining sugar until smooth. In another large bowl, beat cream until stiff peaks form. Gradually fold into cream cheese mixture.

» Spoon half of the cream cheese mixture into prepared pan. Spread with half of strawberry mixture to within 1 in. of edges. Cover; refrigerate remaining strawberry mixture.

» Arrange remaining ladyfingers over top. Spoon remaining cream cheese mixture over ladyfingers. Cover; refrigerate overnight. Remove sides of pan. Serve with reserved strawberry mixture.

Yield: 14 servings.

traditional cheesecake

Here's a basic cheesecake that tastes great alone or dressed up with any number of easy garnishes.

Taste of Home Test Kitchen

1 cup graham cracker crumbs

1 tablespoon sugar

3 tablespoons cold butter

FILLING:

4 packages (8 ounces each) cream cheese, softened

1-1/4 cups sugar

1 tablespoon lemon juice

2 teaspoons vanilla extract

3 eggs, lightly beaten

» In a small bowl, combine cracker crumbs and sugar; cut in butter until crumbly. Grease the sides only of a 9-in. springform pan; press crumb mixture onto bottom of pan. Place on a baking sheet. Bake at 350° for 10 minutes. Cool on a wire rack.

» In a large bowl, beat cream cheese and sugar until smooth. Beat in lemon juice and vanilla. Add eggs; beat on low speed just until combined. Pour filling onto crust. Return pan to baking sheet.

» Bake at 350° for 45-55 minutes or until center is almost set. Cool on a wire rack for 10 minutes. Carefully run a knife around edge of pan to loosen; cool 1 hour longer.

» Refrigerate overnight. Remove the sides of the pan. Garnish as desired.

Yield: 12 servings.

blueberry swirl cheesecake

This recipe is my favorite way to use blueberries, and I make it often for get-togethers. My family is happy to see it on the dessert table.

Cathy Medley • Clyde, Ohio

1-1/2 cups fresh blueberries

1/4 cup sugar

1 tablespoon lemon juice

2 teaspoons cornstarch

1 tablespoon cold water

CRUST:

1 cup graham cracker crumbs (about 16 squares)

2 tablespoons sugar

2 tablespoons butter, melted

FILLING:

3 packages (8 ounces each) cream cheese, softened

1 cup sugar

1 cup (8 ounces) sour cream

2 tablespoons all-purpose flour

2 teaspoons vanilla extract

4 eggs, lightly beaten

» In a small saucepan, combine the blueberries, sugar and lemon juice. Cook and stir over medium heat for 5 minutes or until the berries are softened. Combine cornstarch and water until smooth; stir into the blueberry mixture. Bring to a boil; cook and stir for 2 minutes or until thickened. Remove from the heat; cool to room temperature. Transfer to a blender; cover and process until smooth. Set aside.

» For crust, in a small bowl, combine the crumbs and sugar; stir in the butter. Press onto the bottom of a greased 9-in. springform pan. Place pan on a baking sheet. Bake at 350° for 10 minutes. Cool on a wire rack.

» In a large bowl, beat the cream cheese and sugar until smooth. Beat in the sour cream, flour and vanilla. Add eggs; beat on low speed just until combined. Pour filling over crust. Drizzle with blueberry mixture; cut through batter with a knife to swirl.

» Return pan to baking sheet. Bake at 350° for 1 hour or until center is almost set. Cool on a wire rack for 10 minutes. Carefully run a knife around the edge of pan to loosen; cool 1 hour longer. Refrigerate overnight. Remove sides of pan.

Yield: 12 servings.

peanut butter cup cheesecake

I said I'd bring dessert to a holiday party and tried this recipe. I'm sure you'll agree it tastes as luscious as it looks!

Dawn Lowenstein • Hatboro, Pennsylvania

1-1/4 cups graham cracker crumbs

1/4 cup sugar

1/4 cup crushed cream-filled chocolate sandwich cookies

6 tablespoons butter, melted

3/4 cup creamy peanut butter

FILLING:

3 packages (8 ounces each) cream cheese, softened

1 cup sugar

1 cup (8 ounces) sour cream

1-1/2 teaspoons vanilla extract

3 eggs, lightly beaten

1 cup hot fudge ice cream topping, divided

6 peanut butter cups, cut into small wedges

» In a large bowl, combine cracker crumbs, sugar, cookie crumbs and butter. Press onto the bottom and 1 in. up the sides of a greased 9-in. springform pan. Place on a baking sheet.

» Bake at 350° for 7-9 minutes or until set. Cool on a wire rack. In a microwave-safe bowl, heat peanut butter on high for 30 seconds or until softened. Spread over crust to within 1 in. of edges.

» In a large bowl, beat cream cheese and sugar until smooth. Beat in sour cream and vanilla. Add eggs; beat on low speed just until combined. Pour 1 cup into a bowl; set aside. Pour remaining filling over peanut butter layer.

» In a microwave, heat 1/4 cup fudge topping on high for 30 seconds or until thin; fold into reserved cream cheese mixture. Carefully pour over filling; cut through with a knife to swirl.

» Return pan to baking sheet. Bake at 350° for 55-65 minutes or until center is almost set. Cool on a wire rack for 10 minutes. Carefully run a knife around edge of the pan to loosen; cool 1 hour longer.

» Microwave remaining fudge topping for 30 seconds or until warmed; spread over cheesecake. Garnish with peanut butter cups. Refrigerate overnight. Remove sides of pan.

Yield: 12-14 servings.

EDITOR'S NOTE: Reduced-fat or generic brands of peanut butter are not recommended for this recipe.

cooling cheesecakes

It is recommended to cool a cheesecake for 10 minutes, then carefully run a knife between the cheesecake and pan to loosen it from the sides. If it's not loosened at this point, part of the cheesecake may stick to the sides, causing the cheesecake to crack as it cools further.

» For frosting, in a microwave-safe bowl, melt candy bar; stir until smooth. Cool to room temperature. Gradually stir in whipped topping. Frost top of cheesecake; garnish with almonds.

Yield: 12 servings.

candy bar cheesecake

I am a cheesecake fanatic, and when I found this one, featuring Butterfinger candy bars, I knew it was for me. Our pastor's wife asked me to share the recipe so she could make it to impress her family back home...she could not believe something so elegant-looking was so easy to prepare.

Melissa Pirtle • Fresno, California

2 cups chocolate wafer crumbs (about 35 wafers)

1/3 cup butter, melted

4 packages (8 ounces each) cream cheese, softened

1 cup sugar

3 tablespoons heavy whipping cream

1-1/2 teaspoons vanilla extract

5 eggs, lightly beaten

3 Butterfinger candy bars (2.1 ounces each), frozen and chopped

TOPPING:
1 Butterfinger candy bar (2.1 ounces), frozen and chopped

2 tablespoons butterscotch ice cream topping

» In a small bowl, combine the wafer crumbs and butter. Press onto the bottom and 1-1/2 in. up the sides of greased 9-in. springform pan; set aside.

» In a large bowl, beat cream cheese and sugar until smooth. Beat in cream and vanilla. Add eggs; beat on low speed just

frosted chocolate chip cheesecake

Heavenly is a good description for this luscious dessert, conveniently made a day ahead. When I don't have a candy bar on hand, I melt 3/4 cup of chocolate chips to use in the frosting. Whipped cream can be used in place of the whipped topping.

Arlene Butler • Ogden, Utah

2 cups chocolate wafer crumbs

6 tablespoons butter, melted

FILLING:
3 packages (8 ounces each) cream cheese, softened

1 cup sugar

1 teaspoon vanilla extract

3 eggs, lightly beaten

1 cup (6 ounces) miniature semisweet chocolate chips

FROSTING:
1 milk chocolate candy bar (4 ounces), chopped

2 cups whipped topping

1/4 cup sliced almonds, toasted

» In a small bowl, combine wafer crumbs and butter. Press onto the bottom and 1-1/2 in. up the sides of a greased 9-in. springform pan. Chill for 15 minutes or until set.

» In a large bowl, beat the cream cheese, sugar and vanilla until smooth. Add eggs; beat on low speed just until combined. Stir in chocolate chips. Pour into crust.

» Place pan on a baking sheet. Bake at 325° for 55-60 minutes or until center is almost set. Cool on a wire rack for 10 minutes. Carefully run a knife around edge of pan to loosen; cool 1 hour longer. Cover and refrigerate overnight. Remove sides of pan.

until combined. Fold in chopped candy bars. Pour into crust. Place pan on a baking sheet.

» Bake at 325° for 60-70 minutes or until the center is almost set. Cool on a wire rack for 10 minutes. Carefully run a knife around the edge of the pan to loosen; cool 1 hour longer. Refrigerate overnight.

» Sprinkle chopped candy bar over cheesecake; drizzle with butterscotch topping.

Yield: 12 servings.

americana peanut cheesecake

Need a simple, creamy no-bake cheesecake? We recommend you try this recipe. It's the ultimate indulgence!

Peanut Advisory Board • Canton, Georgia

1 cup graham cracker crumbs

3/4 cup plus 2 tablespoons chopped salted peanuts, divided

1/3 cup butter, melted

4 packages (3 ounces each) cream cheese, softened

2/3 cup creamy peanut butter

1 can (14 ounces) sweetened condensed milk

1/3 cup lemon juice

1 teaspoon vanilla extract

1-1/2 cups whipped topping

» In a small bowl, combine the cracker crumbs, 3/4 cup peanuts and butter. Press onto the bottom and 1 in. up the sides of a greased 9-in. springform pan. Cover and refrigerate for 20 minutes.

» Meanwhile, in a large bowl, beat cream cheese and peanut butter until smooth. Beat in the milk, lemon juice and vanilla. Fold in the whipped topping. Pour over crust. Sprinkle with remaining peanuts. Cover and refrigerate for at least 8 hours. Refrigerate overnight. Remove sides of pan.

Yield: 12 servings.

tiramisu cheesecake dessert

I wasn't a big fan of tiramisu until I tried this recipe with its distinctive cheesecake- and coffee-flavored layers. It's one of my favorite desserts to make during the fall.

Christie Nelson • Taylorville, Illinois

1 package (12 ounces) vanilla wafers

5 teaspoons instant coffee granules, divided

3 tablespoons hot water, divided

4 packages (8 ounces each) cream cheese, softened

1 cup sugar

1 cup (8 ounces) sour cream

4 eggs, lightly beaten

1 cup whipped topping

1 tablespoon baking cocoa

» Layer half of wafers in a greased 13-in. x 9-in. baking dish. In a small bowl, dissolve 2 teaspoons coffee granules in 2 tablespoons hot water. Brush wafers with half of coffee; set remaining mixture aside.

» In a large bowl, beat cream cheese and sugar until smooth. Beat in sour cream. Add eggs; beat on low speed just until combined. Divide batter in half. Dissolve remaining coffee granules in remaining hot water; stir into one portion of batter. Spread over wafers. Layer with remaining wafers; brush with reserved coffee. Top with remaining batter.

» Bake at 325° for 40-45 minutes or until center is almost set. Cool on a wire rack for 10 minutes. Carefully run a knife around edge of dish to loosen; cool 1 hour longer. Refrigerate overnight. Remove sides of pan.

» Spread with whipped topping; dust with cocoa.

Yield: 12 servings.

black forest cheesecake

A friend gave me this recipe, and it quickly became popular at our house. I enjoy making it when we entertain.

Patricia Plett • Blumenort, Manitoba

1-1/4 cups chocolate wafer crumbs

1/4 cup butter, melted

2 envelopes unflavored gelatin

1 cup water

1 can (21 ounces) cherry pie filling

1/2 teaspoon almond extract

2 packages (8 ounces each) cream cheese, softened

1/3 cup sugar

2 ounces semisweet chocolate, melted and cooled

1 teaspoon brandy extract or vanilla extract

1 cup heavy whipping cream, whipped

Maraschino cherries and additional whipped cream and melted chocolate for garnish, optional

» Combine crumbs and butter; press into the bottom and up the sides of a 9-in. springform pan. Chill for 15 minutes.

» In a small saucepan, sprinkle gelatin over cold water; let stand for 1 minute. Heat over low heat, stirring until gelatin is completely dissolved. Combine 1/3 cup gelatin mixture with pie filling and almond extract; pour into crust and chill until set.

» In a large bowl, beat cream cheese and sugar until smooth. Beat in the melted chocolate, brandy extract and remaining gelatin. Fold in whipped cream; spread over cherry layer. Chill at least 3 hours.

» Remove sides of pan. Garnish with the whipped cream, cherries and chocolate if desired.

Yield: 12-16 servings.

white chocolate raspberry cheesecake

As a dairy farmer's wife, I have experience making cheesecake. In fact, most anything containing milk products is tasty in my book. If I'm out of cream cheese, it's time to go to the grocery store!

Wendy Barkman • Breezewood, Pennsylvania

1-1/2 cups graham cracker crumbs

1/4 cup sugar

1/3 cup butter, melted

FILLING:

3 packages (8 ounces each) cream cheese, softened

3/4 cup sugar

1/3 cup sour cream

3 tablespoons all-purpose flour

1 teaspoon vanilla extract

3 eggs, lightly beaten

1 package (10 to 12 ounces) white baking chips

1/4 cup seedless raspberry jam

» In a small bowl, combine the graham cracker crumbs, sugar and butter. Press onto the bottom of a greased 9-in. springform pan; set aside.

» In a large bowl, beat cream cheese and sugar until smooth. Beat in the sour cream, flour and vanilla. Add eggs; beat on low speed just until combined. Fold in the chips. Pour over crust.

» In a microwave-safe bowl, melt the raspberry jam; stir until smooth. Drop by teaspoonfuls over batter; cut through batter with a knife to swirl.

» Place pan on a double thickness of heavy-duty foil (about 16 in. square). Securely wrap foil around pan. Place in a large baking pan; add 1 in. of hot water to larger pan.

» Bake at 325° for 80-85 minutes or until center is just set. Cool on a wire rack for 10 minutes. Carefully run a knife around edge of pan to loosen; cool 1 hour longer. Cover and refrigerate overnight. Remove sides of pan.

Yield: 12 servings.

check your springform pan

For best results, a springform pan should seal tightly and not be warped. If in doubt about the seal, securely wrap heavy-duty foil around the outside of the pan to prevent leaks.

layered hazelnut cheesecake

A creamy topping accents each beautiful slice of this outstanding dessert. It's spectacular-looking as well as scrumptious.

Taste of Home Test Kitchen

1-1/2 cups crushed vanilla wafers

1/4 cup butter, melted

4 packages (8 ounces each) cream cheese, softened

1-3/4 cups sugar

2 teaspoons vanilla extract

4 eggs, lightly beaten

4 ounces finely chopped hazelnuts, toasted

1/3 cup semisweet chocolate chips, melted

TOPPING:

2/3 cup white baking chips

3 tablespoons water

1 teaspoon light corn syrup

1/2 teaspoon instant coffee granules

1/4 cup chopped hazelnuts, toasted

» In a small bowl, combine the wafer crumbs and butter; press onto the bottom of a greased 9-in. springform pan.

» In a large bowl, beat the cream cheese, sugar and vanilla until smooth. Add eggs; beat on low speed just until combined.

» Divide batter into thirds. Into one portion, stir in hazelnuts. Pour over crust. Refrigerate for 20 minutes or until set. Into second portion, gradually stir in melted chocolate. Spoon over bottom layer. Refrigerate for 45 minutes or until set.

» Spoon remaining batter over top. Place pan on a baking sheet. Bake at 350° for 50-60 minutes or until center is almost set. Cool on a wire rack for 10 minutes. Carefully run a knife around the edge of pan to loosen; cool 1 hour longer. Cover and refrigerate overnight.

» For topping, combine the white chips, water, corn syrup and coffee granules in a small saucepan; cook and stir over low heat until smooth. Cool to room temperature. Serve topping with cheesecake; garnish with hazelnuts.

Yield: 12 servings.

lemony white chocolate cheesecake

Although it takes some time to prepare this eye-catching cheesecake, the combination of tangy lemon and rich white chocolate is hard to beat. It's always a hit!

Marlene Schollenberger • Bloomington, Indiana

1-1/4 cups all-purpose flour

2 tablespoons confectioners' sugar

1 teaspoon grated lemon peel

1/2 cup cold butter, cubed

FILLING:
4 packages (8 ounces each) cream cheese, softened

1-1/4 cups sugar

10 ounces white baking chocolate, melted and cooled

2 tablespoons all-purpose flour

2 tablespoons heavy whipping cream

2 tablespoons lemon juice

2 teaspoons grated lemon peel

2 teaspoons vanilla extract

4 eggs, lightly beaten

» Place a 9-in. springform pan on a double thickness of heavy-duty foil (about 18 in. square). Securely wrap foil around pan; set aside.

» In a small bowl, combine the flour, confectioners' sugar and peel; cut in butter until crumbly. Press onto the bottom and 1 in. up the sides of prepared pan. Place on a baking sheet.

Bake at 325° for 25-30 minutes or until golden brown. Cool on a wire rack.

» In a large bowl, beat cream cheese and sugar until smooth. Beat in the white chocolate, flour, cream, lemon juice, lemon peel and vanilla. Add eggs; beat on low speed just until combined. Pour into crust.

» Place pan in a large baking pan; add 1 in. of hot water to larger pan. Bake at 325° for 65-85 minutes or until center is just set and top appears dull.

» Remove pan from water bath. Cool on a wire rack for 10 minutes. Carefully run a knife around edge of pan to loosen; cool 1 hour longer. Refrigerate overnight. Remove sides of pan.

Yield: 12 servings.

pineapple cheesecake

With its make-ahead convenience, this fruit-topped cheesecake often appears on my holiday menus. It never fails to impress guests.

Lorraine Caland • Thunder Bay, Ontario

1-1/4 cups graham cracker crumbs

1/4 cup sugar

1/3 cup butter, melted

FILLING:
3 packages (8 ounces each) cream cheese, softened

1/4 cup sugar

1-1/2 cups (12 ounces) sour cream

3/4 cup sweetened condensed milk

3 to 4 teaspoons grated orange peel

3 teaspoons vanilla extract

5 eggs, separated

TOPPING:
1/4 cup sugar

4 tablespoons cold water, divided

1 can (20 ounces) crushed pineapple, drained

1 tablespoon cornstarch

» In a small bowl, combine the graham cracker crumbs, sugar and butter. Press onto the bottom of a greased 10-in. springform pan; set aside.

» In a large bowl, beat cream cheese and sugar until smooth. Beat in the sour cream, milk, orange peel and vanilla. Add eggs yolks; beat on low speed just until combined.

» In a small bowl, beat egg whites until stiff peaks form; fold into cream cheese mixture. Pour over crust.

» Place pan on a baking sheet. Bake at 325° for 70-75 minutes or until center is almost set. Cool on a wire rack for 10 minutes. Carefully run a knife around edge of pan to loosen; cool 1 hour longer. Cover and refrigerate for at least 6 hours or overnight. Remove sides of pan.

» For topping, combine sugar and 2 tablespoons water in a small saucepan. Bring to a boil over medium heat; cook for 2 minutes. Stir in pineapple. In a small bowl, combine cornstarch and remaining water until smooth; stir into pineapple mixture. Bring to a boil; cook and stir for 2 minutes or until thickened. Cool completely. Spread topping over cheesecake.

Yield: 12 servings.

banana cheesecake

We have banana trees in our backyard that bear fruit virtually all year. After making banana bread, muffins and cookies, I still had some of our bountiful crop left, so I decided to try this recipe.

Sera Smith • West Palm Beach, Florida

3/4 cup all-purpose flour

3/4 cup finely chopped pecans

3 tablespoons sugar

2 tablespoons brown sugar

1-1/2 teaspoons vanilla extract

6 tablespoons butter, melted

FILLING:

1 cup mashed ripe bananas

2 tablespoons lemon juice

2 packages (8 ounces each) cream cheese, softened

1-1/4 cups sugar

1 cup (8 ounces) sour cream

2 tablespoons cornstarch

1-1/4 teaspoons vanilla extract

1/8 teaspoon salt

3 eggs, lightly beaten

TOPPING:

1 cup (8 ounces) sour cream

1/4 cup sugar

1/4 teaspoon vanilla extract

1 cup assorted fresh fruit

» Combine the first five ingredients; stir in butter. Press onto the bottom of a greased 9-in. springform pan; place on a baking sheet. Bake at 350° for 10 minutes or until lightly browned. Cool on a wire rack.

» Combine bananas and lemon juice; set aside. In a large bowl, beat cream cheese and sugar until smooth. Beat in the sour cream, cornstarch, vanilla and salt. Add eggs; beat on low speed just until combined. Fold in banana mixture. Pour into crust. Place pan on a baking sheet.

» Bake at 350° for 50-60 minutes or until center is almost set. Let stand for 5 minutes. Combine sour cream, sugar and vanilla; spread over top of cheesecake. Bake 5 minutes longer.

» Cool on a wire rack for 10 minutes. Carefully run a knife around edge of pan; cool 1 hour longer. Refrigerate overnight. Garnish with fruit.

Yield: 12-14 servings.

softening cream cheese

If cream cheese is not softened before it's beaten for a cheesecake, you may end up with lumps in the baked product. The simplest way to soften cream cheese is to let it stand at room temperature for 30 minutes before using. It can also be softened in the microwave...just make sure to remove the foil packaging before warming.

» In a small bowl, combine the cracker crumbs, nuts and sugar. Stir in butter. Press onto the bottom of a greased 9-in. springform pan. Place on a baking sheet. Bake at 350° for 10 minutes or until lightly browned. Cool on a wire rack.

» In a small saucepan, sprinkle gelatin over cold water; let stand for 1 minute. Heat over low heat, stirring until gelatin is completely dissolved; cool slightly.

» In a large bowl, beat cream cheese and marshmallow creme until smooth. Beat in cranberry sauce. Add cooled gelatin; mix well.

» In a small bowl, beat cream until stiff peaks form. Fold into cream cheese mixture. Pour over crust. Refrigerate for 8 hours or overnight.

» In a microwave-safe bowl, sprinkle gelatin over cold water; let stand for 1 minute. Microwave on high for 1-2 minutes, stirring every 20 seconds, until gelatin is completely dissolved. Whisk until slightly frothy.

» Lightly brush mixture over all sides of berries. Place on a wire rack over waxed paper; sprinkle with superfine sugar. Let stand at room temperature for up to 24 hours (do not refrigerate or the sugar will dissolve).

» Just before serving, carefully run a knife around edge of pan to loosen. Remove the sides of the pan. Spoon sugared cranberries over cheesecake.

Yield: 12 servings.

mallow cranberry cheesecake

Specks of cranberry sauce dot this cool and creamy cheesecake. The sugared cranberries on top are optional.

Gloria Colton • Russell, New York

3/4 cup graham cracker crumbs

1/2 cup finely chopped macadamia nuts

2 tablespoons sugar

1/4 cup butter, melted

1 envelope unflavored gelatin

1/4 cup cold water

2 packages (8 ounces each) cream cheese, softened

1 jar (7 ounces) marshmallow creme

1 can (14 ounces) whole-berry cranberry sauce

1 cup heavy whipping cream

SUGARED CRANBERRIES:

1 envelope unflavored gelatin

1/4 cup cold water

1 package (12 ounces) fresh cranberries or frozen cranberries, thawed

2/3 cup superfine sugar

blueberry cheesecake

Savor the best of the blues with this crowd-pleasing cheesecake. It's a luscious treat for everyday dinners and special occasions alike.

Dick Deacon • Lawrenceville, Georgia

40 vanilla wafers, crushed

1 cup finely chopped pecans

1/3 cup butter, melted

FILLING:

2 packages (8 ounces each) cream cheese, softened

1/2 cup butter, softened

1-1/2 cups sugar

2 cups (16 ounces) 4% cottage cheese

2 cups (16 ounces) sour cream

6 tablespoons cornstarch

6 tablespoons all-purpose flour

4-1/2 teaspoons lemon juice

1 teaspoon vanilla extract

4 eggs, lightly beaten

BLUEBERRY GLAZE:

3-1/2 cups fresh blueberries, divided

1 cup sugar

2 tablespoons cornstarch

» In a large bowl, combine the wafer crumbs, pecans and butter. Press onto the bottom and 2 in. up the sides of a greased 10-in. springform pan. Place on a baking sheet. Bake at 375° for 8 minutes. Cool on a wire rack. Reduce heat to 325°.

» In a large bowl, beat the cream cheese, butter and sugar until smooth. Process cottage cheese in a blender until smooth; beat into a cream cheese mixture. Beat in the sour cream, cornstarch, flour, lemon juice and vanilla. Add eggs; beat on low speed just until combined. Pour over crust.

» Return pan to baking sheet. Bake at 325° for 70-80 minutes or until center is almost set. Cool on a wire rack for 10 minutes. Carefully run a knife around edge of pan to loosen; cool 1 hour longer. Refrigerate overnight.

» For glaze, puree 2-1/2 cups blueberries in a food processor; press through a fine mesh sieve, reserving 1 cup juice. Discard pulp and seeds.

» In a small saucepan, combine sugar, cornstarch and reserved blueberry juice until smooth. Bring to a boil; cook and stir for 2 minutes or until thickened. Refrigerate the mixture until it is completely cooled.

» Remove sides of pan. Spread glaze over cheesecake. Sprinkle with remaining blueberries.

Yield: 14-16 servings.

2 tablespoons all-purpose flour, divided

2 eggs, lightly beaten

1-1/2 cups chopped peeled apples

1/2 teaspoon ground cinnamon

» Place a greased 9-in. springform pan on a double thickness of heavy-duty foil (about 18 in. square). Securely wrap the foil around the pan.

» In a small bowl, combine cracker crumbs, 1/4 cup sugar and butter. Press onto the bottom and 1 in. up the sides of prepared pan. Place on a baking sheet. Bake at 350° for 10 minutes or until lightly browned. Cool on a wire rack.

» In a heavy saucepan over medium-low heat, cook and stir caramels and milk until melted and smooth. Pour 1 cup over crust; sprinkle with 1/4 cup pecans. Set remaining caramel mixture aside.

» In a large bowl, beat the cream cheese, 1 tablespoon flour and remaining sugar until smooth. Add eggs; beat on low speed just until combined. Combine the apples, cinnamon and remaining flour; fold into cream cheese mixture. Pour into crust.

» Place springform pan in a large baking pan; add 1 in. of hot water to larger pan. Bake for 40 minutes. Reheat reserved caramel mixture if necessary; gently spoon over cheesecake. Sprinkle with remaining pecans.

» Bake 10-15 minutes longer or until center is just set. Remove pan from water bath. Cool on a wire rack for 10 minutes. Carefully run a knife around edge of pan to loosen; cool 1 hour longer. Refrigerate overnight.

Yield: 12 servings.

caramel apple cheesecake

This recipe won the Grand Prize in an apple recipe contest. With caramel both on the bottom and over the top, this cheesecake is ooey-gooey good!

Lisa Morman • Minot, North Dakota

1-1/2 cups cinnamon graham cracker crumbs (about 8 whole crackers)

3/4 cup sugar, divided

1/4 cup butter, melted

1 package (14 ounces) caramels

2/3 cup evaporated milk

1/2 cup chopped pecans, divided

2 packages (8 ounces each) cream cheese, softened

pumpkin cheesecake deluxe

I developed this recipe out of my love for cheesecake and my family's love for pumpkin pie. I made it for Thanksgiving and every morsel was devoured. My family wished I had made two!

Andrea Quiroz • Chicago, Illinois

3/4 cup chopped pecans, toasted

32 gingersnap cookies, coarsely crushed

3 tablespoons brown sugar

6 tablespoons butter, melted

FILLING:
3 packages (8 ounces each) cream cheese, softened

1 cup packed brown sugar

1-1/2 cups canned pumpkin

1/2 cup heavy whipping cream

1/4 cup maple syrup

3 teaspoons vanilla extract

1 teaspoon ground cinnamon

1/2 teaspoon ground ginger

1/4 teaspoon ground cloves

4 eggs, lightly beaten

Sweetened whipped cream, optional

Pecan brittle, optional

» Place a greased 9-in. springform pan on a double thickness of heavy-duty foil; securely wrap foil around pan. Place pecans in a food processor; cover and process until ground. Add the gingersnaps, brown sugar and butter; cover and pulse until blended. Press crumbs onto the bottom and 1 in. up the sides of the prepared pan; set aside.

» In a large bowl, beat cream cheese and brown sugar until smooth. Beat in the pumpkin, cream, syrup, vanilla and spices. Add eggs; beat on low speed just until combined. Pour into crust. Place springform pan in a large baking pan; add 1 in. of hot water to larger pan.

» Bake at 325° for 60-70 minutes or until center is just set and top appears dull. Remove pan from water bath. Cool on wire rack for 10 minutes. Carefully run a knife around edge of pan to loosen; cool 1 hour longer. Chill overnight. Remove sides of pan.

» Garnish with whipped cream and pecan brittle if desired.

Yield: 12 servings.

chocolate caramel cheesecake

Layers of caramel and nuts complement this dessert's chocolate flavor, proving you can bake terrific cheesecakes that don't have a lot of fat.

Tamara Trouten • Fort Wayne, Indiana

6 whole reduced-fat graham crackers, crushed

3 tablespoons butter, melted

25 caramels

1/4 cup fat-free evaporated milk

1/4 cup chopped pecans

2 packages (8 ounces each) reduced-fat cream cheese

1/3 cup sugar

1/3 cup semisweet chocolate chips, melted and cooled

2 eggs, lightly beaten

» In a small bowl, combine graham cracker crumbs and butter. Press onto the bottom of a 9-in. springform pan coated with cooking spray. Place on a baking sheet. Bake at 350° for 5-10 minutes or until set. Cool on a wire rack.

» In a small saucepan over low heat, stir caramels and milk until smooth. Pour over crust. Sprinkle with pecans.

» In a large bowl, beat cream cheese and sugar until smooth. Beat in melted chocolate. Add eggs; beat on low speed just until combined. Pour over caramel layer. Place pan on baking sheet.

» Bake at 350° for 30-35 minutes or until center is almost set. Cool on a wire rack for 10 minutes. Carefully run a knife around edge of pan to loosen; cool 1 hour longer. Chill for 4 hours or overnight. Remove sides of pan.

Yield: 12 servings.

mocha truffle cheesecake

I went through a phase when I couldn't get enough cheesecake or coffee, so I created this rich dessert. Its brownie-like crust and creamy mocha layer really hit the spot. It's excellent for get-togethers because it can be made in advance.

Shannon Dormady • Great Falls, Montana

1 package (18-1/4 ounces) devil's food cake mix

6 tablespoons butter, melted

1 egg

1 to 3 tablespoons instant coffee granules

FILLING/TOPPING:

2 packages (8 ounces each) cream cheese, softened

1 can (14 ounces) sweetened condensed milk

2 cups (12 ounces) semisweet chocolate chips, melted and cooled

3 to 6 tablespoons instant coffee granules

1/4 cup hot water

3 eggs, lightly beaten

1 cup heavy whipping cream

1/4 cup confectioners' sugar

1/2 teaspoon almond extract

» In a large bowl, combine the cake mix, butter, egg and coffee granules until well blended. Press onto the bottom and 2 in. up the sides of a greased 10-in. springform pan.

» In another large bowl, beat cream cheese until smooth. Beat in milk and melted chips. Dissolve coffee granules in water. Add coffee to cream cheese mixture. Add eggs; beat on low speed just until combined. Pour into crust. Place the pan on a baking sheet.

» Bake at 325° for 50-55 minutes or until center is almost set. Cool on a wire rack for 10 minutes. Carefully run a knife around edge of pan to loosen; cool 1 hour longer. Chill overnight. Remove sides of pan.

» Just before serving, in a large bowl, beat cream until soft peaks form. Beat in confectioners' sugar and extract until stiff peaks form. Spread over top of cheesecake.

Yield: 12-16 servings.

» Place an ungreased 9-in. springform pan on a double thickness of heavy-duty foil (about 18 in. square). Securely wrap foil around pan.

» In a small bowl, combine cracker crumbs, pecans and brown sugar; stir in butter. Press onto bottom and 1-1/2 in. up the sides of prepared pan. Place on a baking sheet. Bake at 350° for 5 minutes. Cool on a wire rack.

» In a large bowl, beat the cream cheese, sugar and vanilla until smooth. Add eggs; beat on low speed just until combined. Fold in chocolate chips. Pour into crust. Place in a larger baking pan; add 1 in. of hot water to larger pan.

» Bake at 325° for 1-1/2 hours or until center is just set and top appears dull. In a small bowl, combine sour cream and sugar until smooth; spoon over hot cheesecake and spread to cover. Bake for 5 minutes longer or until topping is just set.

» Remove springform pan from water bath. Cool on a wire rack for 10 minutes. Carefully run a knife around edge of pan to loosen; cool 1 hour longer. Refrigerate overnight. Remove sides of pan. Garnish with candies.

Yield: 16 servings.

apricot cheesecake tarts

Dark chocolate and the tart taste of apricots help make these tiny cheesecakes something special for any dessert buffet.

Alicia Montalvo Pagan • New Bedford, Massachusetts

3 ounces bittersweet chocolate, chopped

1/2 teaspoon shortening

1 package (1.9 ounces) frozen miniature phyllo tart shells

1 package (3 ounces) cream cheese, softened

2 tablespoons confectioners' sugar

2 tablespoons sour cream

2 teaspoons apricot nectar

3 dried apricots, cut into thin strips

1 to 1-1/2 teaspoons grated chocolate

» In a microwave, melt bittersweet chocolate and shortening; stir until smooth. Brush over the bottom and up the sides of tart shells. Refrigerate for 15 minutes or until chocolate is set.

» Meanwhile, in a small bowl, beat the cream cheese and confectioners' sugar until smooth. Beat in sour cream and apricot nectar. Spoon into shells. Cover and chill for at least 20 minutes. Just before serving, top with apricot strips and grated chocolate.

Yield: 15 tartlets.

holiday cheesecake

Make Christmas dazzle with this showstopping cheesecake. Each slice is loaded with fun, festive candy toppings.

Taste of Home Cooking School • Greendale, Wisconsin

1-1/2 cups graham cracker crumbs

1/2 cup pecan, toasted and finely chopped

2 tablespoons light brown sugar

6 tablespoons butter, melted

FILLING:
4 packages (8 ounces each) cream cheese, softened

1 cup sugar

3 teaspoons vanilla extract

4 eggs, lightly beaten

1 cup (6 ounces) miniature semisweet chocolate chips

TOPPING:
2 cups (16 ounces) sour cream

1/4 cup sugar

Assorted candies

> » Spread half of the cream cheese mixture over crust. Top with half of the peach mixture; repeat layers. Sprinkle with reserved crumb mixture. Cover and refrigerate for 8 hours or overnight. Remove sides of pan.

Yield: 12 servings.

praline cheesecake

This cheesecake is a stunning with its pretty wafer crust, creamy center and the ooey-gooey caramel-pecan topping cascading down the sides.

Laurel Leslie • Sonora, California

1-1/2 cups crushed vanilla wafers (about 45 wafers)

1/4 cup sugar

1/4 cup butter, melted

16 whole vanilla wafers

FILLING:
3 packages (8 ounces each) cream cheese, softened

1 cup sugar

1/2 cup sour cream

1 teaspoon vanilla extract

3 eggs, lightly beaten

TOPPING:
25 caramels

2 tablespoons milk

1/2 cup chopped pecans, toasted

> » In a small bowl, combine the wafer crumbs, sugar and butter. Press onto the bottom of a greased 9-in. springform pan. Stand whole wafers around edge of pan, pressing lightly into crumbs; set aside.

> » In a large bowl, beat cream cheese and sugar until smooth. Beat in sour cream and vanilla. Add eggs; beat on low speed just until combined. Pour into the crust. Place the pan on a baking sheet.

> » Bake at 325° for 55-60 minutes or until center is almost set. Cool on a wire rack for 10 minutes. Carefully run a knife around edge of pan to loosen; cool 1 hour longer. Refrigerate overnight. Remove sides of pan.

> » Place caramels and milk in a microwave-safe bowl. Microwave, uncovered, on high for 1 minute; stir until smooth. Drizzle the caramel mixture over cheesecake; sprinkle with pecans.

Yield: 12 servings.

EDITOR'S NOTE: This recipe was tested in a 1,100-watt microwave.

peaches and cream torte

This is the dessert I make when I'm craving something cool and fruity. It's a lovely ending to any meal. The cream cheese adds zing to the fluffy filling.

Elva Roberts • Summerside, Prince Edward Island

2 cups graham cracker crumbs

1/3 cup packed brown sugar

1/2 cup butter, melted

FILLING:
1 can (29 ounces) sliced peaches

1-1/4 cups sugar, divided

2 tablespoons cornstarch

1 package (8 ounces) cream cheese, softened

2 cups heavy whipping cream

> » In a small bowl, combine graham cracker crumbs and brown sugar; stir in butter. Set aside 1/4 cup for topping. Press remaining crumb mixture onto the bottom and 1 in. up the sides of a greased 9-in. springform pan.

> » Place pan on a baking sheet. Bake at 350° for 10 minutes. Cool on a wire rack.

> » Drain peaches, reserving syrup in a 2-cup measuring cup. Add enough water to measure 1-1/2 cups. In a large saucepan, combine 1/4 cup sugar and cornstarch; stir in syrup mixture until smooth. Add peaches. Bring to a boil over medium heat; cook and stir for 2 minutes or until thickened. Cool to room temperature, stirring occasionally.

> » Meanwhile, in a large bowl, beat cream cheese and remaining sugar until smooth. In a small bowl, beat cream until stiff peaks form; fold into cream cheese mixture.

1/2 cup white baking chips

2 teaspoons canola oil

Raspberries, optional

Mint leaves, optional

triple-layer chocolate cheesecake

Nothing is as wonderful as cheesecake! This one features a delicious chocolate crust and white chocolate flavor. It is so impressive, guests will want the recipe.

Caryn Wiggins • Columbus, Indiana

1 package (9 ounces) chocolate wafer cookies, crushed

3/4 cup sugar, divided

1/2 cup butter, melted

2 packages (8 ounces each) cream cheese, softened, divided

1 teaspoon vanilla extract, divided

3 eggs

2 ounces semisweet chocolate, melted and cooled

1-1/3 cups sour cream, divided

1/3 cup packed dark brown sugar

1 tablespoon all-purpose flour

1/4 cup chopped pecans

1 package (3 ounces) cream cheese, softened

1/4 teaspoon almond extract

GLAZE:
5 ounces semisweet chocolate, divided

1/4 cup heavy whipping cream

» Combine the wafer crumbs, 1/4 cup sugar and butter. Press onto the bottom and 2 in. up the sides of 9-in. springform pan; set aside.

» In a small bowl, beat one 8-oz. package cream cheese, 1/4 cup sugar and 1/3 teaspoon vanilla until smooth. Lightly beat 1 egg; add to cream cheese mixture and beat on low speed just until combined. Stir in melted chocolate and 1/3 cup sour cream. Spoon over crust.

» In another bowl, beat second 8-oz. package of cream cheese, brown sugar, flour and 1/3 teaspoon vanilla until smooth. Lightly beat 1 egg; add to cream cheese mixture and beat on low speed just until combined. Stir in pecans. Carefully spoon over chocolate layer. Place pan on a baking sheet.

» Beat 3-oz. package of cream cheese, almond extract, and remaining sugar, sour cream and vanilla until smooth. Lightly beat remaining egg; add to the cream cheese mixture and beat on low speed just until combined. Carefully spoon over the pecan layer.

» Bake at 325° for 55-60 minutes or until center is almost set. Cool on a wire rack for 10 minutes. Carefully run a knife around edge of pan to loosen; cool 1 hour longer. Refrigerate overnight.

» For glaze, chop 3 oz. semisweet chocolate and place in a small bowl. In a small saucepan, bring cream just to a boil. Pour over chocolate; whisk until smooth. Remove sides of springform pan; spread glaze over top of cheesecake to within 1/2 in. of edges. Refrigerate until serving.

» For the chocolate curls, melt remaining semisweet chocolate; spread with a spatula into a very thin layer on a baking sheet. Chill for 2 minutes or until set. Microwave white chips and oil at 70% power for 1 minute; stir. If necessary, microwave at additional 10-15 second intervals, stirring until melted. Spread with a spatula into a very thin layer on a second baking sheet. Chill for 2 minutes or until set.

» To make curls, push a metal spatula firmly along the baking sheet, under the chocolate, so the chocolate curls as it is pushed. (If chocolate is too firm to curl, let stand a few minutes at room temperature; refrigerate again if it becomes too soft.) Use a toothpick to carefully place each chocolate curl on a waxed paper-lined baking sheet. Refrigerate curls until ready to use.

» Just before serving, remove side of pan. Arrange the chocolate curls on top of cheesecake. Garnish with raspberries and mint if desired.

Yield: 12 servings.

chocolate berry cheesecake

A fruity sauce accents this fudgy creation, making it perfect for a special occasion.

Lisa Varner • Charleston, South Carolina

1 cup crushed chocolate wafers (about 20 wafers)

2 tablespoons butter, melted

3 packages (8 ounces each) cream cheese, softened

1/2 cup sugar

2 cups (12 ounces) semisweet chocolate chips, melted and cooled

1/2 cup heavy whipping cream

1 tablespoon cornstarch

1 teaspoon vanilla extract

4 eggs, lightly beaten

RASPBERRY SAUCE:

2 tablespoons sugar

2 teaspoons cornstarch

1/2 cup cranberry juice

1 package (12 ounces) frozen unsweetened raspberries, thawed

» Place a greased 9-in. springform pan on a double thickness of heavy-duty foil (about 18 in. square). Securely wrap the foil around the pan.

» In a small bowl, combine wafer crumbs and butter. Press onto the bottom of prepared pan; set aside.

» In a large bowl, beat cream cheese and sugar until smooth. Beat in the chocolate, cream, cornstarch and vanilla. Add eggs; beat on low just until combined. Pour filling over crust. Place springform pan in a large baking pan; add 1 in. of hot water to larger pan.

» Bake at 325° for 55-60 minutes or until center is just set and top appears dull. Remove springform pan from water bath. Cool on a wire rack for 10 minutes. Carefully run a knife around edge of pan to loosen; cool 1 hour longer. Refrigerate overnight.

» In a small saucepan, combine the sugar, cornstarch and cranberry juice until smooth. Bring to a boil over medium heat; cook and stir for 1 minute. Remove from heat; stir in raspberries. Cool completely. Serve cheesecake with raspberry sauce.

Yield: 12-14 servings.

cannoli cheesecake

Combining two of our favorite desserts, this is a traditional holiday treat in my Italian family. We're always certain to pass down the recipe to the next generation.

Marie McConnell • Shelbyville, Illinois

3 cartons (15 ounces each) ricotta cheese

1-1/2 cups sugar

1/2 cup all-purpose flour

3 teaspoons vanilla extract

2 teaspoons grated orange peel

7 eggs, lightly beaten

1/3 cup miniature semisweet chocolate chips

1/4 cup chopped pistachios

» Place a greased 9-in. springform pan on a double thickness of heavy-duty foil (about 18 in. square). Securely wrap foil around pan; set aside.

» In a large bowl, beat ricotta cheese and sugar until smooth. Beat in the flour, vanilla and orange peel. Add eggs; beat on low speed just until combined. Pour into prepared pan; sprinkle with chocolate chips. Place in a large baking pan; add 1 in. of hot water to larger pan.

» Bake at 350° for 65-75 minutes or until center is almost set. Remove pan from water bath. Cool on a wire rack for 10 minutes. Carefully run a knife around edge of pan to loosen; cool 1 hour longer.

» Refrigerate overnight. Remove the sides of the pan. Sprinkle with pistachios.

Yield: 12 servings.

cheesecake with raspberry sauce

It is a family tradition to make this as the finale for our Christmas dinner. And when my daughter was away from home, I made this for her birthday—I shipped it with candles on dry ice.

Jeanette Volker • Walton, Nebraska

1-3/4 cups graham cracker crumbs

1/4 cup sugar

1/3 cup butter, melted

FILLING:

5 packages (8 ounces each) cream cheese, softened

1 cup sugar

1 cup (8 ounces) sour cream

1/2 cup heavy whipping cream

2 teaspoons vanilla extract

7 eggs, lightly beaten

SAUCE/TOPPING:

1 package (12 ounces) frozen unsweetened
   raspberries, thawed

1/2 cup sugar

2 cups heavy whipping cream

1/2 cup confectioners' sugar

1 teaspoon vanilla extract

»   Place a greased 10-in. springform pan on a double thickness of heavy-duty foil (about 18 in. square). Securely wrap the foil around the pan.

»   In a small bowl, combine cracker crumbs and sugar; stir in butter. Press onto the bottom and 1 in. up the sides of prepared pan. Place on a baking sheet. Bake at 350° for 5-8 minutes. Cool on a wire rack.

»   In a large bowl, beat cream cheese and sugar until smooth. Beat in the sour cream, heavy cream and vanilla. Add eggs; beat on low speed just until combined. Pour into crust. Place springform pan in a large baking pan; add 1 in. of hot water to larger pan.

»   Bake at 350° for 50-60 minutes or until center is just set and top appears dull. Remove springform pan from water bath. Cool on a wire rack for 10 minutes. Carefully run a knife around edge of pan to loosen. Cool 1 hour longer. Refrigerate overnight. Remove sides of pan.

»   For sauce, place raspberries and sugar in a food processor; cover and process until blended. For topping, in a small bowl, beat heavy cream until it begins to thicken. Add confectioners' sugar and vanilla; beat until soft peaks form. Serve cheesecake with raspberry sauce and topping.

Yield: 16 servings.

lemon mascarpone cheesecake

This is a beautiful treat for Easter because of its light color and mild lemon flavor. Folks enjoy it so much that I often make it year-round.

Lorraine Caland • Thunder Bay, Ontario

1-1/2 cups biscotti crumbs (about 8 biscotti)

1/3 cup butter, melted

FILLING:

2 packages (8 ounces each) cream cheese, softened

2 cartons (8 ounces each) Mascarpone cheese

3/4 cup sugar

1/4 cup lemon juice

3 tablespoons all-purpose flour

1 tablespoon grated lemon peel

2 teaspoons vanilla extract

4 eggs, lightly beaten

TOPPING:

3/4 cup coarsely chopped dried apricots

1/2 cup boiling water

3/4 cup cold water

1/4 cup sugar

1/4 cup orange marmalade

2 ounces white baking chocolate

» In a small bowl, combine biscotti crumbs and butter. Press onto the bottom and 1 in. up the sides of a greased 9-in. springform pan.

» Place on a baking sheet. Bake at 350° for 8-10 minutes or until lightly browned.

» In a large bowl, beat cheeses and sugar until smooth. Beat in the lemon juice, flour, lemon peel and vanilla. Add eggs; beat on low speed just until combined. Pour into crust.

» Return the pan to baking sheet. Bake at 350° for 45-55 minutes or until the center is almost set. Cool on a wire rack for 10 minutes. Carefully run a knife around edge of pan to loosen. Cool for 30 minutes.

» Meanwhile, soak apricots in boiling water for 10 minutes. Drain and discard liquid. In a small saucepan, bring the apricots, cold water and sugar to a boil. Reduce heat; simmer, uncovered, for 12-14 minutes or until water is absorbed. Remove from the heat; stir in marmalade. Cool to room temperature.

» Carefully spread topping over cheesecake; cool 30 minutes longer. Refrigerate overnight. Remove sides of pan.

» In a microwave, melt white chocolate; stir until smooth. Drizzle over cheesecake. Let stand for 15 minutes.

Yield: 14 servings.

rhubarb swirl cheesecake

I love cheesecake and my husband loves chocolate, so this dessert is a favorite. The tart rhubarb complements the sweet flavors perfectly!
Carol Witczak • Tinley Park, Illinois

2-1/2 cups thinly sliced fresh or frozen rhubarb

1/3 cup plus 1/2 cup sugar, divided

2 tablespoons orange juice

1-1/4 cups graham cracker crumbs

1/4 cup butter, melted

3 packages (8 ounces each) cream cheese, softened

2 cups (16 ounces) sour cream

8 ounces white baking chocolate, melted and cooled

1 tablespoon cornstarch

2 teaspoons vanilla extract

1/2 teaspoon salt

3 eggs, lightly beaten

» In a large saucepan, bring rhubarb, 1/3 cup sugar and orange juice to a boil. Reduce heat; cook and stir until thickened and rhubarb is tender. Set aside.

» Place pan on a double thickness of heavy-duty foil (about 16 in. square). Securely wrap foil around pan; set aside.

» In a small bowl, combine cracker crumbs and butter. Press onto the bottom of a greased 9-in. springform pan. Place on a baking sheet. Bake at 350° for 7-9 minutes or until lightly browned. Cool on a wire rack.

» In a large bowl, beat the cream cheese and remaining sugar until smooth. Beat in the sour cream, white chocolate, cornstarch, vanilla and salt until smooth. Add eggs; beat just until combined.

» Pour half of the filling into crust. Top with half of the rhubarb sauce; cut through batter with a knife to gently swirl rhubarb. Layer with remaining filling and rhubarb sauce; cut through top layers with a knife to gently swirl rhubarb. Place springform pan in a large baking pan; add 1 in. of hot water to larger pan.

» Bake at 350° for 60-70 minutes or until center is just set and top appears dull. Remove springform pan from water bath. Cool on a wire rack for 10 minutes. Carefully run a knife around edge of pan to loosen; cool 1 hour longer. Cover and refrigerate overnight. Remove sides of pan.

Yield: 12-14 servings.

EDITOR'S NOTE: If using frozen rhubarb, measure rhubarb while still frozen, then thaw completely. Drain in a colander, but do not press liquid out.

Sweet Potato Tart • Tart Cherry Lattice
Pie • Bumbleberry Pie • Caramel-Crunch
Apple Pie • Black 'n' Blue Berry Crumb
Pie • Walnut-Streusel Pumpkin Pie •
Apple Pie Bars • Cherry-Berry Peach
Pie • Florida Pie • Strawberry Tartlets

pies

• Triple-Fruit Pie • Decadent Brownie
Pie • Dutch Apple Pie • Classic Pie
Pastry • Two-Layer Silk Pie • Custard
Meringue Pie • Fresh Raspberry Pie
Butterscotch Peach Pie • Chocolate
Hazelnut Tart • Dixie Pie • Marshmallow-
Almond Key Lime Pie • Two-Layer
Silk Pie • Lemonade Meringue Pie •

sweet potato tart

I love making desserts, and by modifying the recipes to reduce the fat, our family can enjoy them more often. You'd never guess this trimmed-down tart, with its delightful pecan crust and creamy filling, is on the light side.

Kate Gaudry • La Jolla, California

1-1/2 cups all-purpose flour

1/2 cup packed brown sugar

1/4 cup cold butter, cubed

2 tablespoons chopped pecans, toasted

1 egg

FILLING:

1 can (15-3/4 ounces) sweet potatoes

1/2 cup packed brown sugar

1/2 cup fat-free milk

2 egg whites

1/3 cup reduced-fat plain yogurt

1 tablespoon all-purpose flour

1/2 teaspoon ground cinnamon

1/4 teaspoon ground ginger

1/4 teaspoon ground nutmeg

1/8 teaspoon ground cloves

Whipped topping, optional

» In a food processor, combine the flour, brown sugar, butter and pecans. Cover and pulse until blended. Add egg, pulsing until mixture forms a soft dough. Press onto the bottom and up the sides of a 9-in. fluted tart pan with removable bottom.

» Place pan on a baking sheet. Bake at 400° for 8-10 minutes or until crust is lightly browned. Cool on a wire rack. Reduce heat to 350°.

» Drain sweet potatoes, reserving 1/4 cup liquid. Place potatoes in a food processor; cover and process until pureed. Add the brown sugar, milk, egg whites, yogurt, flour, spices and reserved liquid; cover and process until blended.

» Pour into crust. Bake for 30-35 minutes or until a knife inserted near the center comes out clean. Cool on a wire rack. Store in the refrigerator. Garnish with whipped topping if desired.

Yield: 12 servings.

tart cherry lattice pie

Whenever my mom is invited to a potluck, everyone requests she bring her homemade double-crust fruit pies. In the summer, she uses fresh tart cherries for this treat. I love a slice topped with fluffy whipped cream.

Pamela Eaton • Monclova, Ohio

1-1/3 cups sugar

1/3 cup all-purpose flour

4 cups fresh or frozen unsweetened pitted tart cherries, thawed and drained

1/4 teaspoon almond extract

Pastry for double-crust pie (9 inches)

2 tablespoons butter, cut into small pieces

» In a large bowl, combine sugar and flour; stir in cherries and extract. Line a 9-in. pie plate with bottom pastry; trim to 1 in. beyond edge of plate. Pour filling into crust. Dot with butter.

» Roll out remaining pastry; make a lattice crust. Trim, seal and flute edges. Cover edges loosely with foil.

» Bake at 400° for 40-50 minutes or until crust is golden brown and filling is bubbly. Remove foil. Cool on a wire rack.

Yield: 6-8 servings.

This sweet apple pie will make you the hit of every get-together. It's even better served warm with a scoop of vanilla ice cream.

Barbara Nowakowski • Mesa, Arizona

caramel-crunch apple pie

28 caramels

2 tablespoons water

5 cups thinly sliced peeled tart apples (about 2 pounds)

1 unbaked pastry shell (9 inches)

3/4 cup all-purpose flour

1/3 cup sugar

1/2 teaspoon ground cinnamon

1/3 cup cold butter, cubed

1/2 cup chopped walnuts

» In a heavy saucepan, combine caramels and water. Cook and stir over low heat until melted; stir until smooth.

» Arrange a third of the apples in pastry shell; drizzle with a third of the caramel mixture. Repeat layers twice. In a small bowl, combine the flour, sugar and cinnamon; cut in butter until crumbly. Stir in walnuts. Sprinkle over pie.

» Bake at 375° for 40-45 minutes or until apples are tender (cover edges with foil during the last 15 minutes to prevent overbrowning if necessary). Cool on a wire rack for 1 hour. Store in the refrigerator.

Yield: 6-8 servings.

» Roll out one portion of dough between two large sheets of waxed paper into a 17-in. x 12-in. rectangle. Transfer to an ungreased 15-in. x 10-in. x 1-in. baking pan. Press pastry onto the bottom and up the sides of pan; trim pastry even with top edge.

» In a large bowl, toss the apples, sugar, flour, cinnamon and nutmeg; spread over crust. Roll out remaining pastry to fit top of pan; place over filling. Trim edges; brush edges between pastry with water or milk; pinch to seal. Cut slits in top.

» Bake at 375° for 45-50 minutes or until golden brown. Cool on a wire rack. Combine glaze ingredients until smooth; drizzle over bars before cutting.

Yield: about 2 dozen.

apple pie bars

This is the only one of the many wonderful desserts that my mother handed down to me. These bars, with their flaky crust and delicious fruit filling, are the perfect way to serve apple pie to a crowd.

Janet English • Pittsburgh, Pennsylvania

4 cups all-purpose flour

1 teaspoon salt

1 teaspoon baking powder

1 cup shortening

4 egg yolks

2 tablespoons lemon juice

8 to 10 tablespoons cold water

FILLING:

7 cups finely chopped peeled apples

2 cups sugar

1/4 cup all-purpose flour

2 teaspoons ground cinnamon

Dash ground nutmeg

GLAZE:

1 cup confectioners' sugar

1 tablespoon 2% milk

1 tablespoon lemon juice

» In a large bowl, combine flour, salt and baking powder. Cut in shortening until mixture resembles coarse crumbs. In a small bowl, whisk egg yolks, lemon juice and water; gradually add to flour mixture, tossing with a fork until dough forms a ball. Divide in half. Chill for 30 minutes.

cherry-berry peach pie

I had an overabundant supply of cherries one year, so I adapted several recipes to use them up. I knew this pie was a keeper when I received phone calls from both my mother and grandmother complimenting me on my creation.

Amy Hartke • Elgin, Illinois

2-1/2 cups all-purpose flour

2 tablespoons sugar

1/2 teaspoon salt

1 cup cold butter, cubed

4 to 6 tablespoons cold water

FILLING:

2 cups fresh or frozen sliced peaches, thawed

1-3/4 cups pitted fresh dark sweet cherries or 1 can (15 ounces) pitted dark sweet cherries, drained

1 cup fresh or frozen blueberries, thawed

1 teaspoon almond extract

1 teaspoon vanilla extract

1-1/2 cups sugar

1/4 cup all-purpose flour

1/4 cup quick-cooking tapioca

1/2 teaspoon salt

1/2 teaspoon ground nutmeg

1 tablespoon butter

» In a large bowl, combine the flour, sugar and salt; cut in butter until crumbly. Gradually add water, tossing with a fork until dough forms a ball. Divide dough in half. Roll out one portion to fit a 9-in. deep-dish pie plate; transfer to pie plate. Trim pastry even with edge of plate; set aside.

» In a large bowl, combine the fruits and extracts. Combine the sugar, flour, tapioca, salt and nutmeg; sprinkle over fruit and gently toss to coat. Let stand for 15 minutes.

» Spoon filling into crust. Dot with butter. Roll out remaining pastry; make a lattice crust. Seal and flute edges.

» Bake at 375° for 50-55 minutes or until crust is golden brown and filling is bubbly. Cover edges with foil during the last 15 minutes to prevent overbrowning if necessary. Cool on a wire rack.

Yield: 6-8 servings.

walnut-streusel pumpkin pie

I made this pie from combining a few favorite recipes. I love streusel and pumpkin pie so putting them together worked perfectly.

Deborah Paulson • Deer Park, Washington

Pastry for single-crust pie (9 inches)

1 can (15 ounces) solid-pack pumpkin

1 can (14 ounces) sweetened condensed milk

1/2 cup sugar

1/2 cup packed dark brown sugar

2 eggs

1 tablespoon all-purpose flour

1-1/2 teaspoons ground cinnamon

1/2 teaspoon salt

1/2 teaspoon ground nutmeg

1/4 teaspoon ground ginger

CREAM CHEESE FILLING:

1 package (8 ounces) cream cheese, softened

1/4 cup sugar

1/2 teaspoon vanilla extract

1 egg, lightly beaten

TOPPING:

1/2 cup old-fashioned oats

1/2 cup packed dark brown sugar

1/2 cup chopped walnuts

1/4 cup all-purpose flour

1/2 teaspoon ground cinnamon

1/2 teaspoon ground nutmeg

1/4 cup cold butter, cubed

» Line a 9-in. deep-dish pie plate with the pastry; trim and flute edges. Set aside.

» In a bowl, beat pumpkin, milk, sugars, eggs, flour, cinnamon, salt, nutmeg and ginger until blended. Pour into crust.

» In a small bowl, beat the cream cheese, sugar and vanilla until smooth. Add egg; beat on low speed just until combined. Gently spread over pumpkin layer.

» In a bowl, combine oats, brown sugar, walnuts, flour, cinnamon and nutmeg; cut in butter until crumbly. Sprinkle over filling.

» Cover edges loosely with foil. Bake at 400° for 15 minutes. Reduce heat to 350°; bake 50-55 minutes longer or until a knife inserted near the center comes out clean. Remove foil. Cool on a wire rack. Refrigerate leftovers.

Yield: 10 servings.

triple-fruit pie

This refreshing pie features juicy slices of peaches, apricots and nectarines and a homemade golden-brown crust. It's irresistible at a warm-weather events.

Janet Loomis • Terry, Montana

2 cups all-purpose flour

1 teaspoon salt

3/4 cup shortening

5 tablespoons cold water

1-2/3 cups each sliced peeled peaches, nectarines and apricots

1 tablespoon lemon juice

1/2 cup packed brown sugar

1/4 teaspoon ground ginger

1/4 teaspoon ground cinnamon

1 tablespoon butter

» In a small bowl, combine flour and salt; cut in shortening until crumbly. Gradually add water, tossing with a fork until dough forms a ball. Divide in half. On a lightly floured surface, roll out one portion to fit a 9-in. pie plate. Transfer pastry to plate; trim to 1/2 in. beyond edge.

» In a large bowl, combine the peaches, nectarines, apricots and lemon juice. Combine the brown sugar, ginger and cinnamon; sprinkle over fruit and toss gently to coat. Pour into crust; dot with butter.

» Roll out remaining pastry to fit top of pie; make decorative cutouts. Set cutouts aside. Place top crust over filling. Trim, seal and flute edges. Moisten cutouts with a small amount of water; place on top of pie.

» Cover edges loosely with foil. Bake at 375° for 25 minutes. Uncover; bake 25-30 minutes longer or until crust is golden brown and filling is bubbly. Cool on a wire rack.

Yield: 6-8 servings.

black 'n' blue berry crumb pie

Here's a very simple recipe for a mouthwatering, fresh pie that features two kinds of berries and is simply delicious! The brown-sugar crumb topping adds buttery old-time flavor and crunch to this summery dessert classic.

Linda Palmer • Greenville, Ohio

1 sheet refrigerated pie pastry

3 cups fresh blackberries

2 cups fresh blueberries

3/4 cup sugar

1/4 cup cornstarch

1/8 teaspoon ground nutmeg

TOPPING:

1/2 cup all-purpose flour

1/4 cup packed brown sugar

1/4 cup cold butter

» Unroll pastry into a 9-in. pie plate. Trim pastry to 1/2 in. beyond edge of plate; flute edges.

» In a large bowl, combine the blackberries and blueberries. Combine the sugar, cornstarch and nutmeg; sprinkle over berries and toss gently. Pour into crust.

» In a small bowl, combine flour and brown sugar; cut in butter until crumbly. Sprinkle over filling.

» Bake at 375° for 55-60 minutes or until set (cover edges with foil during the last 15 minutes to prevent over browning if necessary). Cool on a wire rack.

Yield: 6-8 servings.

chocolate crunch pie

I received the recipe for this rich, chocolaty pie from an aunt of a good friend. It yields two pies, which always seem to disappear quickly at large gatherings.

Jo Ellen Greenhaw • Athens, Alabama

2 unbaked pastry shells (9 inches)

4 eggs

2 cups sugar

1 cup butter, cubed

1 cup (6 ounces) semisweet chocolate chips

1 cup chopped pecans

1 cup flaked coconut

1 teaspoon vanilla extract

» Line unpricked pastry shells with a double thickness of heavy-duty foil. Bake at 450° for 8 minutes. Remove from oven and set aside; remove foil. Reduce heat to 350°.

» In a large heavy saucepan over medium heat, whisk eggs and sugar until blended. Add butter and chocolate chips; cook, whisking constantly, until mixture is thickened and coats the back of a metal spoon. Stir in the pecans, coconut and vanilla.

» Pour into pie shells. Cover edges of pastry with foil. Bake at 350° for 20-25 minutes or until puffed.

Yield: 2 pies (6-8 servings each).

florida pie

I put winter in its place with this light and lovely orange meringue creation that tastes just as sun-kissed as it looks.

Muriel Boyd • Roscoe, Illinois

1 cup sugar

5 tablespoons cornstarch

1-1/2 cups orange juice

3 egg yolks, lightly beaten

2 large navel oranges, peeled, sectioned and finely chopped

2 tablespoons butter

1 tablespoon grated orange peel

1 tablespoon lemon juice

1 pastry shell (9 inches), baked

MERINGUE:

3 egg whites

2 tablespoons sugar

» In a small saucepan, combine sugar and cornstarch. Stir in orange juice until smooth. Cook and stir over medium-high heat until thickened and bubbly. Reduce heat; cook and stir 2 minutes longer.

» Remove from the heat. Stir a small amount of hot filling into egg yolks; return all to the pan, stirring constantly. Bring to a gentle boil; cook and stir for 2 minutes. Remove from the heat. Stir in the oranges, butter and orange peel. Gently stir in lemon juice. Pour into pastry shell.

» In a small bowl, beat egg whites on medium speed until soft peaks form. Gradually add sugar, 1 teaspoon at a time, beating on high until stiff glossy peaks form and sugar is dissolved. Spread evenly over hot filling, sealing edges to crust.

» Bake at 350° for 15 minutes or until meringue is golden brown. Cool on a wire rack for 1 hour. Refrigerate for at least 3 hours before serving. Refrigerate leftovers.

Yield: 8 servings.

strawberry tartlets

This elegant-looking dessert is easy to prepare, and the cute wonton "cups" can be made in advance. They're a different way to present fresh strawberries when entertaining.

Joy Van Meter • Thornton, Colorado

12 wonton wrappers

3 tablespoons butter, melted

1/3 cup packed brown sugar

3/4 cup Mascarpone cheese

2 tablespoons honey

2 teaspoons orange juice

3 cups fresh strawberries, sliced

Whipped cream and fresh mint, optional

» Brush one side of each wonton wrapper with butter. Place brown sugar in a shallow bowl; press buttered side of wontons into sugar to coat. Press wontons sugared side up into greased muffin cups.

» Bake at 325° for 7-9 minutes or until edges are lightly browned. Remove to a wire rack to cool.

» In a small bowl, combine the cheese, honey and orange juice. Spoon about 1 tablespoon into each wonton cup. Top with strawberries. Garnish with whipped cream and mint if desired.

Yield: 1 dozen.

decadent brownie pie

I have no doubt you'll love this favorite of mine. This is the richest brownie you'll ever taste. You can dress it up with different toppings to suit your tastes.

Stephanie Vozzo • Belvidere, New Jersey

2/3 cup butter, softened

1-1/4 cups sugar

1/2 cup light corn syrup

2 eggs

1-1/4 cups all-purpose flour

1/2 cup baking cocoa

1/2 teaspoon salt

3 tablespoons 2% milk

2 cups chopped walnuts

GANACHE:
1 cup heavy whipping cream

8 ounces semisweet chocolate, chopped

Mint Andes candies, fresh raspberries, fresh mint leaves, caramel ice cream topping and whipped cream, optional

» In a large bowl, cream butter and sugar until light and fluffy. Beat in corn syrup. Add eggs, one at a time, beating well after each addition. Combine the flour, cocoa and salt; gradually add to creamed mixture alternately with milk, beating well after each addition. Fold in walnuts.

» Spread into a greased 10-in. springform pan. Bake at 325° for 55-60 minutes or until a toothpick inserted 1 in. from side of pan comes out clean. Cool on a wire rack.

» For ganache, in a small saucepan, bring cream to a boil. Remove from the heat; stir in chocolate until melted. Cool completely. Remove sides of springform pan. Place a wire rack over waxed paper; set brownie on rack.

» Pour ganache over the brownie; spread over top and let drip down sides. Let stand until set. Cut into wedges; garnish with desired toppings. Store in the refrigerator.

Yield: 10-12 servings.

It's hard to resist this pretty pie. Best of all, I can throw it together and set it in the refrigerator a day early.

Jean Shourds • Sault Sainte Marie, Michigan

velvety orange gelatin pie

1 package (.3 ounce) sugar-free orange gelatin

1/2 cup boiling water

1 can (14 ounces) fat-free sweetened condensed milk

1 cup (8 ounces) reduced-fat sour cream

3 tablespoons grated orange peel

1 carton (8 ounces) frozen reduced-fat whipped topping, thawed

1 extra-servings-size graham cracker crust (9 ounces)

» In a large bowl, dissolve gelatin in boiling water. Stir in the milk, sour cream and orange peel. Fold in the whipped topping. Spoon into crust. Cover and refrigerate for at least 4 hours.

Yield: 10 servings.

cranberry walnut tart

Both attractive and delicious, this flaky tart combines a tender golden brown crust with a sweet filling that might remind you of baklava. It's a holiday favorite at our house.

Patricia Harmon • Baden, Pennsylvania

2-1/2 cups all-purpose flour

1 cup cold butter, cubed

1/4 cup sugar

2 egg yolks

3 tablespoons cold water

1 tablespoon lemon juice

1/2 teaspoon grated lemon peel

FILLING:
1 cup sugar

1/4 cup butter, cubed

1/4 cup water

2/3 cup heavy whipping cream

3 tablespoons honey

1/2 teaspoon salt

2 cups chopped walnuts

1/2 cup dried cranberries

1 egg white, lightly beaten

1 teaspoon coarse sugar

» Place the flour, butter and sugar in a food processor; cover and process until mixture resembles coarse crumbs. Add the egg yolks, water, lemon juice and peel; cover and process until

dough forms a ball. Divide dough in half; wrap in plastic wrap. Refrigerate for 1 hour or until firm.

» In a small saucepan, bring the sugar, butter and water to a boil; cook and stir for 1 minute. Cook, without stirring, until mixture turns a golden amber color, about 7 minutes.

» Remove from the heat; gradually stir in the cream. Return to heat; stir in honey and salt until smooth. Stir in walnuts and cranberries. Bring to a boil. Reduce heat; simmer, uncovered, for 5 minutes. Remove from the heat; cool to room temperature.

» On a lightly floured surface, roll out one portion of dough into an 11-in. circle. Transfer to an ungreased 9-in. fluted tart pan with a removable bottom; trim pastry even with edge. Add filling.

» Roll out remaining dough to fit top of tart; place over filling. Trim and seal edges. Cut slits in pastry.

» Brush with the egg white; sprinkle with coarse sugar. Bake at 400° for 20-25 minutes or until the filling is bubbly. Cool on a wire rack.

Yield: 10-12 servings.

dutch apple pie

Everything about this dessert makes it the top request for family gatherings. The delightful crust cuts beautifully to reveal wonderful pieces of diced apple.

Brenda DuFresne • Midland, Michigan

2 cups all-purpose flour

1 cup packed brown sugar

1/2 cup quick-cooking oats

3/4 cup butter, melted

FILLING:

2/3 cup sugar

3 tablespoons cornstarch

1-1/4 cups cold water

3 cups diced peeled tart apples

1 teaspoon vanilla extract

» In a large bowl, combine the flour, brown sugar, oats and butter; set aside 1 cup for topping. Press remaining crumb mixture into an ungreased 9-in. pie plate; set aside.

» For filling, combine the sugar, cornstarch and water in a large saucepan until smooth; bring to a boil. Cook and stir for 2 minutes or until thickened. Remove from the heat; stir in apples and vanilla.

» Pour into crust; top with reserved crumb mixture. Bake at 350° for 40-45 minutes or until crust is golden brown. Cool on a wire rack.

Yield: 6-8 servings.

peanut butter praline pie

The peanut butter flavor comes through nicely in this pie, and it has a creamy consistency. My clan can't get enough of it.

Mary Ellen Friend • Ravenswood, West Virginia

1-1/2 cups crushed vanilla wafers (about 45 wafers)

6 tablespoons baking cocoa

1/3 cup confectioners' sugar

1/4 cup butter, melted

PRALINE LAYER:

1/4 cup packed brown sugar

2 tablespoons sugar

1 tablespoon cornstarch

1/3 cup butter, cubed

2 tablespoons water

1/2 cup chopped pecans

FILLING:

1 package (3 ounces) cook-and-serve vanilla pudding mix

2 cups 2% milk

1 package (10 or 11 ounces) peanut butter chips

1 cup whipped topping

Pecan halves and additional whipped topping

» In a large bowl, combine the wafer crumbs, cocoa and confectioners' sugar; stir in butter. Press into a 9-in. pie plate. Bake at 350° for 10 minutes. Cool on a wire rack.

» In a large saucepan, combine the sugars and cornstarch. Add butter and water. Bring to a boil over medium heat; cook and stir for 1 minute or until thickened. Stir in pecans. Pour into crust; refrigerate.

» Meanwhile, in a large saucepan, combine pudding mix and milk. Cook and stir over medium heat until mixture comes to a boil. Remove from the heat. Stir in peanut butter chips until smooth. Cover and refrigerate for 1 hour.

» Fold in whipped topping; spoon over praline layer. Refrigerate until set. Garnish with pecans and additional whipped topping.

Yield: 6-8 servings.

pick of the apples

Granny Smith is a crisp, tart apple that would be suitable for the Dutch Apple Pie recipe. Other options would be Braeburn and Empire apples, which have a sweet-tart flavor. Cortland and Rome Beauty apples are mildly tart and would also be good choices.

strawberry custard pies

These pies were a spring special at a restaurant where I used to work. Whoever was the cook that day had to bake them the first thing in the morning and again in the afternoon, as soon as the strawberries were ready.

Caroline Park • Pritchard, British Columbia

4-1/2 cups sugar

3/4 cup cornstarch

4-1/2 cups cold water

3 packages (3 ounces each) strawberry gelatin

1 tablespoon lemon juice

6 packages (3 ounces each) cook-and-serve vanilla pudding mix

6 pastry shells (9 inches), baked

3 pounds fresh strawberries, halved

Whipped cream, optional

» In a large saucepan, combine sugar and cornstarch; gradually stir in the water until smooth. Bring to a boil; cook and stir for 2 minutes or until thickened. Remove from the heat. Stir in gelatin and lemon juice until gelatin is dissolved. Cool to room temperature.

» Prepare pudding mixes according to package directions. Pour into pastry shells. Top with the strawberries. Carefully spoon gelatin mixture over berries. Refrigerate until set. Garnish with whipped cream if desired.

Yield: 6 pies (8 servings each).

pumpkin chiffon dessert

This pumpkin dessert is full of delicious flavors you'll love. It's a perfect ending to a family dinner.

Lynn Baker • Osmond, Nebraska

1 cup finely crushed gingersnaps (about 24)

3 tablespoons butter, melted

2 envelopes unflavored gelatin

1/2 cup fat-free milk

1/2 cup sugar

1 can (15 ounces) solid-pack pumpkin

1/2 teaspoon salt

1/2 teaspoon ground cinnamon

1/4 teaspoon ground ginger

1/4 teaspoon ground cloves

1 carton (8 ounces) frozen fat-free whipped topping, thawed

Additional whipped topping, optional

» In a small bowl, combine cookie crumbs and butter. Press onto the bottom of a greased 9-in. springform pan; set aside.

» In a large saucepan, combine gelatin and milk; let stand for 5 minutes. Heat milk mixture to just below boiling; remove from the heat. Stir in sugar until dissolved. Add the pumpkin, salt, cinnamon, ginger and cloves; mix well. Fold in whipped topping. Pour over crust. Refrigerate until set, about 3 hours.

» Remove sides of pan just before serving. Garnish with additional whipped topping if desired.

Yield: 16 servings.

classic pie pastry

Just four ingredients are all you need to create a fabulous flaky pie crust. The double-crust recipe should be used when making a lattice-topped pie.

Taste of Home Test Kitchen

INGREDIENTS FOR SINGLE-CRUST PIE:
1-1/4 cups all-purpose flour

1/2 teaspoon salt

1/3 cup shortening

4 to 5 tablespoons cold water

INGREDIENTS FOR DOUBLE-CRUST PIE:
2 cups all-purpose flour

3/4 teaspoon salt

2/3 cup shortening

6 to 7 tablespoons cold water

» In a small bowl, combine flour and salt; cut in shortening until mixture is crumbly. Gradually add water, tossing with a fork until a ball forms. Cover and refrigerate for 30 minutes or until easy to handle.

» For a single crust, roll out pastry on a lightly floured surface to fit a 9-in. or 10-in. pie plate. Transfer pastry to pie plate. Trim pastry to 1/2 in. beyond edge of plate; flute edges. Fill or bake shell according to recipe directions.

» For a double crust, divide dough in half so one ball is slightly larger than the other. Roll out larger ball on a lightly floured surface to fit a 9-in. or 10-in. pie plate. Transfer pastry to pie plate. Trim pastry even with edge of plate. Add filling. Roll out remaining pastry to fit top of pie; place over filling. Trim, seal and flute edges. Cut slits in top. Bake according to recipe directions.

**Yield: 1 pastry for a single
or double-crust pie (9 or 10 inches).**

dixie pie

When Mom baked this old-fashioned sugar pie, everyone would clamor for second servings. We love the combination of cinnamon, coconut, nuts and raisins. She'd sometimes toss in a few chocolate chips for variety.

Sandra Pichon • Memphis, Tennessee

Pastry for two single-crust pies (9 inches)

1-1/2 cups raisins

1 cup butter, softened

1 cup sugar

1 cup packed brown sugar

6 eggs

2 teaspoons vanilla extract

2 to 4 teaspoons ground cinnamon

1 cup chopped nuts

1 cup flaked coconut

Whipped topping and additional chopped nuts, optional.

» Line two 9-in. pie plates with pastry. Trim pastry to 1/2 in. beyond edge of plate; flute edges. Line crusts with a double thickness of heavy-duty foil. Bake at 450° for 10 minutes. Discard foil. Cool on wire racks.

» Place raisins in a saucepan and cover with water; bring to a boil. Remove from heat; set aside. In a large bowl, cream butter and sugars until light and fluffy. Beat in eggs, vanilla and cinnamon until blended.

» Drain raisins. Stir the raisins, nuts and coconut into creamed mixture (mixture will appear curdled). Pour into the crusts.

» Bake at 350° for 30-35 minutes or until set. Cool on wire racks. Garnish with whipped topping and nuts if desired.

Yield: 2 pies (6-8 servings each).

two-layer silk pie

This luscious recipe eases event preparations because it yields two scrumptious pies that chill overnight. My clan loves the smooth, silky texture. The combination of chocolate and peanut butter satisfies even the strongest sweet-tooth craving.

Maryann Thomas • Clay City, Kentucky

2 unbaked pastry shells (9 inches)

2-1/2 cups cold 2% milk

1 package (5.9 ounces) instant chocolate pudding mix

1 can (14 ounces) sweetened condensed milk

1/2 cup creamy peanut butter

1 carton (12 ounces) frozen whipped topping, thawed

Chocolate curls and chopped peanuts, optional

» Line unpricked pastry shells with a double thickness of heavy-duty foil. Bake at 450° for 8 minutes. Remove foil; bake 5 minutes longer. Cool on wire racks.

» In a large bowl, whisk milk and pudding mix for 2 minutes. Let stand until soft-set. Spread into crusts.

» In another large bowl, beat condensed milk and peanut butter until smooth. Set aside 2 cups whipped topping for garnish; cover and refrigerate.

» Fold remaining whipped topping into peanut butter mixture. Spread over pudding layer. Refrigerate for 6 hours or until set.

» Garnish with reserved whipped topping; top with chocolate curls and peanuts if desired.

Yield: 2 pies (6-8 servings each).

cranberry pear pie

When our family is invited to holiday gatherings, this pie usually comes with us. The recipe is very versatile. You can make it with a double crust or replace the pears with baking apples. Serve it with ice cream or whipped topping.

Helen Toulantis • Wantagh, New York

Pastry for single-crust pie (9 inches)

2 tablespoons all-purpose flour

1/2 cup maple syrup

2 tablespoons butter, melted

5 cups sliced peeled fresh pears

1 cup fresh or frozen cranberries

TOPPING:
1/2 cup all-purpose flour

1/4 cup packed brown sugar

1 teaspoon ground cinnamon

1/3 cup cold butter, cubed

1/2 cup chopped walnuts

» Line a 9-in. pie plate with pastry; trim and flute edges. Set aside. In a bowl, combine the flour, syrup and butter until smooth. Add pears and cranberries; toss to coat. Spoon into crust.

» For topping, combine the flour, brown sugar and cinnamon; cut in butter until crumbly. Stir in walnuts. Sprinkle over filling.

» Cover edges of crust loosely with foil to prevent overbrowning. Bake at 400° for 15 minutes. Reduce heat to 350°. Remove foil; bake 35-40 minutes longer or until crust is golden brown and filling is bubbly. Cool on a wire rack.

Yield: 6-8 servings.

custard meringue pie

Each bite of this light and fluffy dessert will nearly melt in your mouth. The cracker-crumb crust holds a creamy vanilla filling topped with an airy meringue and a sprinkling of more crumbs. Everyone will crave a second slice!

Nancy Holland • Morgan Hill, California

1-1/4 cups crushed Holland Rusks or graham crackers

1/4 cup sugar

1/2 teaspoon ground cinnamon

6 tablespoons butter, melted

FILLING:
2/3 cup sugar

1/4 cup cornstarch

1/2 teaspoon salt

3 cups 2% milk

3 egg yolks, lightly beaten

1 tablespoon butter, softened

1-1/2 teaspoons vanilla extract

MERINGUE:
3 egg whites

1/4 teaspoon cream of tartar

1/8 teaspoon almond extract

6 tablespoons sugar

» In a small bowl, combine the first four ingredients; set aside 2 tablespoons. Press remaining crumb mixture onto the bottom and up the sides of an ungreased 9-in. pie plate.

» Bake at 350° for 10-12 minutes or until golden brown. Cool on a wire rack.

» In a large saucepan, combine the sugar, cornstarch and salt. Stir in the milk until smooth. Bring to a boil; cook and stir for 2 minutes. Remove from the heat.

» Stir in a small amount of hot filling into egg yolks; return all to pan, stirring constantly. Bring to a gentle boil; cook and stir for 2 minutes. Remove from the heat. Stir in butter and vanilla. Pour filling into crust.

» In a small bowl, beat the egg whites, cream of tartar and extract on medium speed until soft peaks form. Gradually beat in sugar, 1 tablespoon at a time, on high until high stiff peaks form and sugar is dissolved. Spread evenly over hot filling, sealing to crust. Sprinkle with reserved crumbs.

» Bake at 350° for 12-15 minutes or until golden brown. Cool on a wire rack for 1 hour. Refrigerate for at least 3 hours before serving. Store leftovers in the refrigerator.

Yield: 6-8 servings.

foolproof pie shells

I received this recipe from my 94-year-old sister. She suggested using an egg, cold water and cider vinegar to keep the crust moist. The recipe is ideal when you need to bake several pies for an event.

Bob Campbell • Lincoln, Nebraska

4 cups all-purpose flour

1 tablespoon sugar

2 teaspoons salt

1-3/4 cups shortening

1 egg

1/2 cup cold water

1 tablespoon cider vinegar

» In a large bowl, combine the flour, sugar and salt; cut in shortening until crumbly. Whisk the egg, water and vinegar; gradually add to flour mixture, tossing with a fork until dough forms a ball. Divide into four portions. Cover and refrigerate for at least 1 hour.

» On a lightly floured surface, roll out each portion of dough to fit a 9-in. pie plate. Transfer pastry to pie plates. Trim each pastry to 1/2 in. beyond edge of plate; flute edges. Fill or bake shells according to recipe directions.

Yield: 4 pie shells.

raspberry cheesecake pie

This creamy cheesecake pie with a raspberry layer makes a light and lovely finale to a heavy meal.

Steve Josserand • Decatur, Illinois

2 packages (8 ounces each) cream cheese, softened

1/2 cup sugar

1/2 teaspoon vanilla extract

2 eggs, lightly beaten

1 chocolate crumb crust (8 inches)

1-1/2 teaspoons unflavored gelatin

2 tablespoons cold water

1/2 cup seedless raspberry jam

1 cup heavy whipping cream

2 tablespoons confectioners' sugar

» In a large bowl, beat the cream cheese, sugar and vanilla until smooth. Add the eggs; beat on low speed just until combined. Pour into crust. Bake at 325° for 25-30 minutes or until the center is almost set. Cool on a wire rack for 1 hour. Refrigerate overnight.

» In a small saucepan, sprinkle gelatin over cold water; let stand for 1 minute. Cook over low heat, stirring until gelatin is completely dissolved. Stir in jam. Refrigerate for 10 minutes.

» In small bowl, beat cream until it begins to thicken. Gradually add confectioners' sugar; beat until stiff peaks form. Remove 1/2 cup for garnish; cover and refrigerate.

» Gently stir 3/4 cup whipped cream into raspberry mixture just until blended. Fold in the remaining whipped cream; spread over cheesecake. Refrigerate for at least 1 hour. Garnish with reserved whipped cream.

Yield: 6-8 servings.

eggnog cream pies

I created this recipe for my brother, who just happens to love eggnog. He was delighted, to say the least, when he tasted this sweet treat.

Anna Long • Modesto, California

2 unbaked pastry shells (9 inches)

4 ounces cream cheese, softened

1/2 cup confectioners' sugar

1 teaspoon ground allspice

1 teaspoon ground nutmeg

2 cartons (one 8 ounces, one 12 ounces) frozen whipped topping, thawed, divided

3-3/4 cups cold eggnog

3 packages (3.4 ounces each) instant cheesecake or vanilla pudding mix

Additional ground nutmeg

» Line unpricked pastry shells with a double thickness of heavy-duty foil. Bake at 450° for 8 minutes. Remove foil; bake 5 minutes longer. Cool on wire racks.

» In a small bowl, beat the cream cheese, confectioners' sugar, allspice and nutmeg until smooth. Fold in the 8-oz. carton of whipped topping. Spoon into crusts.

» In a large bowl, whisk eggnog and pudding mixes for 2 minutes. Let stand for 2 minutes or until soft-set. Spread over cream cheese layer. Top with remaining whipped topping; sprinkle with additional nutmeg. Cover and refrigerate for 8 hours or overnight.

Yield: 2 pies (8 servings each).

EDITOR'S NOTE: This recipe was tested with commercially prepared eggnog.

Packed with peanuts and gooey with caramel, this do-ahead treat is one sweet dream of a dessert to serve company. With an easy cookie crust and scrumptious candy bar layers, it goes together quickly and will disappear just as fast!

Taste of Home Test Kitchen

caramel peanut fantasy

2 cups crushed vanilla wafers (about 60 wafers)

1/3 cup butter, melted

20 caramels

15 miniature Snickers candy bars

1/2 cup caramel ice cream topping

1/2 cup heavy whipping cream, divided

2 cups salted peanuts, chopped

3/4 cup semisweet chocolate chips

» In a small bowl, combine wafer crumbs and butter. Press onto the bottom of a greased 9-in. springform pan. Place on a baking sheet. Bake at 350° for 8-10 minutes. Cool on a wire rack.

» In a heavy saucepan, combine the caramels, candy bars, caramel topping and 1/4 cup cream; cook and stir over low heat until smooth and blended. Remove from the heat; stir in peanuts. Spread over crust. Cover and refrigerate for 1 hour.

» In a microwave, melt chocolate chips and remaining cream; stir until smooth. Spread over caramel layer. Cover and refrigerate for 1 hour or until serving. Refrigerate leftovers.

Yield: 12 servings.

» Divide dough in half. On a lightly floured surface, roll out one portion to fit a 9-in. pie plate. Transfer pastry to pie plate; trim to 1 in. beyond edge of plate.

» In a large bowl, combine the blueberries, sugar, flour, lemon peel and salt; spoon into crust. Drizzle with lemon juice; dot with butter. Roll out remaining pastry; place over filling. Seal and flute edges. Cut slits in top crust.

» Bake at 400° for 40-45 minutes or until crust is golden brown and filling is bubbly. Cool on a wire rack. Store in refrigerator.

Yield: 6-8 servings.

butterscotch peach pie

When peach season arrives, this delicious old-fashioned pie is sure to be on the table. The recipe has been in our family for over 60 years, and I still make it every summer. Butterscotch buffs love it.

Barbara Moyer • Tiffin, Ohio

2 cups all-purpose flour

1 teaspoon salt

3/4 cup shortening

4 to 5 tablespoons cold water

FILLING:

3/4 cup packed brown sugar

2 tablespoons all-purpose flour

blueberry pie with lemon crust

Mom and I have fun baking and creating new treats together. This is a sensational example of one of our keepers. I hope one day to be a great baker like she is.

Sara West • Broken Arrow, Oklahoma

2 cups all-purpose flour

1 teaspoon salt

1/2 teaspoon grated lemon peel

2/3 cup shortening

1 tablespoon lemon juice

4 to 6 tablespoons cold water

FILLING:

4 cups fresh blueberries

3/4 cup sugar

3 tablespoons all-purpose flour

1/2 teaspoon grated lemon peel

Dash salt

1 to 2 teaspoons lemon juice

1 tablespoon butter

» In a large bowl, combine the flour, salt and lemon peel. Cut in shortening until crumbly. Add lemon juice. Gradually add water, tossing with a fork until a ball forms. Cover and refrigerate for 1 hour.

1/3 cup light corn syrup

3 tablespoons butter, melted

2 tablespoons lemon juice

1/4 teaspoon almond extract

8 medium peaches, peeled and sliced

» In a large bowl, combine flour and salt; cut in shortening until crumbly. Gradually add water, tossing with a fork until dough forms a ball. Cover and refrigerate for 30 minutes or until easy to handle.

» For filling, in a small saucepan, combine brown sugar and flour. Stir in corn syrup and butter until blended. Bring to a boil; cook and stir for 2 minutes or until thickened. Remove from the heat; stir in lemon juice and extract. Place peaches in a large bowl; add syrup mixture and toss to coat.

» Divide dough in half so one ball is slightly larger than the other. Roll out larger ball to fit a 9-in. pie plate. Transfer pastry to plate; trim pastry even with edge. Add filling. Roll out remaining pastry; make a lattice crust. Trim, seal and flute edges. Cover edges loosely with foil.

» Bake at 375° for 25 minutes. Uncover; bake 20-25 minutes longer or until crust is golden brown and filling is bubbly. Cool on a wire rack.

Yield: 8 servings.

crumb-topped cherry pie

This pie was my dad's favorite and one my mom made frequently to go along with Sunday dinner.

Sandy Jenkins • Elkhorn, Wisconsin

1-1/4 cups all-purpose flour

1/2 teaspoon salt

1/2 cup canola oil

2 tablespoons 2% milk

FILLING:

1-1/3 cups sugar

1/3 cup all-purpose flour

2 cans (14-1/2 ounces each) pitted tart cherries, drained

1/4 teaspoon almond extract

TOPPING:

1/2 cup all-purpose flour

1/2 cup sugar

1/4 cup cold butter, cubed

1 cup heavy whipping cream

1 tablespoon confectioners' sugar

1/8 teaspoon vanilla extract

» In a small bowl, combine the flour and salt. Combine the oil and milk; stir into the flour mixture with a fork just until blended. Pat evenly onto the bottom and up the sides of a 9-in. pie plate; set aside.

» In a large bowl, combine all the filling ingredients; pour into the crust.

» For topping, combine flour and sugar; cut in butter until crumbly. Sprinkle over filling.

» Bake at 425° for 35-45 minutes or until crust is golden brown and filling is bubbly. Cool on a wire rack.

» Just before serving, in a small bowl, beat cream until it begins to thicken. Add confectioners' sugar and vanilla; beat until soft peaks form. Serve with pie.

Yield: 6-8 servings.

a sparkling crust

To give some pizzazz to the top pie crust or pie crust edge, brush with a combination of one egg beaten with 1 tablespoon water. Then sprinkle with coarse sugar before baking.

chocolate hazelnut tart

This tart looks like it takes a lot of time to prepare but it couldn't be more deceiving! I like to serve it with vanilla or coffee ice cream.

Gilda Lester • Millsboro, Delaware

6 tablespoons butter, softened

2 tablespoons cream cheese, softened

1/3 cup confectioners' sugar

1 teaspoon grated lemon peel

1 cup all-purpose flour

FILLING:
4 eggs

3/4 cup sugar

1/2 cup chocolate syrup

1/4 cup dark corn syrup

1 cup chopped hazelnuts, toasted

1 cup (6 ounces) miniature semisweet chocolate chips

Whipped cream and chocolate shavings, optional

» In a bowl, beat the butter, cream cheese, confectioners' sugar and lemon peel until creamy. Beat in flour just until combined.

» Shape dough into a disk. Wrap in plastic wrap; refrigerate for 30 minutes or until easy to handle.

» Roll dough into an 11-in. circle. Press onto the bottom and up the sides of an ungreased 9-in. fluted tart pan with a removable bottom. Bake at 350° for 18-22 minutes or until lightly browned. Cool on a wire rack.

» In a small bowl, combine the eggs, sugar, chocolate syrup and corn syrup. Pour into crust. Combine hazelnuts and chocolate chips; sprinkle over filling. Place pan on a baking sheet.

» Bake for 25-30 minutes or until center is almost set (center will set when cool). Cool on a wire rack.

» Garnish with whipped cream and chocolate shavings if desired. Refrigerate leftovers.

Yield: 12 servings.

banana cream pie

Cream pies are my mom's specialty, and this dreamy dessert has a wonderful banana flavor. It looks so pretty topped with almonds... and it cuts easily, too.

Jodi Grable • Springfield, Missouri

1 cup sugar

1/4 cup cornstarch

1/2 teaspoon salt

3 cups 2% milk

2 eggs, lightly beaten

3 tablespoons butter

1-1/2 teaspoons vanilla extract

2 large firm bananas

1 pastry shell (9 inches), baked

1 cup heavy whipping cream, whipped

1 tablespoon sliced almonds, toasted

» In a large saucepan, combine the sugar, cornstarch, salt and milk until smooth. Cook and stir over medium-high heat until thickened and bubbly. Reduce heat; cook and stir 2 minutes longer. Remove from the heat. Stir a small amount of hot filling into eggs; return all to the pan. Bring to a gentle boil; cook and stir 2 minutes longer.

» Remove from the heat. Gently stir in butter and vanilla. Press plastic wrap onto surface of custard; cover and refrigerate for 30 minutes.

» Slice the bananas into pastry shell; pour custard over top. Spread with whipped cream; sprinkle with almonds. Chill for 6-8 hours or overnight. Refrigerate leftovers.

Yield: 6-8 servings.

This has been in my party recipe collection for over 30 years and never fails to satisfy my guests. I can always rely on these fancy treats to please even the fussiest eater.

Jessica Feist • Pewaukee, Wisconsin

lemon curd tartlets

3 eggs

1 cup sugar

1/2 cup lemon juice

1 tablespoon grated lemon peel

1/4 cup butter, cubed

1 package (1.9 ounces) frozen miniature phyllo tart shells, thawed

Fresh raspberries, mint leaves and/or sweetened whipped cream, optional

» In a small heavy saucepan over medium heat, whisk the eggs, sugar, lemon juice and peel until blended. Add butter; cook, whisking constantly, until mixture is thickened and coats the back of a metal spoon. Transfer to a small bowl; cool for 10 minutes. Cover and refrigerate until chilled.

» Just before serving, spoon the lemon curd into tart shells. Garnish with the raspberries, mint and/or cream if desired. Refrigerate leftovers.

Yield: 15 tartlets.

cranberry custard meringue pie

I love to serve this treat around the holidays when my family is around. My grandchildren call it the red pie with the fluff topping.

Lee Bremson • Kansas City, Missouri

3 eggs, separated

Pastry for single-crust pie (9 inches)

1-3/4 cups fresh or frozen cranberries

1 tablespoon grated orange peel

1-1/4 cups plus 6 tablespoons sugar, divided

1 cup water

Dash salt

Dash ground cinnamon

4 teaspoons plus 1/4 cup cornstarch, divided

1/4 cup orange juice

2 cups 2% milk, divided

1 tablespoon butter

1 teaspoon vanilla extract

1/4 teaspoon cream of tartar

» Place egg whites in a small bowl; let stand at room temperature for 30 minutes.

» Meanwhile, line a 9-in. pie plate with pastry; trim and flute edges. Line pastry shell with a double thickness of heavy-duty foil. Bake at 450° for 8 minutes. Remove foil; bake 5 minutes longer. Cool on a wire rack.

» In a small saucepan, combine the cranberries, orange peel, 1/2 cup sugar, water, salt and cinnamon. Cook over medium heat until berries pop, about 15 minutes. Combine 4 teaspoons cornstarch and orange juice until smooth; stir into cranberry mixture. Bring to a boil; cook and stir for 1-2 minutes or until thickened. Remove from the heat; set aside.

» In another small saucepan, heat 3/4 cup sugar and 1-3/4 cups milk until bubbles form around sides of pan. In a small bowl, combine the remaining cornstarch and milk. Whisk in egg yolks until blended. Add a small amount of hot milk mixture; return all to the pan, whisking constantly.

» Whisk vigorously over medium heat as mixture begins to thicken (mixture will become very thick). Bring to a boil; whisk 2 minutes longer. Remove from the heat; whisk in butter and vanilla. Transfer custard to crust; spread evenly with reserved cranberry mixture.

» Add cream of tartar to egg whites; beat on medium speed until soft peaks form. Gradually beat in the remaining sugar, 1 tablespoon at a time, on high until stiff glossy peaks form and sugar is dissolved. Spread evenly over filling, sealing edges to crust. Bake at 350° for 12-15 minutes or until meringue is golden brown. Cool on a wire rack for 1 hour. Refrigerate overnight.

Yield: 8 servings.

raspberry pear tart

Fetch the forks! Guests will be eager to dig into this festive tart. Destined to become a favorite on the dessert buffet, it looks and smells as delightful as it tastes.

Bernice Janowski • Stevens Point, Wisconsin

1-2/3 cups all-purpose flour

2/3 cup sugar

2/3 cup cold butter

1/3 cup chopped macadamia nuts

FILLING:

3 medium pears, peeled and thinly sliced

1/2 cup sugar

2 tablespoons cornstarch

1 teaspoon ground cinnamon

1 teaspoon grated lemon peel

2 cups fresh or frozen raspberries

TOPPING:

1/2 cup all-purpose flour

1/2 cup packed brown sugar

1 teaspoon grated lemon peel

1/4 cup cold butter

1/3 cup chopped macadamia nuts

» In a large bowl, combine flour and sugar; cut in butter until mixture resembles coarse crumbs. Stir in nuts. Press onto the bottom and up the sides of an ungreased 11-in. fluted tart pan with removable bottom.

» In a large bowl, combine the pears, sugar, cornstarch, cinnamon and lemon peel. Add raspberries; toss gently. Pour into crust. Bake at 425° for 25 minutes.

» For topping, in a bowl, combine flour, brown sugar and lemon peel; cut in butter until crumbly. Stir in nuts. Sprinkle over filling. Bake 15-20 minutes longer or until filling is bubbly and topping is golden brown. Cool on a wire rack. Refrigerate leftovers.

Yield: 16 servings.

bumbleberry pie

This recipe makes one of the flakiest crusts ever and is sure to impress! The filling is also delicious with the different berries and rhubarb.

Suzanne Alberts • Onalaska, Wisconsin

1-1/2 cups all-purpose flour

1 teaspoon salt

1 teaspoon sugar

1 cup cold butter

1/4 cup cold water

FILLING:

1 medium tart apple, peeled and diced

1 cup diced fresh or frozen rhubarb, thawed

1 cup fresh or frozen raspberries, thawed and drained

1 cup fresh or frozen blueberries, thawed and drained

1 cup sliced fresh or frozen strawberries, thawed and drained

1 cup sugar

1/2 cup all-purpose flour

1 tablespoon lemon juice

» In a small bowl, combine the flour, salt and sugar. Cut in butter until mixture resembles coarse crumbs. Gradually add water, tossing with a fork until a ball forms. Cover and chill for 1 hour.

» On a lightly floured surface, roll out half of the dough to fit a 9-in. pie plate. Transfer pastry to pie plate. Trim pastry to within 1 in. beyond edge of plate.

» In a large bowl, combine the filling ingredients; pour into crust. Roll out the remaining pastry; make a lattice crust. Seal and

flute edges. Cover edges loosely with foil.

» Bake at 400° for 20 minutes. Reduce heat to 350°; remove foil. Bake 40-45 minutes longer or until crust is golden brown and filling is bubbly. Cool on a wire rack.

Yield: 6-8 servings.

strawberry pie

This strawberry pie is perfect for any occasion. It's particularly good topped with vanilla ice cream!

Michelle Isenhoff • Wayland, Michigan

1 unbaked pastry shell (9 inches)

3/4 cup sugar

2 tablespoons cornstarch

1 cup water

1 package (3 ounces) strawberry gelatin

4 cups sliced fresh strawberries

Fresh mint, optional

» Line unpricked pastry shell with a double thickness of heavy-duty foil. Bake at 450° for 8 minutes. Remove foil; bake 5 minutes longer. Cool on a wire rack.

» In a small saucepan, combine the sugar, cornstarch and water until smooth. Bring to a boil; cook and stir for 2 minutes or until thickened. Remove from the heat; stir in gelatin until dissolved. Refrigerate for 15-20 minutes or until slightly cooled.

» Arrange strawberries in the crust. Pour the gelatin mixture over berries. Refrigerate until set. Garnish with mint if desired.

Yield: 6-8 servings.

marshmallow-almond key lime pie

It's great to see that many grocers now carry key limes, which give this treat its distinctive sweet-tart flavor.

Judy Castranova • New Bern, North Carolina

1 cup all-purpose flour

3 tablespoons brown sugar

1 cup slivered almonds, toasted, divided

1/4 cup butter, melted

1 tablespoon honey

1 can (14 ounces) sweetened condensed milk

1 package (8 ounces) cream cheese, softened, divided

1/2 cup key lime juice

1 tablespoon grated key lime peel

Dash salt

1 egg yolk

1-3/4 cups miniature marshmallows

4-1/2 teaspoons butter

1/2 cup heavy whipping cream

» Place the flour, brown sugar and 1/2 cup almonds in a food processor. Cover and process until blended. Add melted butter and honey; cover and process until crumbly. Press onto the bottom and up the sides of a greased 9-in. pie plate. Bake at 350° for 8-10 minutes or until crust is lightly browned. Cool on a wire rack.

» In a large bowl, beat the milk, 5 ounces cream cheese, lime juice, peel and salt until blended. Add egg yolk; beat on low speed just until combined. Pour into crust.

» Bake for 15-20 minutes or until center is almost set. Cool on a wire rack. In a large saucepan, combine marshmallows and butter. Cook and stir over medium-low heat until melted. Remove from the heat and transfer to a bowl. Add cream and remaining cream cheese; beat until smooth. Cover and refrigerate until chilled.

» Beat marshmallow mixture until light and fluffy. Spread over pie; sprinkle with remaining almonds.

Yield: 8 servings.

ginger pear pie

The flavors of ginger and lemon make this pear pie exceptional.

Delilah Stauffer • Mt. Pleasant Mills, Pennsylvania

3 tablespoons cornstarch

1/4 teaspoon ground ginger

1/2 cup water

1/2 cup dark corn syrup

1 teaspoon lemon juice

1/8 teaspoon grated lemon peel

4 large pears, peeled and thinly sliced

1 tablespoon butter

1 unbaked pastry shell (9 inches)

TOPPING:
1/2 cup all-purpose flour

1/4 cup packed brown sugar

1/8 teaspoon ground ginger

1/4 cup cold butter, cubed

1/4 cup chopped pecans

» In a large saucepan, combine the cornstarch and ginger. Stir in the water, corn syrup, lemon juice and peel until smooth. Gently stir in pears. Bring to a boil over medium heat; cook and stir for 1 minute or until thickened. Remove from the heat; add butter. Pour into pastry shell.

» For topping, combine the flour, brown sugar and ginger in a small bowl; cut in butter until crumbly. Stir in pecans. Sprinkle over pears. Bake at 425° for 20-25 minutes or until filling is bubbly and topping is browned. Cool on a wire rack.

Yield: 6 servings.

A relative shared this recipe with me. The wonderful meringue crust is tender and crispy. I love peaches so this pie one of my favorite summertime desserts.

Beatrice Crutchfield • Norcross, Georgia

coconut peach pie

3 egg whites

Dash salt

3/4 cup plus 2 tablespoons sugar, divided

1-1/4 cups flaked coconut, toasted, divided

1/3 cup chopped almonds, toasted

3-1/2 cups sliced peeled peaches (about 6 medium)

1 cup heavy whipping cream

» In a large bowl, beat egg whites and salt on medium speed until foamy. Gradually add 3/4 cup sugar, 1 tablespoon at a time, beating on high until stiff peaks form. Fold in 1 cup coconut and almonds. Spread onto the bottom and up the sides of a greased 9-in. pie plate.

» Bake at 350° for 30 minutes or until light golden brown. Cool completely on a wire rack.

» Arrange peaches in crust. In a bowl, beat cream with remaining sugar until stiff peaks form. Spread over peaches; sprinkle with remaining coconut. Refrigerate for 1 hour before slicing.

Yield: 6-8 servings.

sour cream cherry pie

If I can beat the birds to our cherry tree, I'll make this luscious pie. Otherwise, strawberries or blueberries can be substituted. It's especially good served warm with vanilla bean ice cream.

Betty Wingo • Marshall, Arkansas

3 cups pitted frozen tart cherries, thawed, drained and patted dry

1 unbaked pastry shell (9 inches)

1 tablespoon butter

1-3/4 cups plus 2 tablespoons sugar, divided

1 cup all-purpose flour

1/2 teaspoon salt

2 eggs, lightly beaten

1 cup (8 ounces) sour cream

1 tablespoon lemon juice

» Arrange cherries evenly in the pastry shell. Dot with butter. In a large bowl, combine 1-3/4 cups sugar, flour and salt. Stir in the eggs, sour cream and lemon juice; mix well. Spread evenly over cherries. Sprinkle with remaining sugar.

» Bake at 400° for 10 minutes. Reduce the heat to 350°; bake 30 minutes longer or until topping is set. Cool for 1 hour on a wire rack. Refrigerate for 3-4 hours before cutting. Refrigerate leftovers.

Yield: 8 servings.

apple blackberry pie

After a blackberry-picking trip, we decided to include a few in an apple pie we were making. It was the best we'd ever tasted!

Dorian Lucas • Corning, California

2 cups all-purpose flour

1 teaspoon sugar

1 teaspoon salt

1 teaspoon ground cinnamon

2/3 cup cold butter, cubed

4 to 6 tablespoons cold water

FILLING:

5 cups thinly sliced peeled tart apples (about 6 medium)

1 cup fresh blackberries

1/2 cup packed brown sugar

4-1/2 teaspoons cornstarch

1 teaspoon ground cinnamon

1 teaspoon ground nutmeg

» In a large bowl, combine the flour, sugar, salt and cinnamon; cut in butter until crumbly. Gradually add water, tossing with a fork until dough forms a ball. Divide dough in half. Roll out one portion to fit a 9-in. pie plate; place pastry in plate and trim even with edge.

» In a large bowl, combine apples and blackberries. Combine the brown sugar, cornstarch, cinnamon and nutmeg; add to fruit mixture and toss to coat. Pour into crust.

» Roll out remaining pastry to fit top of pie; place over filling. Trim, seal and flute edges. Cut slits in pastry. Add decorative cutouts if desired. Cover edges loosely with foil.

» Bake at 450° for 10 minutes. Reduce heat to 350°; remove foil. Bake 40-50 minutes longer or until lightly browned and filling is bubbly. Cool on a wire rack. Store in the refrigerator.

Yield: 6-8 servings.

rolling out pie crust

Pie crust can be rolled out between two sheets of waxed paper. When the crust is rolled out, peel off the top sheet, then flip it over into the pie plate and peel off the remaining waxed paper.

berry cream pie

I found this recipe in an old cookbook and made it for a family gathering. The pie was gone in no time.

Sue Yaeger • Boone, Iowa

FILLING:

1/2 cup sugar

3 tablespoons cornstarch

3 tablespoons all-purpose flour

1/2 teaspoon salt

2 cups 2% milk

1 egg, lightly beaten

1/2 teaspoon vanilla extract

1/2 teaspoon almond extract, optional

1/2 cup heavy whipping cream

1 pastry shell (9 inches), baked

GLAZE:

1/2 cup crushed strawberries

1/2 cup water

1/4 cup sugar

2 teaspoons cornstarch

1-1/2 cups quartered strawberries

1-1/2 cups fresh raspberries

» In a large saucepan, combine the sugar, cornstarch, flour and salt; gradually stir in milk until smooth. Cook and stir over medium-high heat until thickened and bubbly. Reduce heat; cook and stir 2 minutes more.

» Remove from the heat and stir a small amount of hot filling into egg; return all to the saucepan, stirring constantly. Bring to a gentle boil; cook and stir for 2 minutes. Remove from the heat; gently stir in the vanilla and almond extract if desired. Cool to room temperature.

» In a small bowl, beat cream until stiff peaks form; fold into filling. Pour into pastry shell. Chill for at least 2 hours.

» About 2 hours before serving, prepare the glaze. In a large saucepan, combine crushed strawberries and water; cook for 2 minutes. Combine sugar and cornstarch; gradually add to the pan. Cook and stir until thickened and clear; strain. Cool for 20 minutes.

» Meanwhile, arrange quartered strawberries and raspberries over filling; pour glaze evenly over berries. Refrigerate for 1 hour.

Yield: 6-8 servings.

pear crunch pie

This pie recipe is one of my favorites. The pecan topping gives it a nice crunch.

Marian Platt • Sequim, Washington

1 cup all-purpose flour

1/2 cup packed brown sugar

1/2 teaspoon ground nutmeg, divided

1/4 teaspoon ground cinnamon

1/2 cup plus 1 tablespoon cold butter, divided

1/2 cup chopped pecans

2 cans (15-1/4 ounces each) pear halves in syrup

1/4 cup sugar

2 tablespoons cornstarch

1/4 teaspoon salt

1 tablespoon lemon juice

1 teaspoon grated lemon peel

1 unbaked pastry shell (9 inches)

» In a large bowl, combine the flour, brown sugar, 1/4 teaspoon of the nutmeg and cinnamon. Cut in 1/2 cup butter until mixture resembles coarse crumbs; stir in nuts. Set aside.

» Drain the pears, reserving 1 cup juice. In a large saucepan, combine the sugar, cornstarch, salt, remaining nutmeg and reserved juice until smooth. Bring to a boil; cook and stir for 2 minutes or until thickened. Remove from the heat; stir in the lemon juice, peel and remaining butter.

» Cut pears in half; arrange in pastry shell. Pour sauce over pears; sprinkle with reserved nut topping. Bake at 375° for 50-55 minutes or until golden brown.

Yield: 6-8 servings.

pineapple sour cream pie

Here's a luscious alternative to lemon meringue pie. The meringue is so creamy and the pineapple filling so refreshing that your family will request it again and again.

P. Lauren Fay-Neri • Syracuse, New York

1/2 cup sugar

2 tablespoons all-purpose flour

1 can (20 ounces) crushed pineapple, undrained

1 cup (8 ounces) sour cream

3 egg yolks, lightly beaten

1 pastry shell (9 inches), baked

MERINGUE:

3 egg whites

1/2 teaspoon vanilla extract

1/4 teaspoon cream of tartar

6 tablespoons sugar

» In a large saucepan, combine sugar and flour. Stir in pineapple and sour cream until combined. Cook and stir over medium-high heat until thickened and bubbly. Reduce heat; cook and stir 2 minutes longer. Remove from the heat.

» Stir a small amount of hot filling into egg yolks; return all to the pan, stirring constantly. Bring to a gentle boil; cook and stir 2 minutes longer. Remove from the heat. Pour into pastry shell.

» In a bowl, beat egg whites, vanilla and cream of tartar on medium speed until soft peaks form. Gradually beat in sugar, 1 tablespoon at a time, on high until stiff glossy peaks form and sugar is dissolved. Spread evenly over hot filling, sealing edges to crust.

» Bake at 350° for 15-18 minutes or until meringue is golden brown. Cool on a wire rack for 1 hour. Refrigerate for at least 3 hours before serving. Refrigerate leftovers.

Yield: 8 servings.

double-crust pear pie

Thanksgiving dinner guests will be pleasantly surprised to see this pretty dessert on the table instead of the usual apple pie. The amount of anise flavor is just right.

Faye Creech • Moore, Oklahoma

2/3 cup sugar

1/4 cup cornstarch

2 teaspoons grated lemon peel

1-1/2 teaspoons crushed aniseed

1-1/2 teaspoons lemon juice

5 cups thinly sliced peeled ripe pears (about 5 medium)

Pastry for double-crust pie (9 inches)

GLAZE:

1/2 cup confectioners' sugar

2 to 3 teaspoons lemon juice

» In a large bowl, combine the sugar, cornstarch, lemon peel, aniseed and lemon juice. Add pears and toss gently.

» Line a 9-in. pie plate with bottom pastry; trim even with edge of plate. Add filling. Roll out remaining pastry to fit top of pie; place over filling. Trim, seal and flute edges. Cut slits in top.

» Bake at 400° for 40-45 minutes or until filling is bubbly and pears are tender. Cover edges with foil during the last 20 minutes to prevent overbrowning. Combine the glaze ingredients; gently spread over hot pie. Cool completely on a wire rack. Store in the refrigerator.

Yield: 6-8 servings.

lemonade meringue pie

Lemonade concentrate and lemon juice give this special pie an excellent citrus flavor. I also like to add some lemon zest on top of the meringue.

Kay Seiler • Greenville, Ohio

3 eggs, separated

1 package (4.6 ounces) cook-and-serve vanilla pudding mix

1-1/4 cups 2% milk

1 cup (8 ounces) sour cream

1/3 cup thawed lemonade concentrate

1 teaspoon lemon juice

1/4 teaspoon cream of tartar

6 tablespoons sugar

1 pastry shell (9 inches), baked

» Place egg whites in a small bowl; let stand at room temperature for 30 minutes. Meanwhile, in a large saucepan, combine the pudding mix, milk and sour cream until smooth. Cook and stir over medium heat until thickened and bubbly, about 5 minutes. Reduce heat; cook and stir 2 minutes longer.

» Remove from the heat. Gradually whisk 1 cup hot filling into egg yolks; return all to the pan. Bring to a gentle boil; cook and stir for 2 minutes. Remove from the heat. Gently stir in lemonade concentrate; keep warm.

» Add lemon juice and cream of tartar to egg whites; beat on medium speed until soft peaks form. Gradually beat in sugar, 1 tablespoon at a time, on high until stiff glossy peaks form and sugar is dissolved.

» Pour warm filling into pastry shell. Spread the meringue over filling, sealing edges to pastry.

» Bake at 350° for 15-20 minutes or until meringue is golden brown. Cool on a wire rack for 1 hour. Refrigerate for at least 3 hours before serving.

Yield: 6-8 servings.

cinnamon apple crumb pie

Here's a dessert any busy hostess will love! It goes together in minutes, and looks and tastes like you really fussed.

Carolyn Ruch • New London, Wisconsin

1 can (21 ounces) apple pie filling

1 unbaked pastry shell (9 inches)

1/2 teaspoon ground cinnamon

4 tablespoons butter, divided

1-1/2 to 2 cups crushed pecan shortbread cookies

» Pour pie filling into pastry shell. Sprinkle with cinnamon and dot with 1 tablespoon butter. Melt remaining butter. Place cookie crumbs in a small bowl; stir in butter until coarse crumbs form. Sprinkle over filling. Cover edges of pastry loosely with foil.

» Bake at 450° for 10 minutes. Reduce heat to 350°; remove foil and bake for 40-45 minutes or until crust is golden brown and filling is bubbly. Cool on a wire rack for at least 2 hours.

Yield: 6-8 servings.

fresh raspberry pie

This pretty pie was practically a staple at our house during the late summer. Our family had raspberry bushes, so the pie was always made with fresh-picked berries.

Emily Dennis • Hancock, Michigan

2 cups all-purpose flour

1 tablespoon sugar

1/2 teaspoon salt

3/4 cup shortening

1 egg, lightly beaten

3 tablespoons cold water

1 tablespoon white vinegar

FILLING:
1-1/3 cups sugar

2 tablespoons quick-cooking tapioca

2 tablespoons cornstarch

5 cups fresh or frozen unsweetened raspberries, thawed

1 tablespoon butter

TOPPING:
1 tablespoon 2% milk

1 tablespoon sugar

» In a large bowl, combine the flour, sugar and salt; cut in shortening until mixture resembles coarse crumbs. Combine the egg, water and vinegar; stir into flour mixture just until moistened. Divide dough in half so that one ball is slightly larger than the other; wrap each in plastic wrap. Refrigerate for 30 minutes or until easy to handle.

» Meanwhile, in another large bowl, combine the sugar, tapioca, cornstarch and raspberries; let stand for 15 minutes.

» On a lightly floured surface, roll out larger ball of dough to fit a 9-in. pie plate. Transfer dough to pie plate; trim even with edge. Add raspberry filling; dot with butter.

» Roll out remaining dough to fit top of pie; place over filling. Trim, seal and flute edges. Cut slits in top. Brush with milk; sprinkle with sugar.

» Bake at 350° for 50-55 minutes or until crust is golden brown and filling is bubbly. Cool on a wire rack.

Yield: 6-8 servings.

pumpkin pies for a gang

When I think of cooking for a crowd this time of year, pumpkin pie always comes to mind. Guests love this traditional treat, and the recipe is perfect for a large gathering...it fills eight pie shells!

Edna Hoffman • Hebron, Indiana

4 packages (15 ounces each) refrigerated pie pastry

16 eggs, lightly beaten

4 cans (29 ounces each) solid-pack pumpkin

1/2 cup dark corn syrup

9 cups sugar

1-1/4 cups all-purpose flour

1 cup nonfat dry milk powder

4 teaspoons salt

4 teaspoons each ground ginger, cinnamon and nutmeg

1 teaspoon ground cloves

8 cups 2% milk

» Unroll pastry; line eight 9-in. pie plates with one sheet of pastry. Flute edges; set aside. In a large bowl, combine the eggs, pumpkin and corn syrup. In another bowl, combine the

dry ingredients; place half in each of two large bowls. Stir half of the pumpkin mixture into each bowl. Gradually stir in milk until smooth.

» Pour into pie shells. Bake at 350° for 60-70 minutes or until a knife inserted near the center comes out clean. Cool on wire racks. Store in the refrigerator.

Yield: 8 pies (6-8 servings each).

I found this tropical custard pie in an old church cookbook. When I sent one to the office with my husband, one of his coworkers said, "It doesn't get any better than this!"

Judi Oudekerk • Buffalo, Minnesota

coconut pineapple pie

1 cup sugar

3 tablespoons all-purpose flour

1 cup light corn syrup

1 cup flaked coconut

1 can (8 ounces) crushed pineapple, undrained

3 eggs, lightly beaten

1 teaspoon vanilla extract

1 unbaked pastry shell (9 inches)

1/4 cup butter, melted

» In a large bowl, combine sugar and flour. Add the corn syrup, coconut, pineapple, eggs and vanilla; mix well. Pour into pastry shell. Drizzle with butter.

» Bake at 350° for 50-55 minutes or until a knife inserted near the center comes out clean. (Cover loosely with foil if the top browns too quickly.) Cool on a wire rack. Chill before cutting. Store in the refrigerator.

Yield: 6-8 servings.

Ice Cream Pretzel Cake • Swirled Sherbet Dessert • Frozen Peach Pies • Country Style Vanilla Ice Cream • Mocha Almond Dessert • Frosty Pistachio Dessert • Ice Cream Cookie Dessert • Cranberry Velvet Freeze • Cherry-Chip Ice Cream

frozen treats

Sandwiches • Coconut Ice Cream Torte • Banana Split Ice Cream Cake • Mint Sundae Brownie Square • Frozen Raspberry Cheesecake • Macaroon Ice Cream Torte • Miniature Napoleans • Peppermint Angel Rolls • Frozen Cheesecake Bites • Nutty Cookies & Cream Dessert • Orange Cream

ice cream pretzel cake

Our family loved a dessert we had at a local restaurant, so I invented my own version for a birthday party. It was a big hit. It's simple to make ahead and just pull out of the freezer when you need it.

Monica Rush • Reading, Pennsylvania

1-1/4 cups crushed pretzels

6 tablespoons cold butter, cubed

3/4 cup hot fudge ice cream topping, warmed

2 packages (7-1/2 ounces each) chocolate-covered miniature pretzels

1/2 gallon vanilla ice cream, softened

1/4 cup caramel ice cream topping

» Place crushed pretzels in a small bowl; cut in butter until crumbly. Press onto the bottom of a greased 9-in. springform pan. Cover and freeze for at least 30 minutes. Spread fudge topping over crust; cover and freeze.

» Set aside 16 chocolate-covered pretzels for garnish. Place remaining pretzels in a food processor; cover and process until crumbly. Transfer to a large bowl; stir in ice cream. Spread over the fudge topping. Drizzle with the caramel topping. Garnish with the reserved pretzels. Cover and freeze for at least 8 hours or overnight.

Yield: 16 servings.

orange cream freezer dessert

With its bold orange taste and cool, smooth texture, this appealing treat is a real crowd-pleaser. People who ask me for the recipe can't believe how easy it is to make. Plus, it serves an extra-large crowd.

Sharon Carroll • Whittier, California

4 cups graham cracker crumbs

3/4 cup sugar

1 cup butter, melted

3-1/2 quarts vanilla ice cream, softened

2 cans (12 ounces each) frozen orange juice concentrate, thawed

» In a bowl, combine cracker crumbs and sugar; stir in butter. Set aside 2 cups for topping. Press remaining crumb mixture into two greased 15-in. x 10-in. x 1-in. pans. Cover and freeze for at least 10 minutes.

» In a large bowl, combine the ice cream and orange juice concentrate until smooth. Spoon over crusts (pans will be full). Freeze for 10 minutes or until partially firm.

» Sprinkle with reserved crumb mixture; gently press down. Cover and freeze for up to 2 months. Remove from the freezer 15 minutes before serving.

Yield: 2 desserts (24 servings each).

Lemon and orange sherbet are swirled over a coconut-pecan crust in this lovely, refreshing dessert. It has a tropical kind of appeal.

Agnes Ward • Stratford, Ontario

swirled sherbet dessert

1 cup crushed vanilla wafers (about 30 wafers)

1/3 cup flaked coconut

1/3 cup chopped pecans

1/4 cup butter, melted

1 pint lemon sherbet, softened

1 pint orange sherbet, softened

» In a small bowl, combine wafer crumbs, coconut, pecans and butter; press onto the bottom of an ungreased 9-in. springform pan. Bake at 350° for 10-12 minutes or until lightly browned. Cool for 10 minutes on a wire rack.

» Arrange scoops of sherbet over crust, alternating flavors. Cut through sherbet with a knife to swirl. Cover and freeze overnight. Remove from the freezer 15 minutes before serving.

Yield: 12 servings.

country-style vanilla ice cream

The creamy texture of this old-fashioned ice cream, with its wonderful vanilla flavor, makes it a winner.

Cyndi Fynaardt • Oskaloosa, Iowa

6 cups milk, divided

2 cups sugar

4 eggs, lightly beaten

1 teaspoon vanilla extract

2 packages (3.4 ounces each) instant vanilla pudding mix

1 carton (8 ounces) frozen whipped topping, thawed

» In a large saucepan, heat 2-1/2 cups milk to 175°; stir in the sugar until dissolved. Whisk a small amount of hot mixture into the eggs. Return all to the pan, whisking constantly. Cook and stir over low heat until mixture reaches at least 160° and coats the back of a metal spoon. Remove from the heat. Cool quickly by placing pan in a bowl of ice water; stir for 2 minutes. Stir in vanilla.

» Place remaining milk in a bowl; whisk in pudding mixes for 2 minutes. Let stand for 2 minutes or until soft-set. Stir into egg mixture. Stir in whipped topping. Press waxed paper onto surface of custard. Refrigerate for several hours or overnight.

» Fill the cylinder of an ice cream freezer two-thirds full; freeze according to manufacturer's directions. Refrigerate remaining mixture until ready to freeze. Transfer to a freezer container; freeze for 2-4 hours before serving.

Yield: 2-1/2 quarts.

frosty pistachio delight

I love the simple make-ahead convenience of this tasty dessert drizzled with fudge topping. Being able to make this pie the night before and then freeze it gives me time to work on all those last-minute holiday dinner details!

Sandie Davenport • Farmer City, Illinois

2-1/2 cups chocolate graham cracker crumbs

2/3 cup butter, melted

1 carton (1-3/4 quarts) vanilla ice cream, softened

2 packages (3.4 ounces each) instant pistachio pudding mix

1 cup plus 2 tablespoons pistachios, chopped, divided

3 drops green food coloring, optional

1 carton (8 ounces) frozen whipped topping, thawed

1 jar (11-3/4 ounces) hot fudge ice cream topping, warmed

» In a small bowl, combine cracker crumbs and butter. Press into a greased 13-in. x 9-in. baking dish. Bake at 350° for 7-9 minutes or until set. Cool on a wire rack.

» In a large bowl, combine the ice cream, pudding mixes, 1 cup pistachios and food coloring if desired. Fold in whipped topping. Spread over the crust. Cover and freeze for at least 4 hours.

» Remove from the freezer 10 minutes before serving. Drizzle with fudge topping; sprinkle with remaining pistachios.

Yield: 15 servings.

frozen peach pies

A frosty peachy filling and a buttery graham cracker crust are the perfect pair. I've found that this pie can be frozen up to three days.

Athena Russell • Florence, South Carolina

2-1/2 cups graham cracker crumbs

1/2 cup plus 2 tablespoons butter, melted

1/4 cup sugar

1 can (14 ounces) sweetened condensed milk

1/4 cup lemon juice

1/4 cup orange juice

1 package (16 ounces) frozen unsweetened sliced peaches

1 tablespoon grated lemon peel

1-1/2 cups heavy whipping cream

» In a small bowl, combine the graham cracker crumbs, butter and sugar; press onto the bottom and up the sides of two greased 9-in. pie plates. Bake at 350° for 10-12 minutes or until lightly browned. Cool on wire racks.

» In a blender, combine the milk, lemon juice, orange juice, peaches and lemon peel; cover and process until smooth. Transfer to a large bowl. In another large bowl, beat cream until stiff peaks form; fold into peach mixture.

» Spoon into crusts. Cover and freeze for at least 4 hours or until firm. Remove from the freezer 15 minutes before serving.

Yield: 2 pies (8 servings each).

mocha almond dessert

Try this recipe for an easy treat that's both luscious and elegant. The perfect blend of mocha and chocolate is in each cool, refreshing slice.

Taste of Home Test Kitchen

1 cup cream-filled chocolate sandwich cookie crumbs

1/4 cup sugar

1/4 cup butter, melted

1 package (8 ounces) cream cheese, softened

1 can (14 ounces) sweetened condensed milk

2/3 cup chocolate syrup

1/2 teaspoon vanilla extract

2 tablespoons instant coffee granules

1 tablespoon hot water

1 cup whipped topping

1/3 cup chopped almonds, toasted

Chocolate-covered coffee beans, optional

» In a small bowl, combine the cookie crumbs, sugar and butter. Press onto the bottom and 1 in. up the sides of a greased 9-in. springform pan; set aside.

» In a large bowl, beat the cream cheese, milk, chocolate syrup and vanilla until smooth. Dissolve coffee granules in hot water; beat into cream cheese mixture. Fold in whipped topping and almonds. Pour over crust. Cover and freeze for 8 hours or overnight.

» Remove from the freezer 10-15 minutes before serving. Carefully run a knife around edge of pan to loosen. Garnish with coffee beans if desired.

Yield: 10-12 servings.

cherry-chip ice cream sandwiches

You can make these marvelous ice cream sandwiches days ahead. My kids created them one afternoon after I made the ice cream.

Sally Hook • Montgomery, Texas

1-1/2 cups 2% milk

1/2 cup sugar

Dash salt

1 cup heavy whipping cream

1 teaspoon vanilla extract

2/3 cup chopped dried cherries

1/2 cup miniature semisweet chocolate chips

10 whole chocolate graham crackers

» In a large saucepan over medium heat, cook and stir the milk, sugar and salt until sugar is dissolved. Remove from the heat; stir in the cream and vanilla. Transfer to a bowl; refrigerate until chilled.

» Line a 13-in. x 9-in. pan with waxed paper; set aside. Fill cylinder of ice cream freezer with milk mixture; freeze according to manufacturer's directions. Stir in cherries and chocolate chips. Spread into prepared pan; cover and freeze overnight.

» Cut or break graham crackers in half. Using waxed paper, lift ice cream out of pan; discard waxed paper. Cut ice cream into squares the same size as the graham cracker halves; place ice cream between cracker halves. Wrap sandwiches in plastic wrap. Freeze until serving.

Yield: 10 servings.

ice cream cookie dessert

Our family loves dessert, and this chocolaty, layered treat is one of Mom's most-requested recipes...and so easy to prepare.

Kimberly Laabs • Hartford, Wisconsin

1 package (18 ounces) cream-filled chocolate sandwich cookies, crushed, divided

1/4 cup butter, melted

1/2 gallon vanilla ice cream, softened

1 jar (16 ounces) hot fudge ice cream topping, warmed

1 carton (8 ounces) frozen whipped topping, thawed

» In a large bowl, combine 3-3/4 cups cookie crumbs and butter. Press into a greased 13-in. x 9-in. dish. Spread with ice cream; cover and freeze until set.

» Drizzle fudge topping over ice cream; cover and freeze until set. Spread with whipped topping; sprinkle with remaining cookie crumbs. Cover and freeze for 2 hours or until firm. Remove from the freezer 10 minutes before serving.

Yield: 12 servings.

» Fill the cylinder of an ice cream freezer two-thirds full; freeze according to the manufacturer's directions. Refrigerate remaining mixture until ready to freeze. When ice cream is frozen, transfer to a freezer container; freeze for 2-4 hours before serving.

Yield: about 4-1/2 quarts.

cranberry velvet freeze

Everyone in my crowd enjoys this frosty treat. I normally serve it at special events.

Pat Seville • Hagerstown, Maryland

2 cans (16 ounces each) whole-berry cranberry sauce

2 cans (one 20 ounces, one 8 ounces) crushed pineapple, drained

1 package (10-1/2 ounces) miniature marshmallows

1 cup green maraschino cherries, quartered

1 cup red maraschino cherries, quartered

1 teaspoon lemon juice

3 cups heavy whipping cream, whipped

» In a bowl, combine cranberry sauce, pineapple, marshmallows, cherries and lemon juice. Fold in whipped cream.

» Spoon into an ungreased 13-in. x 9-in. dish. Cover and freeze overnight. Remove from the freezer 10 minutes before serving.

Yield: 12-16 servings.

rocky road ice cream

My daughters always wants to put this ice cream in cones just like the ice cream shops do. We especially like the marshmallows, chocolate chips and chopped pecans. Sometimes we even add extra chips on top...and whipped cream, too.

Dale Langford • Atwater, California

3 cups whole milk

3 cups half-and-half cream

9 ounces semisweet chocolate, chopped

2-3/4 cups sugar

3/4 teaspoon salt

6 cups heavy whipping cream

3 cups miniature marshmallows

2-1/4 cups miniature semisweet chocolate chips

1-1/2 cups chopped pecans

6 teaspoons vanilla extract

» In a large saucepan, combine the milk and half-and-half; heat to 175°. Add chocolate, sugar and salt; stir until chocolate is melted and sugar is dissolved.

» Remove from the heat. Cool quickly by placing pan in a bowl of ice water; stir for 2 minutes. Cool completely. Transfer to a large bowl; stir in the remaining ingredients. Cover and refrigerate for 30 minutes.

strawberry ice cream dessert

This ice cream dessert is sure to cool you down on a hot, steamy day! If you like, use vanilla or chocolate ice cream for the strawberry.

Teresa Ryherd • Fairbank, Iowa

2 cups graham cracker crumbs

6 tablespoons butter, melted

1 quart strawberry ice cream, softened

1-1/2 cups milk

2 packages (3.3 ounces each) instant white chocolate pudding mix

1 teaspoon vanilla extract

1 carton (16 ounces) frozen whipped topping, thawed, divided

» In a bowl, combine cracker crumbs and butter; set aside 2 tablespoons for garnish. Press remaining crumb mixture onto the bottom of an ungreased 10-in. springform pan. Place on a baking sheet. Bake at 375° for 8 minutes or until edges begin to brown. Cool on a wire rack.

» In a large bowl, combine the ice cream, milk, pudding mixes and vanilla; beat until smooth. Fold in half of the whipped topping. Pour over the crust. Cover and freeze for 1 hour or until firm.

» Spread with remaining whipped topping and sprinkle with reserved crumb mixture. Freeze for at least 3 hours or until firm. Remove from the freezer 15 minutes before serving.

Yield: 12 servings.

banana split ice cream cake

Every time they visit, my children and grandkids request this fantastic frozen cake. It takes time to assemble, but it's worth all the effort when I see all those smiling faces.

Gladys McCollum Abee • McKee, Kentucky

12 ice cream sugar cones, finely crushed

1/2 cup finely chopped walnuts

6 tablespoons butter, melted

CAKE:

1-3/4 quarts low-fat vanilla frozen yogurt, softened, divided

2 medium ripe bananas, mashed

1 teaspoon banana extract, optional

1 jar (16 ounces) hot fudge ice cream topping

1 cup chopped walnuts

1 cup strawberry ice cream topping

1 carton (8 ounces) frozen whipped topping, thawed

» In a small bowl, combine crushed cones, walnuts and butter; press onto the bottom of a greased 9-in. springform pan.

» In another small bowl, combine 3 cups yogurt, bananas and extract if desired. Spread over crust. In a small bowl, combine fudge topping and walnuts; spread over yogurt. Cover and freeze for 2 hours or until firm.

» Top with remaining yogurt; spread with strawberry topping. Cover and freeze for 8 hours or overnight until firm. Garnish with whipped topping.

Yield: 12 servings.

coconut ice cream torte

Guests will ooh and aah when you bring in this fabulous ice cream torte ringed with chocolaty coconut candy bars. This is one summer showstopper busy hostess like: It's super easy, feeds a crowd and can be made days ahead for convenience.

Taste of Home Test Kitchen

18 macaroons, crushed

1/4 cup butter, melted

3/4 cup hot fudge ice cream topping

26 snack-size Mounds or Almond Joy candy bars

1 quart vanilla ice cream, softened

1 quart strawberry ice cream, softened

1/4 cup sliced almonds, toasted

» In a small bowl, combine cookie crumbs and butter. Press onto the bottom of a greased 10-in. springform pan. Freeze for 15 minutes.

» In a microwave, heat hot fudge topping on high for 15-20 seconds or until pourable; spread over crust. Trim one end from each candy bar (save trimmings for another use); arrange candy bars around the edge of pan. Freeze for 15 minutes. Spread the vanilla ice cream over fudge topping; freeze for 30 minutes.

» Spread strawberry ice cream over vanilla layer; sprinkle with almonds. Cover and freeze until firm. May be frozen for up to 2 months. Remove from the freezer 10 minutes before serving. Remove sides of pan.

Yield: 13 servings.

mint sundae brownie squares

I love brownies and this recipe makes a luscious after-dinner treat that's so simple to prepare. Get ready to bring home lots of compliments...and an empty pan!

Edie DeSpain • Logan, Utah

1 package fudge brownie mix (13-inch x 9-inch pan size)

3/4 cup chopped walnuts

1 can (14 ounces) sweetened condensed milk

2 teaspoons peppermint extract

4 drops green food coloring, optional

2 cups heavy whipping cream, whipped

1/2 cup miniature semisweet chocolate chips

1 jar (16 ounces) hot fudge ice cream topping, warmed

1/3 cup chopped salted peanuts

» Prepare brownie mix according to package directions. Stir in the walnuts. Pour into a greased 13-in. x 9-in. baking pan. Bake at 325° for 23-27 minutes or until a toothpick inserted in the center comes out clean (do not overbake). Cool on a wire rack.

» Meanwhile, in a large bowl, combine the milk, extract and food coloring if desired. Fold in whipped cream and chocolate chips. Spread over brownie layer. Cover and freeze for several hours or overnight.

» Let stand at room temperature for 10 minutes before cutting. Drizzle with ice cream topping; sprinkle with peanuts.

Yield: 15 servings.

peppermint angel roll

This is a very festive dessert for holiday events. The angel food cake makes it less heavy than many traditional holiday recipes. My husband loves it, and I adore it because it's so simple and convenient during a hectic season!

Holly Dicke • Plain City, Ohio

1 package (16 ounces) angel food cake mix

1 tablespoon confectioners' sugar

1/2 gallon peppermint ice cream, softened

1 jar (11-3/4 ounces) hot fudge ice cream topping, warmed

Crushed peppermint candies and additional confectioners' sugar, optional

» Prepare cake batter according to package directions. Line a greased 15-in. x 10-in. x 1-in. baking pan with waxed paper and grease the paper. Spread the batter evenly into pan. Bake at 350° for 15-20 minutes or until cake springs back when lightly touched.

» Cool for 5 minutes. Turn cake onto a kitchen towel dusted with confectioners' sugar. Gently peel off waxed paper. Roll up cake in the towel jelly-roll style, starting with a short side. Cool completely on a wire rack.

» Unroll cake and spread ice cream over cake to within 1/2 in. of edges. Roll up again. Cover and freeze until firm.

» Cut into slices; drizzle with hot fudge topping. If desired, garnish with crushed candies and dust with confectioners' sugar.

Yield: 10 servings.

frozen raspberry cheesecake

I got this recipe from my sister years ago and like to fix it when times are rushed. It's fancy enough for the most special occasions but so easy to prepare with ingredients I always have on hand. Try varying the juices and fruits.

Donna Rear • Red Deer, Alberta

1-1/2 cups cream-filled chocolate sandwich cookie crumbs (about 15 cookies)

1/4 cup butter, melted

1 package (8 ounces) cream cheese, softened

3/4 cup confectioners' sugar

1 package (10 ounces) frozen sweetened raspberries, thawed

3/4 cup cranberry-raspberry juice, divided

1 teaspoon lemon juice

2 cups heavy whipping cream, whipped

» Combine cookie crumbs and butter; press onto the bottom of an ungreased 9-in. springform pan. In a large bowl, beat cream cheese and confectioners' sugar until smooth. Beat in the raspberries, 1/2 cup cranberry-raspberry juice and lemon juice until blended. Fold in whipped cream. Pour onto crust.

» Spoon remaining juice over cheesecake; cut through batter with a knife to swirl. Cover and freeze overnight. Remove from the freezer 15 minutes before serving.

Yield: 12 servings.

nutty cookies & cream dessert

1 package (18 ounces) cream-filled chocolate sandwich cookies, crushed

1/2 cup butter, melted

1/2 gallon cookies and cream ice cream, softened

1-1/2 cups salted peanuts, coarsely chopped

2/3 cup hot fudge ice cream topping

2/3 cup caramel ice cream topping

1 carton (8 ounces) frozen whipped topping, thawed

» In a large bowl, combine cookie crumbs and butter; set aside 1 cup. Press remaining crumbs into an ungreased 13-in. x 9-in. dish. Spread with ice cream. Layer with peanuts, ice cream toppings and whipped topping; sprinkle with reserved crumbs. Cover and freeze until firm.

» Remove from the freezer 15 minutes before serving.

Yield: 15 servings.

The flavors of hot fudge, caramel, chocolate cookies and ice cream all combine in every mouthful of this fabulous frozen delight. No matter how big the meal, folks will find room for this treat!

Cheryl Melerski • Harborcreek, Pennsylvania

miniature napoleons

It can be a challenge to come up with an elegant sweet that works well for a large party with friends. These impressive bite-sized desserts are easy to enjoy while mingling.

Taste of Home Test Kitchen

6 tablespoons sugar

2 tablespoons cornstarch

1/4 teaspoon salt

1 cup 2% milk

1 egg yolk, beaten

2 tablespoons butter, divided

1/2 teaspoon vanilla extract

1 sheet frozen puff pastry, thawed

1/2 cup heavy whipping cream

2 ounces semisweet chocolate, chopped

» In a small saucepan, combine the sugar, cornstarch and salt. Stir in milk until smooth. Cook and stir over medium heat until thickened and bubbly. Reduce heat; cook and stir 1 minute longer.

» Remove from heat. Stir a small amount of hot mixture into egg yolk; return all to pan, stirring constantly. Bring to a gentle boil; cook and stir for 1 minute. Remove from the heat. Stir in vanilla. Cool to room temperature without stirring. Refrigerate until chilled.

» Unfold puff pastry; place on an ungreased baking sheet. Prick dough thoroughly with a fork. Bake according to the package directions. Remove to a wire rack to cool.

» In a small bowl, beat cream until stiff peaks form. Fold into custard. Use a fork to split pastry in half horizontally. Spread

filling over the bottom half; replace top. Cover and freeze for 4 hours or until firm.

» Cut into 1-1/2-in. x 1-in. rectangles. In a microwave, melt chocolate and remaining butter; stir until smooth. Drizzle over pastries. Freeze until serving.

Yield: 4-1/2 dozen.

cookie dough ice cream

My grandmother makes a chocolate chip cookie dough cheesecake every time my brother comes home. It inspired me to create this ice cream.

Stacie Wash • Chesterfield, Virginia

3/4 to 1 cup refrigerated chocolate chip cookie dough

CRUST:

2 cups chocolate graham cracker crumbs (about 26 squares)

2 tablespoons sugar

1/2 cup butter, melted

ICE CREAM:

2 cups half-and-half cream

1 cup sugar

2 cups heavy whipping cream

6 teaspoons vanilla extract

12 ounces cream cheese, softened and cubed

» Pinch off small pieces of cookie dough; place on a greased baking sheet. Cover and freeze.

» Meanwhile, for crust, in a bowl, combine cracker crumbs and sugar; stir in butter. Press into a greased 15-in. x 10-in. x 1-in. baking pan. Bake at 350° for 11-15 minutes or until set. Cool on a wire rack. Break into small pieces and set aside.

» For ice cream, in a saucepan, heat half-and-half to 175°; stir in sugar until dissolved. Remove from heat. Cool quickly by placing pan in a bowl of ice water; stir for 2 minutes. Pour into a bowl.

» In a blender, combine the cream, vanilla and cream cheese; cover and process until smooth. Stir into half-and-half mixture. Cover and refrigerate for several hours or overnight.

» Fill the cylinder of an ice cream freezer two-thirds full; freeze according to manufacturer's directions (mixture will be very soft). Refrigerate remaining mixture until ready to freeze.

» In a large bowl, layer a third of the ice cream, cookie dough pieces and crust mixture; repeat layers twice. Swirl ice cream. Freeze for 2-4 hours before serving.

Yield: 2 quarts.

EDITOR'S NOTE: For food safety reasons, use only commercially prepared cookie dough.

frozen cheesecake bites

It only takes one of these fabulous nibbles to cure your cheesecake cravings. But potluck guests are sure to ask for more.

Frank Millard • Janesville, Wisconsin

3 packages (8 ounces each) cream cheese, softened

1-1/4 cups sugar, divided

1-1/2 teaspoons vanilla extract

1/2 teaspoon salt

4 eggs, lightly beaten

9 ounces semisweet chocolate, chopped

3/4 cup heavy whipping cream

1/2 cup graham cracker crumbs

1/2 cup English toffee bits or almond brickle chips, crushed

» Line the bottom of a 9-in. springform pan with parchment paper; coat paper and sides of pan with cooking spray. Set aside. In a large bowl, beat the cream cheese, 1 cup sugar, vanilla and salt until smooth. Add eggs; beat on low speed just until combined. Pour into prepared pan.

» Place on a baking sheet. Bake at 325° for 40-45 minutes or until center is almost set. Cool on a wire rack for 10 minutes. Carefully run a knife around edge of pan to loosen; cool 1 hour longer. Cover and freeze overnight.

» Remove from the freezer and let stand for 30 minutes or until easy to handle. Meanwhile, in a small saucepan over low heat, melt chocolate with cream; stir until blended. Remove from the heat. Transfer to a bowl; cover and refrigerate until mixture reaches spreading consistency, stirring occasionally.

» In a small bowl, combine cracker crumbs and remaining sugar. Using a melon baller, scoop out 1-in. balls of cheesecake; place on parchment paper-lined baking sheets. Top each with a heaping teaspoonful of chocolate mixture. Sprinkle crumb mixture over half of the balls and toffee bits over the remaining balls. Cover and freeze for 2 hours or until firm.

Yield: 5-1/2 dozen.

lemonade dessert

Here's a tasty way to finish off a summer buffet. Adults and kids don't mind standing in line for this easy-to-make treat.

Margaret Linder • Quincy, Washington

1-1/2 cups all-purpose flour

3/4 cup packed brown sugar

3/4 cup cold butter, cubed

3/4 cup chopped pecans

1/2 gallon vanilla ice cream, softened

1 can (12 ounces) frozen pink lemonade concentrate, thawed

» In a small bowl, combine flour and brown sugar; cut in butter until crumbly. Stir in pecans. Spread in a single layer into a greased 15-in. x 10-in. x 1-in. baking pan. Bake at 375° for 9-12 minutes or until golden brown, stirring once. Cool on a wire rack for 10 minutes.

» In a large bowl, beat ice cream and lemonade until blended. Sprinkle half of the crumbles into a greased 13-in. x 9-in. dish. Spread with ice cream mixture; sprinkle with remaining crumbles. Cover and freeze overnight. Remove from the freezer 15 minutes before serving.

Yield: 12-15 servings.

makeover lemon custard ice cream

You'll be delighted with this fantastic light ice cream that matches the wonderful, yet heavier original in taste and texture. I think it'll quickly become a staple for your family.

Linda Tipton • Roanoke Rapids, North Carolina

1-3/4 cups sugar

1/3 cup all-purpose flour

1/4 teaspoon salt

3 cups milk

2 eggs, lightly beaten

2 tablespoons apple jelly

3 cups fat-free half-and-half

1 cup (8 ounces) fat-free sour cream

1 cup lemon juice

» In a large saucepan, combine the sugar, flour and salt. Gradually add milk. Bring to a boil over medium heat; cook and stir for 2 minutes or until thickened. Remove from the heat; cool slightly.

» Whisk a small amount of hot milk mixture into the eggs. Return all to the pan, whisking constantly. Cook and stir until mixture reaches 160° and coats the back of a metal spoon.

» Remove from the heat; stir in jelly until melted. Stir in the half-and-half, sour cream and lemon juice. Cool quickly by placing pan in a bowl of ice water; stir for 2 minutes. Press waxed paper onto surface of custard. Refrigerate for several hours or overnight.

» Fill the cylinder of an ice cream freezer two-thirds full; freeze according to manufacturer's directions. Refrigerate remaining mixture until ready to freeze. When ice cream is frozen, transfer to a freezer container; freeze for 2-4 hours before serving.

Yield: 2 quarts.

frozen chocolate cheesecake tart

I first made this irresistible treat for some dinner guests. They were impressed with its rich flavor and pretty appearance. My husband commented that it was the best tart he ever had.

Heather Bennett • Dunbar, West Virginia

2-1/4 cups crushed chocolate cream-filled sandwich cookies (about 22 cookies)

1/3 cup butter, melted

FILLING:

2 packages (8 ounces each) cream cheese, softened

1/3 cup confectioners' sugar

3 cups white baking chips, melted and cooled

1/3 cup heavy whipping cream

1 teaspoon vanilla extract

1/2 cup miniature semisweet chocolate chips

Chocolate curls, optional

» In a small bowl, combine cookie crumbs and butter. Press onto the bottom and up the sides of a greased 9-in. fluted tart pan with a removable bottom. Cover and freeze for at least 1 hour.

» In a large bowl, beat cream cheese and sugar until smooth.

Beat in the white baking chips, cream and vanilla until well combined. Stir in chocolate chips; pour over crust. Cover and freeze for 8 hours or overnight.

» Uncover and refrigerate 3-4 hours before serving. Garnish with chocolate curls if desired. Refrigerate leftovers.

Yield: 12 servings.

My clan loves any type of frozen dessert. I often make this recipe for special occasions.

Barbara Carlucci • Orange Park, Florida

macaroon ice cream torte

24 macaroon cookies, crumbled

1 quart coffee ice cream, softened

1 quart chocolate ice cream, softened

1 cup milk chocolate toffee bits or 4 (1.4 ounces) Heath candy bars, coarsely chopped

Hot fudge topping, warmed

» Sprinkle a third of the cookies into an ungreased 9-in. springform pan. Top with 2 cups coffee ice cream, a third of the cookies, 2 cups chocolate ice cream and 1/2 cup toffee bits. Repeat layers. Cover and freeze until firm. May be frozen for up to 2 months.

» Remove from the freezer 10 minutes before serving. Cut into wedges; drizzle with hot fudge topping.

Yield: 12-16 servings.

Strawberry Banana Dessert • Raspberry Rhubarb Sauce • Fluffy Lemon Squares • Apple Dumplings • Butter Pecan Sauce • Creamy Orange Gelatin • Pretzel Dessert • White Chocolate Bread Pudding • Chocolate Chip Cookie Delight

more desserts

• Toffee Meringue Torte • Grandma's Baked Rice Custard • Strawberry Puff Pastry Dessert • Chocolate-Hazelnut Cream Puffs • Berry Pavlova • Khrustyky • Chocolate Velvet Dessert • Fruit-Filled Kolaches • Apricot Empanadas • Gran's Granola Parfaits Mini-Apple Turnovers • Sugar Cookie

fluffy lemon squares

These rich bars with a vanilla wafer crust get their sweet-tart flavor from lemon gelatin, sherbet and pudding mix. They're not only fun to make with my grandchildren, but they're delicious, too.

Joyce Speerbrecher • Grafton, Wisconsin

1-1/2 cups crushed vanilla wafers (about 45 wafers)

1/3 cup chopped pecans

6 tablespoons butter, melted

1/2 cup heavy whipping cream

2 packages (3 ounces each) lemon gelatin

1-1/4 cups boiling water

1 package (3.4 ounces) instant lemon pudding mix

1 pint lemon sherbet, softened

» In a small bowl, combine the wafer crumbs, pecans and butter; set aside 1/4 cup for topping. Press remaining crumb mixture into an ungreased 11-in. x 7-in. dish. Cover and refrigerate for 30 minutes.

» Meanwhile, in a small bowl, beat cream until stiff peaks form; set aside. In a large bowl, dissolve gelatin in boiling water. Add pudding mix; beat on low speed for 2 minutes. Add sherbet; beat on low for 1 minute or until soft-set. Gently fold in whipped cream.

» Spread over the crust; sprinkle with reserved crumb mixture. Refrigerate for 1 hour or until set.

Yield: 12 servings.

strawberry banana dessert

Like springtime on a plate, this eye-catching dessert has a bright cheery color and plenty of fruity flavor.

Margaret Kuntz • Bismarck, North Dakota

3 medium firm bananas, sliced

1 prepared angel food cake (8 to 10 ounces), cut into 1-inch cubes

1 pint fresh strawberries, halved

1 package (.6 ounce) sugar-free strawberry gelatin

2 cups boiling water

1-1/2 cups cold water

1 carton (8 ounces) reduced-fat whipped topping, thawed

» Layer banana slices and cake cubes in a 13-in. x 9-in. dish coated with cooking spray. Place strawberries over cake and press down gently.

» In a small bowl, dissolve gelatin in boiling water; stir in cold water. Pour over strawberries. Refrigerate for 3 hours or until set. Frost with whipped topping.

Yield: 16 servings.

raspberry rhubarb sauce

4-1/2 cups sliced fresh or frozen rhubarb

1 cup warm water

1 package (.3 ounce) sugar-free raspberry gelatin

6 cups fat-free vanilla frozen yogurt

» Place rhubarb in a large saucepan. In a small bowl, combine water and gelatin; pour over rhubarb. Bring to a boil; reduce heat and simmer, uncovered, for 5 minutes or until rhubarb is tender.

» Serve warm or chilled over frozen yogurt. Refrigerate leftovers.

Yield: 2-1/2 cups.

I serve this tart, ruby red sauce over ice cream or pound cake for a colorful, refreshing and easy treat. It also perks up a stack of pancakes or waffles for breakfast.

Inge Schermerhorn • Kingston, New Hampshire

new orleans bread pudding

For an extra-special treat, try this sweet and buttery bread pudding. The cowboys we serve it to say it reminds them of home.

Linda Wiese • Payette, Idaho

1/2 cup raisins

1/4 cup unsweetened apple juice

1/2 cup butter, melted, divided

1 tablespoon sugar

4 eggs, lightly beaten

2 cups half-and-half cream

1 cup packed brown sugar

2 teaspoons vanilla extract

1/2 teaspoon salt

1/2 teaspoon freshly ground nutmeg

10 slices day-old French bread (1 inch thick), cubed

SAUCE:
1/2 cup packed brown sugar

2 tablespoons cornstarch

Dash salt

1 cup cold water

1 tablespoon butter

2 teaspoons vanilla extract

» In a small saucepan, combine raisins and juice. Bring to a boil. Remove from the heat; cover and set aside. Brush a shallow 2-1/2-qt. baking dish with 1 tablespoon butter; sprinkle with sugar and set aside.

» In a large bowl, combine the eggs, cream, brown sugar, vanilla, salt and nutmeg. Stir in remaining butter and reserved raisin mixture. Gently stir in bread; let stand for 15 minutes or until bread is softened.

» Transfer to prepared dish. Bake, uncovered, at 350° for 35-40 minutes or until a knife inserted near center comes out clean.

» For sauce, in a small saucepan, combine the brown sugar, cornstarch and salt; gradually add water. Bring to a boil; cook and stir for 1-2 minutes or until thickened. Remove from the heat; stir in butter and vanilla. Serve with bread pudding.

Yield: 12 servings.

creamy orange gelatin

After serving this gelatin at two graduation celebrations in less than a year, it was clear that this was definitely everyone's favorite.

Sue Gronholz • Beaver Dam, Wisconsin

4 packages (3 ounces each) orange gelatin

4 cups boiling water

1 quart vanilla ice cream, softened

1-1/2 cups orange juice

2 cans (11 ounces each) mandarin oranges, drained

» In a large bowl, dissolve gelatin in boiling water. Stir in ice cream and orange juice until blended. Chill until partially set.

» Fold in oranges. Pour into two 6-cup ring molds coated with cooking spray. Refrigerate overnight or until firm. Just before serving, unmold.

Yield: 12 servings.

apple dumplings

Luscious dumplings are a popular fundraiser for the College Hill Presbyterian Church Women's Association. We increase our fresh apple order by a bushel each year to prepare for these fruity delights.

College Hill Presbyterian Church Women's Association
Beaver Falls, Pennsylvania

8 cups all-purpose flour

3 tablespoons baking powder

4-1/2 teaspoons salt

1-1/2 pounds butter-flavored shortening

2 cups 2% milk

24 medium tart apples, peeled and cored

1-1/2 cups sugar

1 teaspoon ground cinnamon

1/2 cup butter

SYRUP:

2-1/2 cups packed brown sugar

1-1/2 cups water

1 cup butter, cubed

1 teaspoon ground cinnamon

» In a large bowl, combine the flour, baking powder and salt; cut in shortening until crumbly. Gradually add milk, tossing with a fork until dough forms a ball. Divide into 24 portions. Cover and refrigerate for at least 1 hour or until easy to handle.

» On a well-floured surface, roll each portion of dough into a 7-in. square. Place an apple on each square. Combine sugar and cinnamon; place 1 tablespoonful into the core of each apple. Dot each with 1 teaspoon butter.

» Gently bring up corners of pastry to center; pinch edges to seal. Place in four greased 13-in. x 9-in. baking dishes. Bake at 350° for 15 minutes.

» Meanwhile, in a large saucepan, combine the syrup ingredients. Bring to a boil; cook and stir until smooth and blended. Pour over apples.

» Bake 35-40 minutes longer or until apples are tender and pastry is golden brown. Serve warm.

Yield: 24 servings.

butter pecan sauce

Try this thick, rich, buttery sauce over ice cream, fried ice cream or slices of angel food cake for a satisfying dessert. It's so delicious!

Delores Goossen • Morris, Manitoba

1/2 cup butter, cubed

3/4 cup sugar

1/4 cup light corn syrup

1 cup heavy whipping cream

1 cup chopped pecans, toasted

1/2 teaspoon vanilla extract

Vanilla ice cream

» In a large heavy saucepan, cook butter over medium heat for 4-6 minutes or until golden brown. Stir in sugar and corn syrup; cook and stir for 2 minutes or until sugar is dissolved. Remove from the heat; gradually stir in cream.

» Bring to a boil. Reduce heat to medium. Cook until the sauce begins to thicken. Remove from the heat. Stir in pecans and vanilla. Serve warm over ice cream.

Yield: 2 cups.

delicious angel food dessert

This is one of my all-time top picks for a dessert. I took it to a family reunion, and everyone raved about it.

Jessie Bradley • Bella Vista, Arkansas

2 cans (20 ounces each) unsweetened crushed pineapple, drained

4 medium firm bananas, sliced

1 loaf-shaped angel food cake (10-1/2 ounces), cut into 1-inch cubes

3 cups cold fat-free milk

2 packages (1 ounce each) sugar-free instant vanilla pudding mix

1 carton (8 ounces) frozen reduced-fat whipped topping, thawed

1/3 cup chopped pecans, toasted

» Place the pineapple in a large bowl; gently fold in bananas. Place cake cubes in a 13-in. x 9-in. dish. Spoon fruit over cake.

» In another large bowl, whisk milk and pudding mixes for 2 minutes. Let stand for 2 minutes or until soft-set. Spread over fruit. Carefully spread whipped topping over pudding. Sprinkle with pecans. Cover and refrigerate for at least 2 hours before serving.

Yield: 15 servings.

black cherry cream parfaits

These parfaits are light and cool but taste incredibly decadent.

Margaret Schmieder • Sparks, Nevada

2 packages (3 ounces each) black cherry gelatin

2 cups boiling water

2 cups black cherry soda, chilled

1 cup heavy whipping cream

1/2 cup confectioners' sugar

1 can (15 ounces) pitted dark sweet cherries, drained

1/2 cup chopped walnuts

» In a large bowl, dissolve gelatin in boiling water. Stir in soda; refrigerate for 2 hours or until partially set.

» In a large bowl, beat the cream until it begins to thicken. Add confectioners' sugar; beat until soft peaks form. Stir cherries and walnuts into gelatin; fold in whipped cream. Spoon into parfait glasses. Chill until firm.

Yield: 10 servings.

pretzel dessert

This is one of my mom's favorites. The salty crust tastes so good with the sweet cream cheese filling.

Erin Frakes • Moline, Illinois

2 cups crushed pretzels

3/4 cup butter, melted

2 tablespoons sugar

FILLING:

1 package (8 ounces) cream cheese, softened

1 cup sugar

1 carton (8 ounces) frozen whipped topping, thawed

TOPPING:

2 packages (3 ounces each) strawberry gelatin

2 cups boiling water

1/2 cup cold water

» In a large bowl, combine the pretzels, butter and sugar. Press into an ungreased 13-in. x 9-in. baking dish. Bake at 350° for 10 minutes. Cool completely.

» In a large bowl, beat cream cheese and sugar until smooth. Stir in whipped topping. Spread over pretzel crust. Cover and refrigerate until chilled.

» For topping, in a small bowl, dissolve gelatin in boiling water. Add cold water; chill until partially set. Carefully pour over filling. Cover and refrigerate for 4-6 hours or until gelatin is firm. Cut into squares.

Yield: 12-16 servings.

pear custard bars

When I take this crowd-pleasing treat to a potluck, I always come home with an empty pan. Cooking and baking come naturally for me—as a farm girl, I helped my mother feed my 10 siblings.

Jeannette Nord • San Juan Capistrano, California

1/2 cup butter, softened

1/3 cup sugar

1/4 teaspoon vanilla extract

3/4 cup all-purpose flour

2/3 cup chopped macadamia nuts

FILLING/TOPPING:

1 package (8 ounces) cream cheese, softened

1/2 cup sugar

1 egg

1/2 teaspoon vanilla extract

1 can (15-1/4 ounces) pear halves, drained

1/2 teaspoon sugar

1/2 teaspoon ground cinnamon

» In a large bowl, cream butter and sugar until light and fluffy. Beat in vanilla. Gradually add flour to creamed mixture. Stir in the nuts.

» Press into a greased 8-in. square baking pan. Bake at 350° for 20 minutes or until lightly browned. Cool on a wire rack.

» In a small bowl, beat cream cheese until smooth. Beat in the sugar, egg and vanilla. Pour over crust.

» Cut pears into 1/8-in. slices; arrange in a single layer over filling. Combine sugar and cinnamon; sprinkle over pears. Bake at 375° for 28-30 minutes (center will be soft-set and will become firmer upon cooling). Cool on a wire rack for 45 minutes.

» Cover and refrigerate for at least 2 hours before cutting. Store in the refrigerator.

Yield: 16 bars.

strawberry angel dessert

This is a wonderful dessert for spring and summer get-togethers, when fresh strawberries are readily available. Every time I make this pretty sensation for a large group of friends, I get plenty of requests for the recipe.

Theresa Mathis • Tucker, Georgia

1-1/2 cups sugar

5 tablespoons cornstarch

1 package (3 ounces) strawberry gelatin

2 cups water

2 pounds fresh strawberries, hulled, divided

1 package (8 ounces) cream cheese, softened

1 can (14 ounces) sweetened condensed milk

1 carton (12 ounces) frozen whipped topping, thawed

1 prepared angel food cake (8 to 10 ounces), cut into
  1-inch cubes

» For glaze, in a large saucepan, combine the sugar, cornstarch and gelatin. Add water and stir until smooth. Cook and stir over medium-high heat until mixture begins to boil. Cook and stir 1-2 minutes longer or until thickened. Remove from the heat; cool completely. Cut half of the strawberries into quarters; fold into glaze.

» In a small bowl, beat cream cheese until smooth. Beat in milk until blended. Fold in whipped topping.

» In a 4-qt. clear glass bowl, layer half of the cake cubes, glaze and cream mixture. Repeat layers. Cut remaining strawberries in half and arrange over the top. Cover and refrigerate for at least 2 hours or overnight.

Yield: 12-16 servings.

toffee meringue torte

This is one of those "Where did you get this recipe?" creations! It's simple to make ahead, so it's perfect for having on hand for a big gathering. This is a wonderful finale to a holiday meal or a decadent item for when guests drop by.

Karen Nemeth • Calgary, Alberta

6 egg whites

2 teaspoons vanilla extract

1/2 teaspoon cream of tartar

1-1/2 cups sugar

1 carton (8 ounces) frozen whipped topping, thawed

4 Butterfinger candy bars (2.1 ounces each), coarsely crushed,
  divided

» Place egg whites in a large bowl; let stand at room temperature for 30 minutes. Using a pencil, draw a 10-in. circle on each of two sheets of parchment paper. Place each sheet, pencil mark down, on a baking sheet or pizza pan; set aside.

» Add vanilla and cream of tartar to egg whites; beat on medium speed until soft peaks form. Gradually beat in the sugar, 1 tablespoon at a time, on high until stiff peaks form.

» Spread into 10-in. circles on prepared pans. Bake at 225° for 50-60 minutes or until set and lightly browned. Turn oven off; leave meringues in oven for 1 to 1-1/4 hours.

» Just before serving, place whipped topping in a large bowl; fold in three candy bars. Place one meringue layer on a serving plate; top with half of topping mixture. Repeat layers. Sprinkle with remaining candy bar.

Yield: 12 servings.

white chocolate bread pudding

A delectable white chocolate sauce is the crowning touch on servings of this comforting cinnamon bread pudding.

Kathy Rundle • Fond du Lac, Wisconsin

16 slices cinnamon bread, crusts removed, cubed

1 cup dried cranberries

3/4 cup white baking chips

3/4 cup chopped pecans

1/4 cup butter, melted

6 eggs

4 cups 2% milk

3/4 cup plus 1 tablespoon sugar, divided

1 teaspoon vanilla extract

1/4 teaspoon ground cinnamon

1/4 teaspoon ground allspice

SAUCE:
2/3 cup heavy whipping cream

2 tablespoons butter

8 ounces white baking chocolate, chopped

» In a greased 13-in. x 9-in. baking dish, layer half of the bread cubes, cranberries, white baking chips and pecans. Repeat layers. Drizzle with butter.

» In a large bowl, beat the eggs, milk, 3/4 cup sugar, vanilla, cinnamon and allspice until blended; pour over bread mixture. Let stand for 15-30 minutes.

» Sprinkle with remaining sugar. Bake, uncovered, at 375° for 55-65 minutes or until a knife inserted near the center comes out clean. Cover loosely with foil during the last 15 minutes if top browns too quickly.

» In a small saucepan, bring cream and butter to a boil. Add chocolate and remove from the heat (do not stir). Let stand for 5 minutes; whisk until smooth. Serve the sauce with warm bread pudding.

Yield: 12 servings (1-1/2 cups sauce).

grandma's baked rice custard

My mother lived a very basic life while growing up in Italy in the early 1900s. But when Easter Sunday arrived, my grandmother would make this dessert as a special treat.

Antonetta Matteo • Smithfield, Rhode Island

14 eggs, lightly beaten

1-1/2 cups sugar

4 cups whole milk

1 carton (15 ounces) ricotta cheese

1-1/2 cups cooked rice

1 can (8 ounces) crushed pineapple, undrained

1 cup evaporated milk

3 teaspoons vanilla extract

Ground cinnamon

» In a large bowl, combine eggs and sugar. Stir in the milk, ricotta cheese, rice, pineapple, evaporated milk and vanilla. Pour into a greased 13-in. x 9-in. baking dish and a greased 11-in. x 7-in. baking dish. Sprinkle with cinnamon.

» Bake, uncovered, at 350° for 40-45 minutes or until a knife inserted near the center comes out clean. Serve warm or cold. Refrigerate leftovers.

Yield: 20-22 servings.

double nut baklava

It may take some time to make this rich, buttery treat, but it's well worth the effort! The blend of coconut, pecans and macadamia nuts makes it irresistible.

Kari Caven • Post Falls, Idaho

1-1/4 cups flaked coconut, toasted

1/2 cup finely chopped macadamia nuts

1/2 cup finely chopped pecans

1/2 cup packed brown sugar

1 teaspoon ground allspice

1-1/4 cups butter, melted

1 package phyllo dough (16 ounces, 14-inch x 9-inch sheet size), thawed

1 cup sugar

1/2 cup water

1/4 cup honey

» In a large bowl, combine the first five ingredients; set aside. Brush a 13-in. x 9-in. baking pan with some of the butter. Unroll the sheets of phyllo dough; trim to fit into pan.

» Layer 10 sheets of phyllo in prepared pan, brushing each with butter. (Keep remaining dough covered with plastic wrap and a damp towel to prevent it from drying out.) Sprinkle with a third of the nut mixture. Repeat layers twice. Top with five phyllo sheets, brushing each with butter. Brush top sheet of phyllo with butter.

» Using a sharp knife, cut into 36 diamond shapes. Bake at 350° for 30-35 minutes or until golden brown. Cool completely on a wire rack.

» In a small saucepan, bring the sugar, water and honey to a boil. Reduce heat; simmer for 5 minutes. Pour hot syrup over baklava. Cover and let stand overnight.

Yield: 3 dozen.

rich hot fudge sauce

I've made this scrumptious topping ever since the early 1980s. It always turns out smooth and yummy. The dark chocolate flavor, with a hint of rum extract, is not overly sweet but will still satisfy a chocoholic's cravings. It's an ideal addition to an ice cream social.

Carol Hunihan • Ann Arbor, Michigan

1 cup heavy whipping cream

3/4 cup butter, cubed

1-1/3 cups packed brown sugar

1/4 cup sugar

Dash salt

1 cup baking cocoa

1/2 cup plus 2 tablespoons light corn syrup

2 ounces unsweetened chocolate

3 teaspoons vanilla extract

1 to 2 teaspoons rum extract

» In a heavy saucepan, combine cream and butter. Cook and stir over medium-low heat until butter is melted. Add the sugars and salt; cook and stir until sugar is dissolved, about 4 minutes. Stir in the cocoa and corn syrup; cook and stir for 3 minutes or until cocoa is blended.

» Add the chocolate; cook and stir 3-4 minutes longer or until the chocolate is melted. Reduce heat to low. Simmer for 12-16 minutes or until desired thickness is reached, stirring constantly. Remove from the heat; stir in extracts. Cool slightly. Serve warm over ice cream. Refrigerate leftovers.

Yield: about 3-1/2 cups.

summer fruit crisp

What says summer more than this simple dessert packed with fresh cherries and juicy peaches? To beat the heat, dollop with a scoop of low-fat frozen yogurt or ice cream.

Beth Garvin • Cisco, Texas

4 cups fresh dark sweet cherries (about 1-1/4 pounds), pitted

4 cups sliced peeled peaches

1/3 cup sugar

2 tablespoons all-purpose flour

1/8 teaspoon salt

TOPPING:

1/2 cup old-fashioned oats

1/2 cup packed brown sugar

1/3 cup all-purpose flour

1/4 cup chopped pecans

1/4 teaspoon salt

1/4 teaspoon ground cinnamon

3 tablespoons cold butter

» In a large bowl, combine the cherries, peaches, sugar, flour and salt. Transfer to a 13-in. x 9-in. baking dish coated with cooking spray.

» For topping, in a small bowl, combine the oats, brown sugar, flour, pecans, salt and cinnamon. Cut in butter until crumbly. Sprinkle over fruit mixture.

» Bake at 400° for 20-25 minutes or until filling is bubbly and topping is golden brown. Serve warm.

Yield: 10 servings.

sugar cookie fruit pizzas

Purchased sugar cookies make a sweet "crust" for these colorful fruit pizzas. Make them throughout the year with a variety of fresh and canned fruits for a flavorful treat.

Marge Hodel • Roanoke, Illinois

1/2 cup sugar

1 tablespoon cornstarch

1/2 cup unsweetened pineapple juice

1/4 cup water

2 tablespoons lemon juice

4 ounces cream cheese, softened

1/4 cup confectioners' sugar

1-3/4 cups whipped topping

12 sugar cookies (3 inches)

1 cup fresh blueberries

1 cup chopped peeled kiwifruit

1/2 cup chopped fresh strawberries

» For glaze, in a small saucepan, combine the sugar, cornstarch, pineapple juice, water and lemon juice until smooth. Bring to a boil; cook and stir for 2 minutes or until thickened. Transfer to a small bowl; refrigerate until cooled but not set.

» In a small bowl, beat cream cheese and confectioners' sugar until smooth; fold in whipped topping. Spread over tops of cookies. Arrange fruit on top; drizzle with glaze. Refrigerate for 1 hour or until chilled.

Yield: 1 dozen.

nut cookie fudge

I've been making this easy and delicious fudge for Christmas for years. It's great to give as a gift. For variation, I sometimes add mint chips or mint extract. It would sell well at bake sales.

Sherry Hamilton • Florissant, Missouri

1-1/2 teaspoons butter, softened

2 cups (12 ounces) semisweet chocolate chips

1 can (14 ounces) sweetened condensed milk

1-1/2 cups crushed cream-filled chocolate sandwich cookies

1 cup chopped nuts

» Line an 8-in. square dish with foil and grease the foil with butter; set aside. In a heavy saucepan, melt chocolate chips and milk over low heat, stirring constantly until smooth. Remove from the heat; stir in cookie crumbs and nuts.

» Spread evenly into prepared dish. Refrigerate for at least 2 hours or until firm. Using foil, lift fudge out of pan. Discard foil; cut fudge into 1-in. squares. Store in an airtight container in the refrigerator.

Yield: about 2 pounds.

thawing puff pastry

It's best to thaw puff pastry at room temperature for 20 minutes before using. Handle the pastry as little as possible to avoid stretching and tearing.

chocolate chip cookie delight

This is a simple recipe for any type of potluck occasion, and the pan always comes home empty.

Diane Windley • Grace, Idaho

1 tube (16-1/2 ounces) refrigerated chocolate chip cookie dough

1 package (8 ounces) cream cheese, softened

1 cup confectioners' sugar

1 carton (12 ounces) frozen whipped topping, thawed, divided

3 cups cold milk

1 package (3.9 ounces) instant chocolate pudding mix

1 package (3.4 ounces) instant vanilla pudding mix

Chopped nuts and chocolate curls, optional

» Let cookie dough stand at room temperature for 5-10 minutes to soften. Press into an ungreased 13-in. x 9-in. baking pan. Bake at 350° for 14-16 minutes or until golden brown. Cool on a wire rack.

» In a large bowl, beat the cream cheese and confectioners' sugar until smooth. Fold in 1-3/4 cups whipped topping. Spread over crust.

» In a large bowl, whisk milk and pudding mixes for 2 minutes; let stand for 2 minutes or until soft-set. Spread over cream cheese layer. Top with remaining whipped topping. Sprinkle with nuts and chocolate curls if desired.

» Cover and refrigerate for 8 hours or overnight until firm.

Yield: 15 servings.

strawberry puff pastry dessert

My failed attempt to make a triple-layer strawberry malt mousse resulted in this scrumptious sensation. I don't use puff pastry often, but it was simple to work with. My husband declared it one of the best desserts he ever had.

Anna Ginsberg • Austin, Texas

1 package (17.3 ounces) frozen puff pastry

5 cups sliced fresh strawberries, divided

6 ounces white baking chocolate, chopped

1 package (8 ounces) cream cheese, softened

1 teaspoon vanilla extract

1 cup confectioners' sugar

1/3 cup malted milk powder

2 cups heavy whipping cream, whipped

Strawberry syrup, optional

» Thaw one puff pastry sheet (save remaining sheet for another use). Unfold pastry; cut lengthwise into three 3-in.-wide strips. Cut each strip into thirds, making nine squares.

» Place 1 in. apart on ungreased baking sheets. Bake at 400° for 11-13 minutes or until golden brown. Remove to wire racks to cool.

» Place 2-1/2 cups strawberries in a blender; cover and puree; set aside. In a large microwave-safe bowl, melt white chocolate; stir until smooth. Cool slightly. Add cream cheese and vanilla; beat until smooth. Beat in the confectioners' sugar and malted milk powder until smooth. Stir in the puree. Fold in whipped cream.

» Split pastry squares in half horizontally. Line an ungreased 13-in. x 9-in. dish with bottom pastry halves, cut side up; spread with 3-1/2 cups strawberry cream. Top with 1 cup of sliced berries. Cover with pastry tops, cut side down.

» Spread with the remaining strawberry cream. Sprinkle with remaining berries. Drizzle with strawberry syrup if desired. Refrigerate leftovers.

Yield: 12 servings.

caramel apple crunch

I combined ingredients from various apple crisp recipes to create this one. I like to use tart apples because they provide a balance to the sweetness of the caramels.

Melissa Williams • Peoria, Illinois

8 cups sliced peeled tart apples

33 caramels, divided

2 tablespoons plus 2 teaspoons 2% milk, divided

3/4 cup all-purpose flour

3/4 cup quick-cooking oats

3/4 cup packed brown sugar

1/2 cup chopped walnuts

1/8 teaspoon salt

Dash ground cinnamon

1/2 cup cold butter, cubed

Vanilla ice cream, optional

» Place the apples in a greased 13-in. x 9-in. baking dish. In a heavy saucepan, melt 25 caramels with 2 tablespoons milk, stirring often; drizzle over apples.

» In a large bowl, combine the flour, oats, brown sugar, walnuts, salt and cinnamon; cut in butter until mixture resembles coarse crumbs. Sprinkle over apples.

» Bake at 375° for 45-50 minutes or until golden brown. Cool for 10 minutes. Meanwhile, in a heavy saucepan, melt remaining caramels with remaining milk, stirring often until smooth. Drizzle over dessert and ice cream if desired.

Yield: 12-16 servings.

chocolate-hazelnut cream puffs

Chocoholic friends and family will know you fussed when they taste these mini chocolate cream puffs filled with creamy, chocolate-hazelnut flavor. These tiny treats are as pretty as a picture and worth every mouthwatering bite.

Mary Lou Wayman • Salt Lake City, Utah

2 packages (3 ounces each) cream cheese, softened

4 tablespoons sugar, divided

2/3 cup chocolate hazelnut spread

1/4 cup heavy whipping cream

1/2 cup chopped hazelnuts or pecans, toasted

1 cup all-purpose flour

3 tablespoons baking cocoa

1 cup water

1/2 cup butter

1/4 teaspoon salt

4 eggs

Confectioners' sugar

» For filling, in a small bowl, beat cream cheese and 2 tablespoons sugar until smooth. Gradually beat in hazelnut spread and cream until blended. Stir in nuts. Cover and refrigerate.

» In another bowl, combine the flour, cocoa and remaining sugar. In a large saucepan, bring water, butter and salt to a boil. Add flour mixture all at once and stir until a smooth ball forms. Remove from the heat; let stand for 5 minutes. Add eggs, one at a time, beating well after each addition. Continue beating until mixture is smooth and shiny.

» Drop by rounded tablespoonfuls 2 in. apart onto greased baking sheets. Bake at 400° for 20-25 minutes or until set and browned. Remove to wire racks. Immediately split puffs open; remove and discard soft dough from inside. Cool completely.

» Spoon filling into the cream puffs; replace tops. Dust with confectioners' sugar. Refrigerate leftovers.

Yield: 2 dozen.

EDITOR'S NOTE: Look for chocolate hazelnut spread in the peanut butter section.

cherry gelatin supreme

When I was growing up, this yummy, easy-to-make dessert was always on the menu at holiday get-togethers. My aunt gave me the recipe, and now when I make it for my family, I think of her.

Janice Rathgeb • Brighton, Illinois

2 cups water, divided

1 package (3 ounces) cherry gelatin

1 can (21 ounces) cherry pie filling

1 package (3 ounces) lemon gelatin

1 package (3 ounces) cream cheese, softened

1/3 cup mayonnaise

1 can (8 ounces) crushed pineapple, undrained

1 cup miniature marshmallows

1/2 cup heavy whipping cream, whipped

2 tablespoons chopped pecans

» In a large saucepan, bring 1 cup water to a boil. Stir in cherry gelatin until dissolved. Stir in pie filling. Pour into an 11-in. x 7-in. dish. Cover and refrigerate for 2 hours or until set.

» In a small saucepan, bring remaining water to a boil. Stir in lemon gelatin until dissolved. In a small bowl, beat the cream cheese and mayonnaise until smooth. Beat in lemon gelatin and pineapple. Cover and refrigerate for 45 minutes.

» Fold in the marshmallows and whipped cream. Spoon over cherry layer; sprinkle with pecans. Cover and refrigerate for 2 hours or until set.

Yield: 12 servings.

coconut cream dessert

This simple, refreshing creation satisfies the sweet tooth. My sister gave me the recipe years ago.

Deanna Richter • Elmore, Minnesota

1 cup all-purpose flour

2 tablespoons sugar

1/2 cup cold butter, cubed

1/2 cup chopped pecans

FILLING:

1 package (8 ounces) cream cheese, softened

1 cup confectioners' sugar

1 carton (12 ounces) frozen whipped topping, thawed, divided

4 cups cold 2% milk

1-1/2 teaspoons coconut extract

3 packages (3.4 ounces each) instant vanilla pudding mix

2 cups flaked coconut, divided

» In a small bowl, combine flour and sugar; cut in butter until crumbly. Stir in the pecans. Press into a greased 13-in. x 9-in. baking dish. Bake at 325° for 20-25 minutes or until edges are lightly browned. Cool on a wire rack.

» In a large bowl, beat the cream cheese and confectioners' sugar until smooth; fold in 1 cup whipped topping. Spread over the crust.

» In another large bowl, whisk the milk, extract and pudding mixes for 2 minutes; let stand for 2 minutes or until soft-set. Fold in 1-1/2 cups coconut. Spread over cream cheese mixture. Top with remaining whipped topping. Toast remaining coconut; sprinkle over top. Refrigerate overnight.

Yield: 15 servings.

chocolate velvet dessert

This creamy concoction is the result of several attempts to duplicate a dessert I enjoyed on vacation. It looks so beautiful on a buffet table that many folks are tempted to forgo the main course in favor of this chocolaty treat.

Molly Seidel • Edgewood, New Mexico

1-1/2 cups chocolate wafer crumbs

2 tablespoons sugar

1/4 cup butter, melted

2 cups (12 ounces) semisweet chocolate chips

6 egg yolks

1-3/4 cups heavy whipping cream

1 teaspoon vanilla extract

CHOCOLATE BUTTERCREAM FROSTING:
1/2 cup butter, softened

3 cups confectioners' sugar

3 tablespoons baking cocoa

3 to 4 tablespoons 2% milk

» In a small bowl, combine wafer crumbs and sugar; stir in butter. Press onto the bottom and 1-1/2 in. up the sides of a greased 9-in. springform pan. Place on a baking sheet. Bake at 350° for 10 minutes. Cool on a wire rack.

» In a large microwave-safe bowl, melt chocolate chips; stir until smooth. Cool. In a small bowl, combine the egg yolks, cream and vanilla. Gradually stir a third of the cream mixture into melted chocolate until blended. Fold in remaining cream mixture just until blended. Pour into crust.

» Place pan on a baking sheet. Bake at 350° for 45-50 minutes or until center is almost set. Cool on a wire rack for 10 minutes. Carefully run a knife around edge of pan to loosen; cool 1 hour longer. Refrigerate overnight.

» In a small bowl, combine the butter, confectioners' sugar, cocoa and enough milk to achieve a piping consistency. Using a large star tip, pipe frosting on dessert.

Yield: 12-16 servings.

khrustyky

This crisp, dainty pastry dusted with confectioners' sugar has an egg flavor similar to cream puffs. I honor my Ukrainian heritage by serving khrustyky on Christmas Eve as part of the traditional feast of 12 dishes. Each dish symbolizes one of the apostles.

Carol Funk • Richard, Saskatchewan

2 eggs

3 egg yolks

1 tablespoon heavy whipping cream

1 tablespoon vanilla extract

2 tablespoons sugar

1-1/2 cups all-purpose flour

1/2 teaspoon salt

Oil for deep-fat frying

Confectioners' sugar

» In a large bowl, beat the eggs, egg yolks, cream and vanilla. Beat in sugar. Combine flour and salt; stir into the egg mixture just until smooth (dough will be soft). Divide into four portions.

» On a well-floured surface, roll out one portion to 1/8-in. thickness. Cut into 1-1/2-in. strips; cut strips diagonally into three pieces. Cut a 1-1/2-in. slit lengthwise into the center of each piece; pull one end of the strip through slit to make a loop. Cover the shaped pieces while rolling out and cut the remaining dough.

» In an electric skillet or deep-fat fryer, heat 2-3 in. of oil to 375°. Fry pastries, a few at a time, until golden brown, turning once. Drain on paper towels. Dust with confectioners' sugar while still warm.

Yield: 1-1/2 dozen pastries.

berry pavlova

A soft, crusty meringue lusciously complements a sweet strawberry-blueberry filling in this pretty dessert.

Nancy Foust • Stoneboro, Pennsylvania

6 egg whites

1/2 teaspoon cream of tartar

1 teaspoon cider vinegar

1 teaspoon vanilla extract

1-1/2 cups sugar

FILLING:

2 packages (3 ounces each) cream cheese, softened

1 cup sugar

1 teaspoon vanilla extract

2 cups heavy whipping cream, whipped

2 cups miniature marshmallows

1 can (21 ounces) blueberry pie filling

1 package (16 ounces) frozen unsweetened strawberries, thawed

» Place egg whites in a large bowl; let stand at room temperature for 30 minutes. Add cream of tartar; beat until foamy. Add vinegar and vanilla; beat until soft peaks form. Gradually beat in sugar, 1 tablespoon at a time, on high until stiff glossy peaks form and sugar is dissolved.

» Spread evenly into a greased 13-in. x 9-in. baking dish. Bake at 225° for 1-1/4 hours; turn off oven and do not open door. Let meringue dry in oven for 1 hour.

» In a large bowl, beat the cream cheese, sugar and vanilla until smooth; gently fold in whipped cream and marshmallows. Spread over meringue. Cover and chill for 12 hours.

» Cut into squares; top with the pie filling and strawberries. Refrigerate leftovers.

Yield: 12 servings.

strawberry pizza

Both strawberry and cheesecake lovers will delight in this fruity treat. My family requests this delectable pizza every strawberry season.

Kara Cook • Elk Ridge, Utah

6 tablespoons butter, softened

1/2 cup sugar

1 egg

1/2 teaspoon vanilla extract

1/4 teaspoon almond extract

1-1/4 cups all-purpose flour

1/2 teaspoon baking powder

1/2 teaspoon salt

FILLING:

1 package (8 ounces) cream cheese, softened

1/2 cup confectioners' sugar

2 cups sliced fresh strawberries

1 cup sugar

1/4 cup cornstarch

2 cups crushed strawberries

» In a large bowl, cream butter and sugar until light and fluffy. Beat in egg and extracts. Combine the flour, baking powder and salt; gradually add to creamed mixture. Cover and refrigerate for 1 hour.

» On a floured surface, roll dough into a 13-in. circle. Transfer to an ungreased 12-in. pizza pan. Build up edges slightly.

» Bake at 350° for 18-22 minutes or until lightly browned. Cool completely.

» In a large bowl, beat cream cheese and confectioners' sugar until smooth. Spread over crust. Arrange sliced strawberries on top.

» In a large saucepan, combine the sugar, cornstarch and crushed berries until blended. Bring to a boil; cook and stir for 2 minutes or until thickened. Cool slightly. Spoon over the strawberries. Refrigerate until serving.

Yield: 12-16 servings.

peppermint stick sauce

Turn ice cream into a special treat with this yummy sauce. Kids and adults alike will love its cool, sweet flavors at ice cream socials.

Kelly Ann Gray • Beaufort, South Carolina

1-1/2 cups crushed peppermint candies

1 cup heavy whipping cream

1 jar (7 ounces) marshmallow creme

» In a heavy saucepan, combine the crushed candies, whipping cream and marshmallow creme. Cook and stir over low heat until candy is completely melted and mixture is smooth. Store in the refrigerator.

Yield: 2-1/4 cups.

cranberry peach cobbler

This cobbler is a little nontraditional but it will soon be at the front of your recipe list because it's an easy and tasty dessert. Serve it warm with French vanilla ice cream.

Graciela Sandvigen • Rochester, New York

1/2 cup butter, melted

2 cans (29 ounces each) sliced peaches

1 package (15.6 ounces) cranberry-orange quick bread mix

1 egg

2 tablespoons grated orange peel, divided

1/3 cup dried cranberries

1/3 cup sugar

» Pour butter into a 13-in. x 9-in. baking dish. Drain peaches, reserving 1 cup juice. Pat peaches dry and set aside. In a large bowl, combine the quick bread mix, egg, 1 tablespoon orange peel and reserved peach juice.

» Drop batter by tablespoonfuls over butter, spreading slightly. Arrange the peaches over the top; sprinkle with cranberries.

Combine the sugar and remaining orange peel; sprinkle over the peaches. Bake at 375° for 45-50 minutes or until golden brown. Serve warm.

Yield: 12-15 servings.

apricot empanadas

1 cup butter, softened

2 packages (3 ounces each) cream cheese, softened

2 cups all-purpose flour

2 teaspoons grated lemon peel

6 tablespoons apricot jam

Cinnamon-sugar

» In a small bowl, cream butter and cream cheese until light and fluffy. Gradually beat in the flour and lemon peel. Shape dough into a ball. Cover and refrigerate overnight.

» Remove the dough from the refrigerator 1 hour before rolling. On a lightly floured surface, roll the dough into a 17-1/2-in. x 12-1/2-in. rectangle; cut into 2-1/2-in. squares. Spoon 1/2 teaspoon jam onto each square. Brush the edges with water; fold pastry over filling, forming a triangle. Seal edges well with a fork.

» Place on greased baking sheets. Sprinkle with cinnamon-sugar. Bake at 375° for 15-18 minutes or until golden brown. Remove to wire racks. Refrigerate leftovers.

Yield: 35 empanadas.

These cute pastries are flaky and tender outside with a flavorful fruit filling inside. They take a little time to make, but you'll know they're worth it when the compliments start flowing.

Jeaune Hadl Van Meter • Lexington, Kentucky

» Pour into a greased 15-in. x 10-in. x 1-in. baking pan. Bake at 400° for 28-30 minutes or until puffed and golden brown. Cool on a wire rack.

» For filling, in a large bowl, beat the cream cheese, milk and pudding mixes until smooth. Spread over the crust; refrigerate for 20 minutes. Spread with whipped topping. Store in the refrigerator. Just before serving, drizzle with chocolate syrup.

Yield: 15 servings.

fancy phyllo cups

Phyllo dough is great for making eye-catching desserts with a little work. Experiment with other preserves for a tasty twist on these fancy, delicious cups.

Cody Geisler • Cohasset, Minnesota

8 sheets phyllo dough (14 inches x 9 inches)

1/3 cup butter, melted

1/2 cup confectioners' sugar

1 cup white baking chips

2 tablespoons 2% milk

1 package (8 ounces) cream cheese, softened

1 carton (8 ounces) frozen whipped topping, thawed

1/2 cup seedless raspberry preserves, room temperature

White chocolate curls, optional

» Place one sheet of phyllo dough on a work surface (keep remaining phyllo covered with plastic wrap and a damp towel to prevent it from drying out); brush sheet with butter and dust with confectioners' sugar. Top with a second sheet of phyllo; brush with butter and dust with sugar.

» Cut into 12 squares. Place one square on top of a second square, alternating corner points; press into a greased muffin cup. Repeat with remaining 10 squares, filling five more muffin cups. Repeat the process three times with remaining phyllo dough, butter and sugar.

» Bake at 350° for 5-6 minutes or until lightly browned. Carefully remove from pans to wire racks to cool.

» In a microwave, melt baking chips with milk; stir until smooth. In a large bowl, beat cream cheese and melted chip mixture until smooth. Fold in whipped topping.

» Spoon or pipe into phyllo cups; drizzle with raspberry preserves. Cover and refrigerate until serving. Garnish with chocolate curls if desired.

Yield: 2 dozen.

cream puff dessert

Inspired by classic cream puffs, this recipe is a wonderful treat. I've served it at Cub Scout banquets, birthday parties and holidays. I'm a regular baker, and this dessert is one of my all-time favorites.

Denise Wahl • Homer Glen, Illinois

1 cup water

1/2 cup butter

1/4 teaspoon salt

1 cup all-purpose flour

4 eggs

FILLING:

1 package (8 ounces) cream cheese, softened

2-1/2 cups cold 2% milk

2 packages (3.4 ounces each) instant vanilla pudding mix

TOPPING:

1 carton (8 ounces) frozen whipped topping, thawed

Chocolate syrup

» In a large saucepan over medium heat, bring the water, butter and salt to a boil. Add flour all at once and stir until a smooth ball forms. Continue beating until smooth and shiny. Remove from the heat; let stand for 5 minutes. Add the eggs, one at a time, beating well after each addition.

peaches 'n' cream pizza

With a crispy crust, this pizza is topped with almond-flavored cream cheese and a tantalizing peach-pie filling. I get rave reviews every time I serve it.

Linda Patrick • Houston, Texas

1 tube (8 ounces) refrigerated crescent roll dough

1 package (8 ounces) cream cheese, softened

1/2 cup sugar

1/2 teaspoon almond extract

1 can (21 ounces) peach pie filling

1/2 cup all-purpose flour

1/4 cup packed brown sugar

3 tablespoons cold butter

1/2 cup sliced almonds

» Separate the crescent dough into eight triangles. Press onto a greased 12-in. pizza pan; seal seams. Bake at 375° for 8-10 minutes or until the crust edges are golden. Cool slightly on a wire rack.

» In a small bowl, beat the cream cheese, sugar and extract until smooth. Spread over crust. Top with the pie filling. In a small bowl, combine flour and brown sugar; cut in butter until crumbly. Sprinkle over peaches. Top with almonds. Bake for 20-25 minutes or until golden brown. Cool. Cut into wedges. Refrigerate leftovers.

Yield: 12-16 servings.

fruit-filled kolaches

Also spelled Kolachkes, these sweet yeast breads have both Polish and Czech roots. This small, flaky pastry is filled with fruit, jam, poppy seeds or nuts.

Mary Pecinovsky • Clamar, Iowa

1-1/4 cups warm water (70° to 80°)

1/2 cup butter, softened

1 egg

1 egg yolk

1 teaspoon lemon juice

1/3 cup nonfat dry milk powder

1/4 cup mashed potato flakes

1/4 cup sugar

1 teaspoon salt

3-3/4 cups plus 3 tablespoons bread flour

2 teaspoons active dry yeast

1 can (12 ounces) apricot or raspberry cake and pastry filling

Additional butter

» In bread machine pan, place the first 11 ingredients in order suggested by manufacturer. Select dough setting (check dough after 5 minutes of mixing; add 1 to 2 tablespoons of water or flour if needed).

» When the cycle is completed, turn dough onto a lightly floured surface. Pat or roll into a 15-in. x 10-in. rectangle. Cover with plastic wrap; let rest for 10 minutes.

» Cut dough into 24 squares. Place a heaping teaspoonful of pastry filling in the center of each square. Overlap two opposite corners of dough over filling; pinch tightly to seal. Place 2 in. apart on greased baking sheets. Cover and let rise in a warm place until doubled, about 1 hour.

» Bake at 425° for 8-10 minutes or until lightly browned. Remove from the oven; brush with additional butter. Remove from pans to wire racks to cool.

Yield: 2 dozen.

EDITOR'S NOTE: We recommend you do not use a bread machine's time-delay feature for this recipe.

mini apple turnovers

These cute little pastries are so yummy. I'm tempted to hoard them for myself when I make a batch, but I always end up sharing.

Merrill Powers • Spearville, Kansas

1 package (8 ounces) cream cheese, softened

3/4 cup butter, softened

1 egg, separated

3 tablespoons cold water, divided

2 cups all-purpose flour

7 cups thinly sliced peeled tart apples (about 6 medium)

3/4 cup sugar

1-1/2 teaspoons ground cinnamon

Additional sugar, optional

Vanilla ice cream, optional

» In a large bowl, beat cream cheese and butter until smooth. Refrigerate the egg white. Beat egg yolk and 2 tablespoons water into the cream cheese mixture. Gradually add flour until well blended. Shape pastry into a ball. Cover and refrigerate for 1 hour.

» Meanwhile, in a large skillet, combine the apples, sugar and cinnamon. Cover and cook over low heat for 8-10 minutes or until apples are tender. Remove from the heat.

» Turn the pastry onto a lightly floured surface. Roll to 1/8-in. thickness; cut into 4-in. circles. Top each circle with apple mixture. Brush edges of pastry with water; fold pastry over filling and seal edges well.

» In a small bowl, whisk egg white and remaining water; brush over pastry. Sprinkle with additional sugar if desired.

» Place turnovers on greased baking sheets. Bake at 375° for 18-22 minutes or until golden brown. Remove to wire racks to cool. Serve with ice cream if desired.

Yield: 2 dozen.

cherry crescents

These light, flaky crescents are so easy to make, and they always get raves at our house. The festive cherry filling is great, but you can substitute other flavors, too.

Leona Luecking • West Burlington, Iowa

2 cups all-purpose flour

1/2 teaspoon salt

1 cup cold butter, cubed

1 egg yolk, lightly beaten

1 cup (8 ounces) sour cream

1 can (21 ounces) cherry pie filling

1/2 teaspoon almond extract

Confectioners' sugar

» In a large bowl, combine flour and salt. Cut in butter until mixture resembles coarse crumbs. Combine egg yolk and sour cream; add to crumb mixture and mix well. Refrigerate for several hours or overnight.

» Coarsely chop cherries in the pie filling; place in a small bowl. Stir in extract; set aside. Divide dough into quarters. On a lightly floured surface, roll each portion into a 12-in. circle. Cut each circle into 12 wedges.

» Place 1 teaspoon filling at the wide end. Roll up from wide end and place point side down 1 in. apart on ungreased baking sheets. Curve ends to form crescent shape.

» Bake at 375° for 20-24 minutes or until golden brown. Immediately remove from pans to wire racks to cool. Dust with confectioners' sugar.

Yield: 4 dozen.

lemon schaum torte

Schaum Torte is a classic Austrian dessert that consists of meringue layers filled with fruit and topped with whipped cream. This modified version conveniently bakes in a 13-inch x 9-inch pan for easy travel.

Cindy Steffen • Cedarburg, Wisconsin

6 egg whites

1 teaspoon vanilla extract

1/8 teaspoon cream of tartar

2 cups sugar, divided

9 egg yolks

1/2 cup lemon juice

1 tablespoon grated lemon peel

4 cups heavy whipping cream

2/3 cup confectioners' sugar

Ground cinnamon

» Place the egg whites in a large bowl and let stand at room temperature for 30 minutes. Add vanilla and cream of tartar. Beat on medium spoon until soft peaks form. Gradually beat in 1 cup sugar, 2 tablespoons at a time, on high speed until stiff glossy peaks form and sugar is dissolved.

» Spread meringue on the bottom and up the sides of a greased 13-in. x 9-in. baking dish. Bake at 275° for 1 hour. Turn oven off and let stand in oven for 1 hour. Do not open door. Remove from the oven; cool on wire rack.

» In a large saucepan, combine egg yolks, lemon juice, lemon peel and remaining sugar. Cook and stir over medium heat until mixture is thickened and coats the back of a metal spoon. Transfer to a small bowl; cool.

» In a chilled bowl, beat cream until it begins to thicken. Add confectioners' sugar; beat until stiff peaks form. Spread half over meringue; cover with lemon mixture. Top with remaining cream mixture. Sprinkle with cinnamon. Refrigerate leftovers.

Yield: 12-15 servings.

beating egg whites

For the highest volume when beating egg whites, follow these tips. Separate the eggs while they are still cold, but let the whites stand at room temperature for 30 minutes before beating. Use clean, dry glass or metal bowls and make sure there is no yolk, fat or oil mixed in with the whites.

caramel chocolate trifle

A highlight of our annual family reunion is the dessert competition. The judges take their jobs very seriously! Last year's first-place winner was this tempting trifle.

Barb Hausey • Independence, Missouri

1 package (9 ounces) devil's food cake mix

2 packages (3.9 ounces each) instant chocolate pudding mix

1 carton (12 ounces) frozen whipped topping, thawed

1 jar (12-1/4 ounces) caramel ice cream topping

1 package (7-1/2 or 8 ounces) English toffee bits or almond brickle chips

» Prepare and bake cake according to package directions for an 8-in. square baking pan. Cool on a wire rack. Prepare pudding according to package directions.

» Cut cake into 1-1/2-in. cubes; place half of the cubes in a 3-qt. trifle bowl or large glass serving bowl; lightly press down to fill in gaps. Top with half of the whipped topping, pudding, caramel topping and toffee bits; repeat layers. Cover and refrigerate until serving.

Yield: 16 servings.

gran's granola parfaits

When my mother-in-law has us over for brunch, I especially enjoy her yogurt parfaits. They are refreshing, light and wholesome. I made a few changes to her recipe and came up with this sweet, crunchy and nutty variation. Yum!

Angela Keller • Newburgh, Indiana

2 cups old-fashioned oats

1 cup Wheaties

1 cup whole almonds

1 cup pecan halves

1 cup flaked coconut

4-1/2 teaspoons toasted wheat germ

1 tablespoon sesame seeds, toasted

1 teaspoon ground cinnamon

1/4 cup butter, melted

2 tablespoons maple syrup

2 tablespoons honey

1 can (20 ounces) pineapple tidbits, drained

1 can (15 ounces) mandarin oranges, drained

1 cup halved green grapes

2 to 3 medium firm bananas, sliced

1 cup sliced fresh strawberries

4 cups (32 ounces) vanilla yogurt

» In a large bowl, combine the first eight ingredients. Combine the butter, syrup and honey; drizzle over oat mixture and stir until well coated. Pour into a greased 13-in. x 9-in. baking pan. Bake, uncovered, at 350° for 30 minutes, stirring every 10 minutes. Cool on a wire rack; crumble into pieces.

» Combine the fruits in a large bowl. For each parfait, layer 2 tablespoons yogurt, 2 tablespoons of granola and 3 round tablespoons fruit in a parfait glass or dessert bowl. Repeat layers. Sprinkle with remaining granola. Serve immediately.

Yield: 16 servings.

palmiers

It takes just two ingredients to make these impressive but easy-to-do French pastries, which are often called palm leaves.

Taste of Home Test Kitchen

1 cup sugar, divided

1 sheet frozen puff pastry, thawed

» Sprinkle a surface with 1/4 cup sugar; unfold puff pastry sheet on surface. Sprinkle with 2 tablespoons sugar. Roll into a 14-in. x 10-in. rectangle. Sprinkle with 1/2 cup sugar to within 1/2 in. of edges. Lightly press into pastry.

» With a knife, very lightly score a line widthwise across the middle of the pastry. Starting at one short side, roll up jelly-roll style, stopping at the score mark in the middle. Starting at the other side, roll up pastry jelly-roll style to score mark. Cut into 3/8-in. slices.

» Place cut side up 2 in. apart on parchment paper-lined baking sheets. Sprinkle lightly with 1 tablespoon sugar.

» Bake at 425° for 12 minutes. Turn pastries over and sprinkle with remaining sugar. Bake 5 minutes longer or until golden brown and glazed. Remove to wire racks to cool completely. Store in airtight containers.

Yield: about 2 dozen.

grandmother's bread pudding

Comforting is the best word to describe this lovely, flavorful bread pudding. And the drizzle of tangy lemon sauce offers a little zing!

Edna Butler • Los Fresnos, Texas

5 eggs

3 cups 2% milk

1-1/4 cups sugar

1 cup half-and-half cream

1/4 cup butter, melted and cooled

2 teaspoons vanilla extract

1 teaspoon almond extract

1/2 teaspoon ground nutmeg

4 cups cubed day-old white bread

4 cups cubed day-old wheat bread

1/3 cup raisins

LEMON SAUCE:

1-1/2 cups sugar

1/3 cup cornstarch

1/4 teaspoon salt

2-1/4 cups cold water

3 egg yolks, beaten

1/3 cup lemon juice

2 tablespoons butter

» In a large bowl, combine the first eight ingredients. Stir in bread cubes and raisins. Transfer to a greased 13-in. x 9-in. baking dish. Bake, uncovered, at 350° for 45-55 minutes or until a knife inserted near the center comes out clean.

» For sauce, combine the sugar, cornstarch, salt and water in a large saucepan until smooth. Bring to a boil over medium heat, stirring constantly. Remove from the heat.

» Stir a small amount of hot filling into egg yolks; return all to the pan, stirring constantly. Bring to a gentle boil; cook and stir for 2 minutes.

» Remove from the heat; gently stir in lemon juice and butter. Serve with bread pudding. Refrigerate leftovers.

Yield: 12-15 servings.

indexes

GENERAL INDEX

This handy index lists the recipes by food category and major ingredients, so you can easily locate the recipes that suit your needs.

CARAMEL (CONTINUED)

CARROTS

CHEESECAKES

CHERRIES

CHOCOLATE

Bars & Brownies

Cakes

Cheesecakes

ALPHABETICAL INDEX

This handy index lists every recipe in alphabetical order, so you can easily find your favorites.